Wheeling to
Healing

Wheeling to
Healing

BROKEN HEART ON A BICYCLE

Understanding and Healing Adverse
Childhood Experiences (ACEs)

JAMES ENCINAS

new 72 media

PUBLISHING

Disclaimer
All content expressed or implied in this book is provided for information purposes only. The information is not intended to specify a means of diagnosing, treating, curing or preventing any type of physical illness or emotional trauma. It is not a substitute for treatment by a qualified medical or healthcare professional who should always be consulted before beginning any health program. The publisher, author, interviewees, doctors and healthcare practitioners referenced in this book expressly disclaim all responsibility for any liability, loss or risk, personal or otherwise, which is incurred as a consequence, directly or indirectly, of the use, effectiveness, safety or application of any of the procedures, treatments, therapies or recommendations mentioned, herein.

ACKNOWLEDGEMENTS

We can only be said to be alive in those moments when
our hearts are conscious of our treasures.

~ THORNTON WILDER ~

To my parents, Wilma and Jaime—your love brought me to the person I am today. I love both of you with a heart full of gratitude.

My sister Patricia and my brother David—thank you with love for sharing this journey with me. Tony, our brother, our gift—may you raise your children with love.

To Nora—you gave us the greatest of all gifts: our daughter Emma.

Emma, you taught me how to love unconditionally—that love will continue forever.

My Grandparents, Medardo, Raquel, Sebastian and Margarita…I know you watch over me from heaven and I thank you always.

Kati, you gave me your love, support and home—the space in which I wrote this book.

To all the human angels who shared their stories with me and whose stories appear in this book, I thank you with love. Your stories changed, informed and transformed me. I am a better person than I was before I met you. Each of you taught me to be conscious of the abundance that exists in my life, the meaning of mercy, the power of compassion, and what it truly means to accept God's grace.

Thank you to the great writers whose wisdom appears in quotations to support the healing of all who read this book.

Thank you to Mary L. Holden, my editor, and to Shannon McElroy and Meghan McIntyre for their work with Mary in finalizing this manuscript for publication.

This book itself has been a journey. I ask, "Where will this road take it?"

Contents

FOREWORD

I n the spring of 2014, James Encinas called to tell me that he was planning to ride his bicycle from California to New Jersey—alone—to meet people along the route, ask about their childhood experiences and then tell them about the CDC-Kaiser Permanente Adverse Childhood Experiences Study and related ACEs science.

He knew of ACEsTooHigh.com, the news site about ACEs that I'd founded, and its companion social network, ACEsConnection.com, which now has more than 10,000 members, and asked if I could introduce him to people who were implementing—or thinking about implementing—trauma-informed and resilience-building practices based on ACEs science. In this book, you'll read about a few of those people.

I also introduced him to Mary L. Holden, a fellow journalist who was one of the first reporters to write about the ACE Study (*Raising Arizona Kids* magazine, April 2010; http://www.raisingarizonakids.com/2010/04/casting-light-shadow-abuse/) and encouraged him to write a book about his life and the experience of the cross-country trip. James took lots of notes then collaborated with Mary to craft his story—and the intriguing stories of the many people that he met along both his life's journey and his bicycle ride.

Wheeling to Healing...Broken Heart on a Bicycle: Understanding and Healing Adverse Childhood Experiences (ACEs) is one of a few recently published books* about childhood trauma and ACEs science, which includes the ACE Study (how toxic stress from childhood trauma damages the brain and body, how these effects can be passed from generation to generation) and resilience research, which shows how our brains are plastic and our bodies want to heal. Through real people, real places, real stories, the book describes a range of experiences in trauma and healing. It also offers information about various healing methods. They are included as points for exploration.

Having experienced the trauma of domestic violence, divorce, living with an alcoholic parent and physical abuse as a child, and the effects of all this on him as an adult, James credits learning about the ACE Study for starting his process of healing. At the age of eight, he emigrated from Bolivia with his mother and siblings to settle in Pennsylvania. The path of his career took him through social work, stage and screen, international business and education. The miles he's traveled, plus the people he's met are vast in number—but they are only a small measure of his life's experience. His goal is to assist others in becoming more loving to themselves and others through the power of words and teaching.

James's journey is a story of how we learn to love and heal— other people and especially ourselves. The only way we can truly love others is to accept and love ourselves and our own journey, however chaotic or unplanned. Generated by James's determination and fueled by his curiosity, this journey on two wheels reveals the process of healing and loving as it progresses through confident pedaling along flat wide, highways in balmy weather as well as through uncertain and painful slogging up steep hills during storms. There are interruptions that lead to accidental uplifting experiences, and planned stops that deteriorate into aggravating and sometimes harmful detours. By consciously having to seek out rest and nourishment in food and companionship in a different way every day, James continued learning about others, and through these experiences, learned to understand and love them and himself.

By putting his remarkable journey to words, we also learn to heal and love, and to make his journey part of our own.

JANE STEVENS
Founder of ACEs Too High (www.acestoohigh.com)
and ACEs Connection (www.acesconnection.com)

*At least two other books regarding ACEs were published in 2016:

Childhood Disrupted: How Your Biography Becomes Your Biology, and How You Can Heal, by Donna Jackson Nakazawa (Atria Books, paperback – July 26, 2016).

The ACEs Revolution! The Impact of Adverse Childhood Experiences, by John Richard Trayser (CreateSpace, paperback – January 25, 2016).

INTRODUCTION

There are only two ways to live your life.
One is as though nothing is a miracle.
The other is as though everything is a miracle.
~ ALBERT EINSTEIN ~

A bicycle provides self-powered transportation. It takes riders to work or school, to visit friends, to run errands or into an adventure. It is exercise. Forward motion. Bicycling is a chance to observe one's personal landscape at a pace that's faster than walking, slower than driving a car.

Bicycles are for fun and transportation. They are not tools for healing. But I used a bicycle to heal emotional wounds embedded in me during childhood. Then I used it as a tool to raise awareness in others of the possibility of healing from early childhood trauma.

My ability and passion to commandeer a bicycle (a Panasonic Villager II) first happened when as a young man I ran away from feelings I'd packed away like oil-soaked rags in a metal box that were nearing spontaneous combustion. Having witnessed many episodes of domestic violence as a child and being unable to find a toehold in life as a responsible adult, I grew frustrated to a point that frightened me. So, at age 23, directionless and unemployed, I left a temporary home in California and returned to my family in New Jersey—on a bicycle.

Here's what happened on a portion of that trip....

On April 4, 1981, dusk was nearing. My body was tired and everything hurt, but I was in the zone—pedaling, cycling—in New Mexico. All my senses, thoughts, intentions and feelings were working together in rhythm toward the town of Tucumcari. I had already logged 100 miles on my bicycle that day and I was running on adrenaline. At a recent stop, I'd checked a map and learned that Tucumcari was fewer than five miles away.

A loud crack of thunder ripped through the sky and forced me back into an awareness of my immediate surroundings. Focused on the road ahead, I'd failed to notice a gathering cluster of ominous clouds. I leaned down over the handlebars and pedaled on, wheeling over the chuckholes and hills of State Highway 18.

The sky above me burst open.

Hail the size of large marbles rained down and bounced off my helmet and the paved two-lane road. Willing my tired legs to pump harder against the storm, I sought comfort in prayer and asked God to protect me from the lightning. I also increased the volume of the country music radio program from Albuquerque that I was listening to on the cheap yellow Walkman headphones I wore over my helmet. Some guy was singing about wanting a girl to love him.

I don't know where the pickup truck came from, but the next thing I did was pick myself up from the side of the road. I was not yet aware of the nasty scrape on my right knee as I caught sight of my ten-speed Panasonic bicycle, partially lodged under four wheels and a chassis.

The driver helped me dislodge my bike and load it onto the empty horse trailer hitched to the truck. He apologized, and gave me a lift into Tucumcari. I nursed my injury and he said that as soon as he saw me on the bike, he'd slammed and pumped the brakes, but because of the rain and hail, and the weight of the horse trailer he was towing, he could not keep the truck from skidding into me.

As he spoke, I was thinking, "I still have over 2,000 miles to go, I'm in New Mexico, and my bike is ruined."

What I did not know then was that I had many more than 2,000 miles and many years to go before I would find relief for the wounds to my spirit. I would take another bicycle trip from California to New Jersey to spread messages of the scientific discoveries about healing from childhood trauma, and, to collect stories from other people about the resilience of the human spirit.

Thirty-three years after that first ride, I was a grade school teacher with panniers packed on my Marin Hydro-Light mountain bike (I'd adapted it for touring). I was ready to hit the pavement for my second cross-country ride to my family in New Jersey. On April 12, 2014, as I followed students through the auditorium of Le Grand Union High School in Merced, California toward the open doors leading out onto the parking lot, my mind was on the person who had taken that first bicycle ride so many years ago—the one with a broken heart—who had run away in search of answers.

Looking at both rides from a new point of discernment and appreciation, my awareness shifted to the thought of life and healing as a process—like pedaling a bicycle. Life, when lived from the heart, is joyful. Joy opens an ability to heal. When the heart is in a healing process, there are times when celebration is necessary. The way I chose to celebrate, and activate even more healing, was with that second cross-country trip on two self-powered wheels.

The concept of living from the heart took me 56 years to grasp. The great poet Rainer Maria Rilke wrote about this simple yet complex lesson in *Letters to a Young Poet* (1929):

> ...*have patience with everything unresolved in your heart and to try to love the questions themselves as if they were locked rooms or books written in a very foreign language. Don't search for the answers, which could not be given to you now, because you would not be able to live them. And the point is, to live everything. Live the questions now. Perhaps then, someday far in the future, you will gradually, without even noticing it, live your way into the answer.*

Rilke's wisdom came to me during middle age. It was this passage that made me understand that if I were patient, diligent, and humble, I would find the answers I sought. I got that the point of life is to live everything in the present moment—even to live the questions now. My lifelong questions were rising to a crescendo I could no longer ignore.

As a child in the darkness of my bedroom, I had asked God "Why?"

That question multiplied, persisted, and never left my mind:

"Why are my parents fighting?"

"Why are so many people suffering?"

"Why couldn't my parents have loved me for who I was?"

"Why does life have to be so difficult?"

"Why do people lack responsibility for themselves?"

"Why do people find it so difficult to honor the self?"

"Why am I on Earth?"

These questions and a quest for their answers were what propelled me onto a bicycle in my early 20s to ride across the country alone. I did not know then I was not yet ready to live the answer. Wanting an answer to "Why are so many people suffering?" I decided to trust the bicycle once again—this time to rally support for my intention to strive toward personal and universal healing.

So, as over 200 young students cheered me on to start the second journey, two thoughts entered my mind: "The weather is perfect!" and "It has so far been a most excellent day." Principal Javier Martinez and student coordinator Andre Griggs adjusted their helmets and prepared to accompany me on their bicycles to the Merced county line. Theirs were chivalrous acts of kindness, solidarity, and support, made even more special by the fact that it had been years since either of these two men had ridden bicycles.

The word *bicycle* shares with the word *book* the letter "b" and two circles: wheels, and the letter "o." This book, which tells my story of dealing with childhood domestic violence, is set into a compilation of similar stories told to me by people I met along the way on that second cross-country bicycle ride—strangers who had become friends long enough for me to collect their stories.

From my bicycle, this book arrived in your life.

With the individuals who told me their stories, I shared two common bonds: we'd all suffered Adverse Childhood Experiences, or ACEs, and we all desired to heal from their effects.

Your body works to heal itself from physical wounds.

Your mind must find a way to heal itself from emotional and spiritual wounds.

I believe that healing is easier than it seems to be.

Your body, mind and spirit are each shaped, developed, and defined both by genetics and, more fully, by the community from which you originated. Your personal identity is embedded in your immediate and extended family, in the schools you attended, groups you joined or are a member of, and in the places in which you learned to worship, meditate, or gained the vocabulary necessary to talk about emotions and spirit energy.

Childhood is a short time yet an individual's traumatic experiences during childhood have lifelong implications. For far too many children, home is not a safe haven. According to the National Coalition Against Domestic Violence and the U.S. Department of Justice, "1 in 15 children are exposed to intimate partner violence each year, and 90 percent of these children are eyewitnesses to this violence." Leading researchers in the field of neuroscience, social psychology, and child development have confirmed that growing up in domestic violence disrupts cognitive development, intensifies social-emotional needs, and leads to high-risk behaviors that influence health during adulthood.

Violence in the home is one of the most pervasive human rights challenges of our time, yet it remains a hidden problem that few countries, states, communities, or families openly confront. A global phenomenon, violence is deep within and also beyond the boundaries of geography, ethnicity, or financial status.

Domestic violence is one type of trauma children experience; there are others. All traumas suffered during childhood affect adult health. Science has tested, and proved, this fact.

In the later years of the 20th century, two medical doctors, Vincent J. Felitti and Robert Anda, studied the effects of childhood trauma on adult health through Southern California's Kaiser Permanente Healthcare System. They developed the ACE (Adverse Childhood Experiences) Evaluation, a short quiz available for free on the internet to any person who is interested. A low score means you experienced few ACEs; a high score means your childhood was traumatic.

Find your ACE Score at www.acestudy.org.

Here is the general list of ACEs:

- Humiliation or emotional abuse of a child by an adult

- Threats of violence toward a child by an adult

- Actual violence, physical punishment or abuse of a child by an adult

- Sexual abuse by a household resident at least five years older

- Victimization by bullies at or after school

- Witnessing abuse by or between adult residents of the child's home

- Parent, parents or other household residents who abused alcohol or drugs

- Parent, parents or another household resident with mental illness

- Parent or parents who separated, divorced, disappeared, were incarcerated or died

- Living in poverty (lack of shelter, food, safety, healthcare, education)

It is easy for a person who did not experience any or few ACEs to get the wrong idea about the lives of people who experienced many of them. Those fortunate enough to have a low ACE score may take pity on those who have high scores. This is not helpful. Pity does little to erase the problem and, in fact, it serves to exacerbate and continue the cycle of violence and trauma by inferring that ACEs happen to "other people," or in other families. The truth is that no one is immune to trauma—especially during childhood. A person who has suffered multiple childhood traumas faces a hard fight for a life of quality and, sometimes, even for survival.

Although my childhood was filled with many adverse experiences—domestic violence, a traumatic head injury, cultural shock, and frustration with social and intellectual barriers—I did not learn about the ACE study until the age of 55.

A couple of weeks before setting off on the bicycle ride from Le Grand Union High School in 2014, I attended a conference titled "Everyday Courage," in Los Angeles. During the keynote speech, Robert Ross, Ph.D., Executive Director of the California Endowment, reported an epidemic of childhood trauma.

He cited studies showing that two out of every three children in America experience some form of trauma. At least one in five are exposed to multiple traumas such as physical, emotional, and/or sexual abuse; seeing alcohol and/or drug abuse in the home; living with a household member who is either on parole or has been released from prison; living with a household member who is chronically depressed, mentally ill, institutionalized, or suicidal. One in five children have witnessed violence in their neighborhood, school or home. Dr. Ross stated that the research shows that traumatic stress blocks bodies and minds from developing in a healthy way.

The good news is that awareness of the significance of childhood trauma minimizes the cycle of violence in homes and communities. It creates new, healthier landscapes for relationships. Increasing public awareness is work that people need to do together. It is work that requires courage.

As long as there are children, there will be ACEs, but they need not have the same impact as they now have on those who have already passed through their own childhood years. By dealing with memories of ACEs, these adults can find paths toward healing. Many methods of healing are available.

Healing from ACEs and moderating their impact on a person's life—and on those whose lives this person may impact—is necessary if people are ever to end the cycles of violence in this world. In order to heal, people must know themselves well enough to find a healing modality that will work most effectively for their individual 'self.' This book contains suggestions for those seeking to heal from ACEs.

The key to finding your own path to lasting healing is to obtain your ACEs score, and then to follow your heart's guidance to a method that will serve you the best.

In the past, psychotherapy ('talk therapy') was accepted as the way to treat and heal emotional trauma. Psychotherapy may help in terms of articulating an individual's feelings, but to completely remove the negative charges associated with emotional scars so that optimum health becomes possible, an active process of engaged, energetic healing must be explored, tested, and allowed to take root.

Global solutions for preventing and minimizing ACEs include building trauma informed communities of parents, families, schools and teachers, health care institutions and health care professionals. But healing happens in a big way after it has taken place on an individual level.

You can help end the cycle of ACEs for yourself, for other children, and for future generations. First, undertake your own healing. Find a way to own your story of suffering, relief and healing. Then participate in activism by telling others about the significance of the ACEs survey. By doing so, you can create new cycles for human lifestyles that will heal all, or at least, many of the people in your life and others who surround you in the world.

CHAPTER 1

How I 'Scored' My ACEs

As a child I felt myself to be alone, and I am still,
because I know things and must hint at things which
others apparently know nothing of, and for the most
part do not want to know.
~ **C.G. JUNG** ~

The place of my birth was La Paz, Bolivia. It was then and is still an enchanted city. Cradled in a valley about 12,000 feet above sea level, the majestic, snowcapped peaks of Mount Illimani and Mount Illampu surround it. At the top of the valley, at about 13,000 feet, sits a plateau called the Altiplano. To the north of this plateau is Lake Titicaca, the highest-altitude navigable lake in the world.

Lake Titicaca is home to one of the world's largest frog types, the Titicaca frog. An endangered species, it faces the possibility of becoming extinct. But that was not the case in the 1970s, when the famous explorer and conservationist Jacques Cousteau, then searching Lake Titicaca for Inca treasure, reported seeing thousands of these frogs, some almost 20 inches long.

My father's father, Sebastian, once told me that the native people believed these frogs had special powers, particularly the power to bring rain. He told me a tale in which the Aymara Indians captured and carried the frogs in ceramic pots to a hillside where the creatures would call in distress. The people thought the frogs' calls sounded to the gods like a plea for rain. Once the downpour began, the pots overflowed and the sacred animals escaped back to the lake.

The frogs in my grandfather's story were one thing, but a real distress call was going on—and it was coming from me. Often, as a child, I cried out to God in prayer from the darkness of my bedroom, imploring Him to stop my father from hurting my mother.

In fact, the trauma in my childhood began before I even learned to pray.

My father, a lawyer, got an appointment as a delegate to the United Nations when I was one year old. His job was to address Bolivia's lack of access to the sea—the result of a peace treaty signed by Bolivian leaders in 1904 after losing a war with Chile. In the treaty, Bolivia relinquished territory to Chile and lost its Pacific coast. My father left for the United States for what was supposed to be a short trip that turned into a year's absence from home.

He'd requested that my mother and I live at his parents' home—on the third floor of grandfather Sebastian's and grandmother Margarita's house—while he was away. The house was very large. Three of my fathers' brothers (my uncles, Walter, Nano, and Hector) and one of his sisters, my aunt Maria, also lived there. Three housekeepers, Vicenta, Leonita, and Leonita's daughter, Maria Eugenia, lived on the property. In a room across from where my mother and I slept lived Fina, one of my grandmother's relatives. Fina was deaf.

My mother tells me that when she would go to see her sister, my aunt Betty, she'd leave me with Fina. I liked that because Fina read to me. During one of these times, Fina got distracted and took her eyes and attention off of me. I took the opportunity to walk to the top of the wooden staircase, three floors up, and called out for my grandmother, Margarita. Since Fina was deaf she did not hear me yelling as I teetered on the top step. My grandmother heard the commotion and tried as best she could to run up the long flights of stairs—but not before I fell—and went tumbling, tumbling down. She was rounding the corner of the final flight of stairs as she scooped me into her arms and back under appropriate supervision.

When I was 2½-years-old, I ran into the living room where a large gathering of family and friends was taking place, seized center stage and, at the top of my lungs, with all the passion I had, belted out a current popular song: *"Que pasa con esa banda?"* Translation: "What's up with that band?" and you can find it in the Spanish language on YouTube. The answer to that question is, *"Lo que pasa es que la banda esta boracha, esta boracha, esta boracha,"* or "What's up is that the band is drunk, the band is drunk, the band is drunk."

I share this story to draw attention to the fact that I was born with *joie de vivre*, a gift I've worked hard to retrieve—one handed down to me through my genes, but one that domestic violence concealed.

When I was 3, we moved to Miraflores in Bolivia, my parents' first home. My baby sister was born right after our move. It was in this home that I experienced childhood trauma in the form of domestic abuse.

Here is one of my early memories. A loud, persistent car horn shattered the night's silence. It took me by surprise, piercing my eardrums. A light came on in the hallway and the harsh sound inter-mingled with my mother's footsteps. Through one partially opened eye, I saw her shadow. I followed her silhouette as she made her way over to my sister's crib. I watched her lean into the crib and wrap the baby in a swaddling blanket. I closed my eyes when she turned in my direction. She kissed me on the forehead. With one finger and a delicate touch she wiped away little droplets of sweat on my nose. She pulled the bedcovers over my shoulders. Having made sure that her two precious babies were snug, safe and sound, my mother made her way to the stairs to go down and open the gates for my father.

I kicked off the sheets and followed her, jarred by cold tiles beneath my feet, to the top of the stairway. My mother did not know I was following her. I looked down from the top of the stairs and watched. She went out of our home and left the front door ajar.

Frozen in place, I stared at the open door as a cacophony of sounds and images played out and threw all my young senses into hyperawareness. I walked right down the stairs into it, transported by pandemonium. Metal gates opened, car tires crunched gravel, car doors slammed shut, headlights pierced the night, and dark, evil shadows came to life before me.

When I stepped outside, the waking nightmare became something even more frightening and horrific. I was now a witness to my father and mother rolling over each other on the ground, locked in battle. He had a hold on her hair; she clawed and screamed as they rolled like toy tops.

From deep within me, fear bloomed and then came out as sound. My mother's screams combined with my own. After a time, my screams were the only sounds.

My parents froze in their tracks—both stared up at me. My mother disengaged herself from my father's grasp and pulled herself to her feet. She pulled her bloody, dirty, and torn nightgown around herself as she ran to me, grabbed me, and lifted me up.

The last image I have of my father that night is one of supplication. Just before she closed the door, I saw him pulling himself to his knees.

From that moment on, I lived much of my life in a state of hyper-arousal. New sights, sounds, and experiences were accompanied by feelings of tension. The rustling of trees, innocuous shadows, darkness, or any unknown gave rise to fear. My view of the world transformed. Instead of feeling joy and sensing wholeness, I saw fractures and felt suspicion.

As time passed, the violence between my parents intensified. My life turned into a roller coaster ride. I never knew when a conflict would erupt so I stayed on the lookout; I was teaching myself to be forever vigilant. My father's rage only grew and my mother became much more combative.

It was at this point that I remember disconnecting from my true self. I'm positive my younger sister and brother followed that same pattern. By now, my family had five participants bound together by blood, fear, and struggle.

Between the births of my sister and brother, there were periods of respite from the domestic violence, but I don't remember them lasting for long. Because of my father's drinking and womanizing, times of peace were ruined. One minute, the five of us could be having a great time, but in the next minute, after a spell of fury, our experience descended into anger's darkness and frustration's shadow.

Right after my fifth birthday, my father returned from one of his business trips and took our family on an outing in the car. I was wearing a mariachi outfit he brought back for me from Mexico. We were happy and making our way along a curvy dirt road when my mother screamed at him: *"Puto cabron! Cobarde! Para el carro!"*

From the back seat, my siblings and I watched as she tried to open the door. My father grabbed her arm in an attempt to keep her in the car.

I figured out that she'd seen red rouge or lipstick on his white collar. My sister sat frozen and my little brother began to cry as I screamed at them to stop.

The car door flew open. My father swerved and slammed on the brakes. My mother fell out of the car and tumbled out into the dirt. My father stopped the car. Having seen our mother fall caused my siblings and me to sob and wail in agony. My father reacted with more violence. He reached his arm back and threatened to hit us while he screamed at us to stop crying. He yelled at my mother, commanding her to get back in the car.

After a while of this back and forth, he told her to go to hell, started the car, and drove a short distance away. I leaned forward, put my hands on his shoulders, and begged him to stop. All three of us were crying and repeating, "*Mami! Mamita, mamita, mamita. Mami!*" My father had no choice but to slow down and stop the car.

When she fell, my mother suffered an injury to her heel. I saw pain on her face as I watched her hobble over to and get back in the car.

As always, after the chaos, we went forward—toward the next violent event.

A few days later my mother packed our clothes, shepherded us into a taxi, and directed the driver to take us to the airport. My father was at work. She had decided to leave him and take us to her parents' home in Sucre, Bolivia. Sucre is the White City, known for its whitewashed architecture.

The flight we took was not direct. It included a stop in Cochabamba to refuel and discharge passengers. Shortly before we landed in

Cochabamba, sparks of fire shot out of one of the two engines. We landed safely, but the aircraft needed repairs. There was no other connecting flight, and we had to spend the night so we went in search of a motel near the airport. We found one with a pool and settled in for some fun. My mother must have taken the picture I still have of us by that pool: my 2-year-old sister, 1-year-old brother and a dog, me, and a kid we'd befriended. In the photo, my little brother is hugging the dog.

That night, a knock at the door wakened us. My mother got out of bed. She put the chain latch on the door before opening it, and by that point I was at her side, leaning next to her. As she opened the door to the width of the chain, I saw my father. His sorry face was looking right back at me. In a controlled, calm voice, he implored her to open the door and let him in.

My body tensed. I could smell her fear and feel my own. He begged her to open the door. She pleaded with him to leave us alone, to please go away. He persisted. He grew insistent, asking her many times to forgive him, crying, saying he was sorry, telling her that he loved her and that he loved and couldn't live without us. On and on he begged her forgiveness…as I was pleading with her not to open the door.

His persistence paid off and he won her over.

As soon as she removed the latch, the door flew open and the night erupted into chaos and pandemonium. Screams and cries of agony and heartbreak filled the room as he threw her against the wall and slapped her hard across the face. Blood streamed from her nose as he dragged her by the hair into the bathroom and tried to close the door.

I remember jumping on his back, my sister was holding onto one of his legs, as our father put our mother's head under the sink faucet and turned on the tap. Unsatisfied with the way she was cleaning the blood off of her nose, he pulled her away from the faucet and forced her down, attempting to stick her head into the toilet, screaming for her to get clean.

When or how it stopped I don't remember. Very early the next morning, with my father passed out on one of the beds, my mother carried my little brother and led me, holding onto my little sister's tiny hand, out the door.

Six months went by before my father was able to gain my mother's forgiveness and work his way back into our lives. During that time we lived a fairytale existence, in the home of my maternal grandparents, Raquel and Medardo Navarro, in Sucre. It was a brief moment in time during which I accrued a stockpile of magnificent and enchanted memories, beautiful and everlasting, which have sustained me, given me resilience, and influenced the person I've become today.

My aunt, Carmen Rosa Navarro, was my mother's youngest sister. She was a refined, delicate flower of a woman and a master storyteller. A consummate scholar, she spoke six different languages and loved reading books; she honored every written page with a sense of reverence and utmost care. Reverence was a trait with which she endowed everything and everyone she came in contact with, especially her mother, my grandmother Raquel. Carmen Rosa was also very shy around adults but she came alive with children when she had a story to share.

Enticed by the promise of chocolate bonbons, I would sit in her room and be delighted and entertained with stories from history of great women and men, stories of fascinating places and events, and biblical stories. My favorites were her poetic, magical stories that transported me into the world of my ancestors. There is power in listening to a story and it is one of the greatest events in the life of a child. I learned this from Carmen Rosa.

To illustrate the magic of my childhood in Sucre, here is a story that depicts the origins of what I earlier described as the *joie de vivre* I was born with. Aunt Carmen Rosa told me of a significant moment in the life of my grandmother, *abuela* Raquel Fuertes Navarro.

Raquel's Story

At the beginning of the 20th century, in the year 1909 in Sucre, there was a great epidemic of typhoid. There was no drug like penicillin—no antibiotics. People died; many of them were children. The archbishop of the city's Catholic diocese also died of this contagion.

Raquel, nine years old at the time, contracted typhoid. Her father, Pablo Fuertes, called a doctor to the family home, a hotel that he owned. The doctor said that Raquel would not see the light of the next day. Pablo trusted the diagnosis and sat by her bedside, weeping for a parent's greatest loss.

A little while later, Dr. Melgarejo passed by the hotel. This doctor was not popular—he was an alcoholic. He stopped in to see his good friend Pablo. It was early in the evening and the doctor's tongue had not yet tasted its first drop of liquor. When he walked into the hotel, Dr. Melgarejo found Pablo with his elbows supported on a table, head bowed in his hands.

Dr. Melgarejo asked what was happening.

Pablo gave him Raquel's prognosis.

Dr. Melgarejo told him that they still could try something, and said, "*Que sera, sera.*" Then he asked for a tub. At that time there were no modern bathrooms; bathtubs were portable. Dr. Melgarejo instructed my great-grandfather to fill the tub with freezing cold water, place a table near the tub, cover the table with a blanket, then get Raquel to come to the tub.

As she stood in front of the tub, the men stripped off her clothing. One man held her by the armpits and the other by her feet as they submerged her in the water. They held her in the cold water for perhaps a minute. Then they removed her from the tub and laid her on the table, wrapped her with the blanket and left her to rest for another few minutes.

They carried out this operation time and time again. Raquel trembled with each dip into the cold water. Thus elapsed the night— the men dipping and Raquel resting—until dawn arrived and her fever descended.

Raquel did see the light of a new day.

When my grandmother related her story to Carmen Rosa, she said that for many weeks after the treatment she was so weak she could not walk or feed herself. She told of how my great-grandfather Pablo stayed by her side, feeding her spoonful after spoonful of chicken soup, until she became strong and had recovered in full from typhoid.

Thanks to the fighting spirit of an alcoholic doctor, Raquel lived to be 98. For the rest of her life, she was blessed with good health and vitality. Her *joie de vivre* was memorable. I believe she passed this quality down to me through the genes of her body—and through the spirit of her soul. My grandmother was a force of nature and bastion of strength. Every good trait she had multiplied when she married her soul's match—my grandfather, Medardo Navarro—a medical doctor.

Because of this story, I believe that in addition to physical genes, humans have a heritage that is spiritual. This spiritual heritage can be of persecution, suffering and even dependence on things like drugs or alcohol in attempts to remove pain. But this spiritual 'genetic' heritage also offers personal power and strength to overcome misfortunes, pain, suffering. It may even allow humans to stop dwelling in misery by repeating the cycles and patterns that bring harm instead of joy.

It is in everyone's *physical* genetic heritage to discover where trauma has informed the kinds of pain that is passed down through generations. And, it is everyone's *spiritual* genetic heritage to discover where resilience occurred and also got passed on to the following generations.

It seems to me that the 'fighting spirit' inside Dr. Melgarejo, Pablo, and my grandmother Raquel was passed on to my mother—and then to me. It is a part of what allowed me to recharge and heal over time on emotional, mental and spiritual levels.

Raquel was a wonderful cook; Medardo was a general practitioner with a kind and good heart. The two did their best to heal and nurture my mother and us children in their home, a huge and magical house in Sucre. Together they provided us with stability and a respite from the storm and the safety, order, and peace that I rarely experienced in the world of my parents. My grandparents' civility and shared mutual love radiated throughout that home and touched everyone who entered. Raquel and Medardo genuinely loved and understood each other. The suffering they'd each known prior to their union was endured before I came into the world, and it served to make them humble, empathetic, compassionate, and caring human beings.

The house of my grandparents was located near the center of Sucre. It had enormous wooden front doors with large, lion-shaped door-knockers made of metal. These doors opened out onto a small park named for Saint Francis. That park was our front yard; it was where we played and enjoyed childhood. Directly across the street stood the church of Saint Francis, one of many churches built in Sucre during the 16th century by the Spanish conquistadors.

I can still remember the feelings of fear, excitement, and wonder that coursed through my veins whenever I entered that church. It was a dark, supernatural, and sacred space that often called out to me to visit it. It was where I learned to pray. At its center was a beautiful golden altar, and along the walls, in dark niches, stood statues of saints and martyrs in various stages of suffering and exultation. These statues were painted in bright colors and some had red tears of blood flowing from their eyes, hands, and feet. There were paintings of joyful angels, as well as images of the fires of Purgatory and pits of Hell. The ceiling of this church was lined with giant spikes.

From Raquel, I learned that Saint Francis was my family's patron saint. She told me the story of how Saint Francis spread his arms like wings and a flock of birds landed there—sparrows, larks, doves, and owls. People gathered to listen to this man who was filled with rapture as he preached to all who had gathered near him. They heard the divine wisdom and joy in his voice. Even though the people in this crowd spoke many different languages, they all understood Saint Francis. She told me he spoke Italian, but every listener understood the sermon because each bird repeated the words of Saint Francis in a different language. The birds acted as translators! It was a miracle.

Every Thursday, my grandfather opened his office to the poor and provided them with medicine and general health consultations, free of charge. His office was located to the right of the main entrance of the house and had its own separate street entrance. On these Thursdays, I remember seeing indigenous men, women, and children in need of care standing in lines that stretched across many city blocks.

My grandmother taught half the people in town how to cook. On a weekly basis, she'd throw open the doors of her industrial-sized kitchen to give free classes. The house of my grandparents was always alive with people. It was a place in which I saw the virtues of charity and service modeled.

Unlike my grandfather's office, a site we were not encouraged to enter, my grandmother's kitchen was one of my favorite places. Pulled there by sounds and smells that excited my senses, I'd sit in a corner, mesmerized by the room's landscape. Even today, that memory lets me see steam emanating from boiling pots and my grandmother standing over a table holding a dead chicken in her powerful hands, forearms bulging as she's plucking its feathers. I also remember being wide-eyed with wonder as she held a turkey between her legs and poured sweet red wine into a funnel shoved down its gullet. All over the patio, dozens of drunken turkeys ran around in circles, falling all over the place. Years later, I learned that wine delivered to turkeys by this method tenderizes the meat.

Not all was carnage in that kitchen. With love, I recall the taste of the pastries my grandmother created. One of my favorite jobs was licking clean the bowl of egg whites beaten to stiff peaks with sugar on days when she baked resplendent lemon meringue pies. When I turned six, my grandmother made a beautiful birthday cake for me. It was in the shape of a swimming pool and it had a diving board, complete with little people! The center of the cake, a blue-green gelatin, looked like water.

I lived in Sucre for six months. Then my father visited, met with my mother and her family, and convinced her to bring us back to Miraflores, south of downtown La Paz and approximately 250 miles away from my grandparents' home. At the age of 6, I remember having conflicting emotions—not wanting to leave my grandparents, but wanting to be with my father.

The love I received from my grandparents and my mother's extended family provided me with the resilience and ability to cope with the powerlessness and lack of safety I experienced growing up in a violent home. I was taught to perceive the world as a threatening place, like so many others who share similar experiences in their pasts. To survive, I developed coping strategies that were neither functional nor healthy. The fighting and hostility in which we lived adversely affected my entire life and the lives of all those around me. Although the physical violence I experienced diminished from the age of eight on, emotional and verbal abuse took its place. My mother was not the only target of this insidious abuse. My father directed it at all of us.

Being the oldest, I received the brunt of it.

The role forced me to act as my mother's shield and defender. Domestic abuse affected the way I learned and developed. For me, and for so many children, suffering trauma affects the ability to learn and figure things out. Trauma suffered by a child compromises academic performance and their enthusiasm to belong to a school's community.

As a result of the violence I experienced as a youth living at home with my father, I had difficulty making friends and maintaining relationships. I developed a low tolerance for stress that resulted in many physical altercations. I engaged in fistfights with anyone I felt was a threat. I walked around feeling angry and defiant, and it led me to seeking out other kids who were just like myself.

The animosity I felt for my father increased as I grew up, and my respect for my mother diminished. In my teenage years, and into early adulthood, I abused drugs and alcohol in order to cope and survive. The traumas of domestic violence I suffered in early childhood had curated and cultivated my self-hatred.

But I did not know that then.

CHAPTER 2

A Story of the Road

Every time I see an adult on a bicycle I no longer
despair for the future of the human race.
~ **H. G. WELLS** ~

After five years of living in Miraflores, and traveling back and forth to the United States, my father got a scholarship to New York University's law school. He did not finish; he ended up taking jobs in international business. Our family stayed behind in Bolivia until I was 8-years-old, when we joined him to live in Lansdowne, Pennsylvania—a Quaker community.

The move was difficult for me. I found myself in a third grade classroom with very little command of English. After six months, I caught up with language, but I did not have support to master academic content and I struggled in many subjects. I felt lost and stayed lost. My younger siblings did not have the same issues with school, and my father struggled with me as I struggled.

There was nothing I could do to rise above this vortex until I fell from a high diving board and suffered a head injury. I spent several days in the hospital. My parents prayed that if I survived, they would put me into a Catholic school because they felt it was their bargain with God.

I survived. My parents kept their promise to God, and Corpus Christi Elementary in Lansdowne was where I spent the rest of my grade school years. The strict rules I endured there, at the hands of the nuns, were not enough to protect me. At the point of graduating from eighth grade, I began abusing alcohol.

Listening to the chatter and laughter of classmates, nuns, and teachers milling around the back yard enjoying the party, I hid in a cluster of bushes on the side of Mrs. Rich's house. On my knees, bent over, clutching my stomach with both hands, I tried to be as quiet as possible as I struggled against nausea. In between bouts of dry heaves, with tears streaming down my face, I prayed that no one would come around the corner and discover me with the half-full bottle of Johnnie Walker Red protruding from a pocket in my jacket.

I'd stolen the bottle from my father's liquor cabinet because I wanted to impress my friends. Mrs. Rich was the eighth grade math teacher at Corpus Christi and the mother of one of my classmates. Most of the graduates and some school staff attended the graduation party she and her husband hosted for their son.

As sick as I was, no one discovered me and I did not get into any trouble. It was the first time I was drunk, but not the last. It was, however, the only time ever I drank whiskey—my father's drink of choice.

In my mid-teens and early 20s, I muddled my way through high school and, fueled by alcohol, perpetuated the vicious cycle that growing up in a violent and abusive home had set in motion—the one in which a child learns to be violent and abusive to both self and others. This cycle leads to unhealthy coping skills (alcohol and drug abuse, belligerent behaviors, depression, anxiety). These states of consciousness then attract others of like mind and create communities that feed the cycle of abuse that starts within the self.

By the time I was a senior in high school, drinking on weekends was already a ritual—one that continued through college. Having completed all final exams just barely passing my freshman year of college, I chose to celebrate by embarking on an alcohol soaked rampage. This celebration ended with me waking up the next morning in a phone booth across the street from the 72 stone steps at the entrance to the Philadelphia Museum of Art.

Those steps are referred to as the 'Rocky Steps' because of their appearance in the film "Rocky." In that movie, the hero is training for a boxing match and runs up those steps to the song "Gonna Fly Now." The message is how hard it is to train before you can take off into something that feels like success. My ending up across from the 'Rocky Steps' was no coincidence; it led to my being banned from the right to live on campus for the remainder of my time at that college.

At that time in my life, a 12-step program would not have been enough for me; even 72 steps were not enough to save me from myself.

Sophomore year of college began for me on a bad foot—literally. Torn ligaments in my right ankle put me on the sidelines with a pair of crutches. I'd suffered the injury in a soccer game at the very beginning of the season, and the coach removed my name from the roster of active players. The injury deprived me of the one thing that had given me some balance throughout high school and freshman year. In fact, if it had not been for soccer I don't know if I would even have gone to college. Playing the game was how I coped, when I wasn't drinking alcohol. Losing the chance to play left a void within me. I had no way to express a large part of myself in a safe way. I had lost the chance to release my troubles in a physical way, and it led me into depression.

At the time, I did not understand depression—I didn't want to understand it. I could only marinate in it. Since then, I've read the words of Sherry Anshara, founder of the QuantumPathic Energy Method*, on the definition of depression: "An emotion that is the deepest disappointment in one's self." In her book, *A Glossary of QuantumPathic Terms*, she added: "...events leading to depression become particles of experience stored in the soul by the body," and that they "...may be changed and healed through energy. Drugs mask or minimize depression but only conscious energy can transform it by finding and igniting the ability within this disability."

At that time, 'energy healing' was still very much in the closet.

For the next several months, it took everything I had to get myself out of bed, hobble to class, get through the day, and hobble back to the rented room where I returned to bed and slept for up to 12 hours. I didn't have a term for it then, but I was depressed. It was something I attempted to manage on my own with alcohol and sleep. When I did come out of my depression, all I wanted to do was get away.

And that's just what I did.

After jumping through a series of hurdles, I was able to get a meeting with the school's academic dean. In the meeting, I talked my way into completing my junior year abroad. I convinced him of my desire to follow in my father's footsteps. I explained how going to Mexico to learn about international relations and experience a different culture would put me back on the right track.

So, at the age of 19, I found myself in Mexico City, where I experienced my first true love, first heartbreak, and lots of Mexican *pulque* and *mescal*—alcoholic distillations from the agave or maguey plant. One particular *mescal* fueled excursion culminated with Don Fortino, the owner of the home I rented in a village at the foot of Popocatépetl—an active volcano located in central Mexico—finding me passed out, face down, on a mound of gravel and rocks. I was living at the foot of this volcano because the young woman I fell in love with was studying social anthropology and had embarked on a six-month anthropological study of the people, forest, and fauna of the region. I took the class just to be near her but soon realized that my feelings for her were not reciprocated. I dealt with the rejection the only way I knew how—with alcohol.

Don Fortino told me he had been passing by on his way to the market and there I was—out cold. So he dismounted his mule, picked me up and laid me across the blanket he used as a saddle, and walked back to the house. There was a beautiful avocado tree outside the window of my room, and for the next two days I nursed a terrible hangover by eating its fruit.

Six months later, still suffering from a broken heart, I returned home and managed to finish my last two years of college to earn a degree in sociology. But I had no sense of purpose. Scrambling for something to do with my life, I made a plan to travel to California to share an apartment with two guys with whom I'd lifeguarded on the Jersey Shore during college summer breaks. We'd stayed in touch and had often talked about getting a place together.

Now they were living in a three-bedroom apartment in the beach town of Carlsbad, working as lifeguards. When I told my parents that I was going to move there, they were opposed to the idea. My father did not believe that lifeguarding constituted a job and felt that it was time I started "growing up." In his eyes, "growing up" meant entering the world of business, a world in which one could make a real living and raise a family.

He asked me to consider an internship with a cousin of his in Venezuela, and he sweetened the offer by bribing me with the promise of a monthly allowance and my own apartment. In my mind, that job was really a repayment to my father for the fact that when this cousin was 4 years old, he was orphaned due to the tragic deaths of his mother and father in an auto accident and my father's parents took him in and raised him as one of their own. At the age of 17 this cousin left my grandparents' home in Bolivia and headed north in search of his fortune. Settling in Venezuela, he worked his way up from the bottom at an import/export company that sold farming supplies. He became its president and was now a millionaire who owned and operated a couple of companies. My father wanted me to go to the one in Caracas.

My plans to head to California evaporated and I soon found myself in Caracas, marking time and being unwilling to learn about a business that was of no interest to me. Even though I was a couple thousand miles from home and on a different continent, I was right back to the same old behaviors—hanging out, drinking, and womanizing with the salesmen who worked for my father's cousin. In fact, the week I landed in Caracas, one of my cousins forced me to experience culture shock by driving me to the city and taking me to a brothel. Never having been in a brothel and not interested in supporting prostitution, I sat on the red velvet couch in the lobby and waited for him. The fact that I did not participate seemed odd to him, but it was a small moment of clarity for me. In that moment, I learned something true (and perhaps good) about myself.

On Fridays after work, my co-workers, the salesmen, took me to the baseball stadium. Baseball is a very popular pastime in Venezuela. On weekends, I traveled to various towns with different salesmen. Most of them had second families in the village towns, and they brought things like shoes for the "other" kids or a dress for wife number two. When the town was celebrating a saint's feast day, the trip activities involved a lot of eating and drinking.

Six months after my arrival in Caracas, I determined that the world of import/export was not for me. I quit and returned home to New Jersey. My father was not at all happy and it created a lot of tension between us—so much so that after a couple of weeks of living in simmering tension with him, I knew I was going to explode.

I packed my bags and flew to California.

My lifeguard buddies and some other friends picked me up at the airport. Everyone but the driver was high on magic mushrooms. Having just come from the parties in Venezuela, I found this welcome to California surreal.

A couple of days later, I went to the California Parks Department office to ask about the date of the required ocean swim test to get a job lifeguarding and learned that no test was scheduled in the foreseeable future. Needing a job, I set out in search of employment.

After two weeks of pounding the streets, the best job I was able to land was as a telemarketer selling pre-fabricated steel buildings. It didn't take long to once again do what I knew—the same thing I'd been doing in Venezuela and had done all the way through high school and college—hang out, get high, and drink alcohol.

Off course, adrift and lost, I was unable to find my way. The questions kept coming:

"What am I doing with my life?"

"Why am I so lost?"

"What do I want to do?"

"What do I want to be?"

"Who am I...really?"

Restless, feeling alone, and needing to feel a connection to someone, I called my friend Dorothy, who lived back east, near my mother. I asked her if she would be willing to fly out to visit and whether she was open to doing me a favor. After telling her that I would pay all expenses, I asked if she would visit my mother, pick up my bicycle, and bring it with her to California. She said she missed me, and the timing was great because her college spring break was soon. She arrived two weeks later with my bicycle in tow and we embarked on a mini-vacation, cruising the coast of sunny southern California in a pink Cadillac I borrowed from one of my housemates.

One evening on our way to catch the sunset at the shore, we spotted a small cave on a cliff overlooking the ocean. It was low tide and we were able to climb up the bluff and go into the cave. Snuggling up in a warm blanket, we watched as the sun set and a full moon rose. The moon was enormous, the sky's stars were brilliant, and the waves that brought in the high tide shimmered like translucent glass. It was a happy moment for me—one that helped confirm what I was about to do for myself—go home.

When our week together was over, Dorothy went back to art school.

It was time for me to embark on my first cross-country bicycle journey.

It was on the eleventh day of my trek that I crossed the mountains of New Mexico and a truck towing a horse trailer ran into me on my bicycle. The man who hit me was nice enough to drive my broken bike and me to a motel in Tucumcari. While I checked in, he left. I never learned his name.

On my own, I found a new rim for the damaged tire and had my knee treated. When I called my parents to tell them that I had suffered a minor accident but would get back on the road in a day, they told me that what I was doing was crazy and reckless. It was no great surprise that they were angry with me—their fear of me having an accident had come to pass. They asked me to leave the crazy idea behind and fly home; they offered an airplane ticket. I thanked them but declined. I wanted to make them understand that I had to do this for myself, that something in me needed to keep on going.

On the road again with a renewed sense of purpose and an ardent goal, (enhanced by having survived a frightening experience) I trekked forward. Through the Oklahoma panhandle into Kansas, I experienced strong head winds and had seven flat tires. One day the winds were so strong that I was standing up on the pedals, struggling to make each revolution, cursing at the top of my lungs, because no matter how hard I pedaled it felt as though I was standing still.

Late one afternoon, worn out by a week of battling the Kansas winds, I came upon an empty Methodist church. I went inside, called out and found no one around, so I gathered the bike and all my gear and went into what seemed to be a children's playroom. Closing the door, I placed my bike against the wall, laid my sleeping bag out over the rubber mat map pieces that outlined the 50 states and slept. I stayed there for two days. Not a soul bothered me. After resting, my legs no longer felt tired.

I crossed into Missouri and on one of my stops there, I met a man sitting by the side of the road playing his guitar. He was singing songs he'd written about people on bicycles who had ridden through the area and crossed his path. His guitar case was open and some bills were resting inside. I threw in a couple of dollars and took his card. When I was leaving he told me that he would write a song about our meeting. I'm not sure if he did, but I now wish I'd told him I'd one day write this book.

On a very hot day in Illinois, I ran out of water and made my way over a gravel road toward a small house next to a red barn. The lady who answered the door allowed me to fill up my water bottles from her tap. After learning about how far I had come and what I was doing, she invited me into her kitchen and made me a delicious breakfast of bacon and eggs with a glass of milk fresh from the cow on her farm.

Twenty-one hundred miles behind me, but with the Appalachian Mountains yet to cross, I arrived in Hazard, Kentucky, on Easter Sunday with thoughts of quitting on my mind. The roads were terrible. I was in the middle of coal country and the coal mining trucks that rumbled by made no attempt to give me a wide berth.

I stopped at a roadside diner with a plan to have a breakfast of bacon and eggs, grits, and corn muffins smothered in gravy, and then call my parents to accept their offer of an airplane ticket that would get me back home. I locked my bike and went inside.

Sometimes the universe, or maybe God, has a strange way of altering plans.

As I was eating, a man and woman entered the diner. They sat at the table next to me. After wishing me a Happy Easter, they asked questions.

"Is that your bicycle outside?"

"What are you doing in Hazard…and on a bicycle?"

"How far did you ride?"

"Where are you going?"

Then, the questions became statements.

"What you're doing is admirable. It's something not many people are able to accomplish."

"Riding across the country alone on a bicycle requires strength and courage. It requires faith."

When their food arrived, they asked me if I would pray with them. I said yes, and after they gave thanks for the food they were about to eat, they asked Jesus to watch over me during my journey.

I thanked them and shared that on the road there is not much for one to do but pedal, think, and talk to God. Throughout the ride, I felt God had been with me and I asked Him lots of questions—questions for which I had no answers.

As they listened to the parts of my story that created my questions, the sun that had been in and out all morning disappeared, the clouds opened up, and it began to rain. This couple told me that it was dangerous to bicycle on the local roads, even without rain, and it didn't look like it was going to be stopping anytime soon. They offered me a place to stay for the night. They also gave me an invitation to join them and the people at their home for Easter dinner, a chance to sit near a warm fire, and share my story with people they knew who had experienced some of the very same things that had created the questions I was grappling with.

At dinner later that evening, I marveled at the generosity of spirit emanating from the couple. Five women and seven children were present; this couple had created a safe haven for them—the couple had converted their home into a shelter for battered, abused women and their children.

Later that night, after having unfolded my sleeping bag near the crackling fire in the fireplace, I got on my knees and prayed that this couple and the women and children they sheltered be kept safe, and I asked God to give me the strength to continue. I believe God answered those prayers as I kept cycling onward.

Leaving Kentucky, I struggled through Virginia and Maryland. I found some relief while pedaling up and coasting down the rolling hills of Pennsylvania. Once I reached the New Jersey border, I felt a sense of inner satisfaction and accomplishment that only exists within my heart. I have no words to describe it with accuracy.

Overcome by the excitement of being so close to home, I snuck onto the New Jersey parkway at exit seven and made it to exit nine before the state police stopped and escorted me off with a reprimand. I can still remember the feeling of euphoria I felt as I rode the last 30 to 40 miles.

Turning onto the street where my family lived, I spotted my father. He was mowing the lawn. Thirty-eight days after departing from Carlsbad and about 3,200 miles later, I'd arrived home. I pulled into the driveway, leaned my bike against the garage, and walked over to my father. With smiles on our faces we exchanged a warm bear hug and went inside where the rest of my family was awaiting my return.

A week or two after I got home from this cross-country bicycle trip, a reporter from the local newspaper contacted me. He asked for an interview and came over to the house. The story he wrote appeared in print on Thursday May 14, 1981. I said, "I feel closer to God than when I began the trip."

Reading that quote today, I am mindful that I had no idea then what I was saying. I wasn't ready to grasp that *feeling* is not quite the same as *action*. Action comes after feeling; feeling provides intent to take action. But the trip I'd made did plant a seed for knowing how to turn feeling into action. My cross-country trip on two wheels facilitated and shaped the new questions I needed to ask myself. I think of the quote by Rilke: "Perhaps, someday far in the future, you will gradually, without even noticing it, live your way into the answer."

The trip galvanized and energized my soul. That energy converted itself into motivation and resolve. After I'd rested, I felt a need to put order in my life and knew it was time for me to move out, get my own apartment, and pay for my own place to live. I needed a job that had some kind of future, so I started making calls and pounding the pavement. The sociology degree I had earned from Saint Joseph's University in Philadelphia was instrumental in helping me get a job as a caseworker with a children's service agency in Staten Island, New York.

That job allowed me to move out of my parents' house, but it only lasted a year because I was ill-prepared for the suffering I witnessed in that line of work. I burned out. I didn't know how to separate myself from those I met who needed so much relief from their suffering. For example, rather than place a teenage girl in what I knew to be an abusive group home, I took her to my parents' house to stay while I searched for a better placement for her. It was not a good idea, and one that could have created a lot of problems for me. I was fortunate that in the chaos of that job, the act went unnoticed.

Shortly after that incident, I went on a job search to look for a placement that would be less draining on my emotions and also offered better pay. I landed a job as a counselor at an inpatient alcohol detox center in Secaucus, New Jersey. My job was to assist patients as they transitioned from the seven-day detox program into a long-term treatment center. I was successful and, as a result, the Jersey City Medical Center, one of the centers to which I referred clients, hired me to work in their alcohol inpatient care facility. That job eventually led to a job at Harbor House in Paterson, New Jersey, in a program for people struggling with mental illness.

A few years after the first bicycle trip, my family welcomed a new member. My mother, at age 48, became pregnant with a son, my fourth sibling. Things seemed to be going well between my parents at the time. My father agreed to have my grandmother Raquel come to live with them so that my mom could go back to work as a high school teacher.

Shortly after my brother's first birthday, I decided to leave my job to enroll in naval officer candidate school in Rhode Island. I did this because of my sense of dissatisfaction in my job, coupled with a yearning for adventure that I'd seen in the movie "An Officer and a Gentleman." In that movie, Richard Gere played a troubled young man who found himself by enrolling in the Navy and attending flight school to become a pilot. I identified with the dysfunctional character Gere played and was excited by the adventure that joining the military seemed to offer.

My experience was not as romantic as Gere's. A year after having joined, I found myself on a pay phone as all those around me celebrated graduation from the officer candidate school. I was calling home, in tears, to tell my parents that I had decided to drop out. I had not performed well on the academic training and I was drinking so much that the choice I was given was to either take an honorable discharge or repeat the program after agreeing to take an anti-alcohol drug regimen and enter a six-week rehab.

My mother answered that call. She said, "How could you do this to me?"

It turned out that my father abhorred the fact that I had joined the military and blamed my mother for my doing so. My father took the phone and said, "Don't worry, son. Come home and we'll work it out."

Once again I returned to my parents' house. This time I was living in the home with my father, mother, grandmother, little brother, sister, and aunt Carmen Rosa who had just moved in to share a room with my grandmother.

Although I was able to return to my job at Harbor House, I had not saved enough to find an apartment. In a short time, the stress and tension of all of us sharing a common space brought an end to the grace we'd celebrated after my little brother's birth.

My little brother turned 3. At the same time, after 28 years of marriage, my mother decided to leave my father.

This time it was for good.

Even though she had left him a number of times during my own childhood, my father had always been able to beg her forgiveness and win her back. But this time it was different. The birth of my brother and the support of her mother and sister had given her the strength to finally leave my father. Even though he had not physically abused her for many years, the emotional and verbal abuse had continued. My mother did not want my little brother to experience what the rest of us had experienced with my father.

My father stayed behind in the house, even though my mother used her inheritance money to purchase it. My mother moved into a two-bedroom railroad apartment near the Metuchen train station. My grandmother, aunt Carmen Rosa, my sister (in college but not away), and our little brother went with her. My other brother was away at college.

I stayed in the house with my father.

The separation and impending divorce altered my life. As the oldest, I felt I'd failed to fulfill my responsibility to look out for my mother's best interest. It was also a matter of principle. I had a deep belief that the house she'd moved out of rightly belonged to my mother.

So, soon after my mother's departure I let my father know that he was not going to be able to take the house away from my mom. I said I would stay in the house as long as it took for him to do the right thing; to move out and let her move back in. My philosophy created a deep animosity. For the next six months, my father and I lived in the large four-bedroom house while barely speaking to one other.

But we did engage with each other on three separate occasions.

The first occurred one autumn day when I came home from work and was surprised to see his car in the garage. The sound of the TV blaring from his room caused me to call out to him. Hearing no response, I made my way upstairs to find his door slightly ajar. Looking through a crack in the door I saw him sitting on a couch in an unbuttoned dress shirt and underwear, glass of scotch in hand, staring up at the ceiling.

I pushed the door open and stood in the doorway. He didn't move and continued to stare at the ceiling. "Are you OK?" I asked.

He took a sip of scotch. After a very long pause, he said, "My father is dead."

My father never shared much regarding his childhood. I don't think that many men of his generation and culture did. Now I know that he had the same kinds of experiences with his father that I'd had as his son. Being the oldest, he'd inherited the role of being his mother's shield.

The only thing I could think to say was, "I'm sorry to hear that." The silence that followed made me uncomfortable and I stepped back, closed the door, and went back downstairs.

The second significant interaction happened early the next year. On the morning of my 26th birthday, I came out of my bedroom and, on my way to the bathroom, I saw him in the kitchen getting ready to leave for work. Seeing me, he put the cup he was carrying down on the table and said, "Happy birthday." Our family ritual consisted of starting all birthday mornings by sitting down together, sharing a birthday cake, singing happy birthday in English and Spanish, and then lighting and blowing out the cake's candles.

I acknowledged him with a nod and continued into the bathroom, where I stayed until I heard the garage door close and his car leave the driveway. I decided to go up the stairs into the kitchen. On the kitchen table he had placed a birthday cake.

And then, one day that summer, the third event happened. Our silent interaction changed forever.

It was a beautiful sunny morning. My friend Gary and I were on the streets of Edison, New Jersey, doing one of our weekly 20-mile training runs. After the cross-country bike ride, I had gotten into triathlons, a distance and endurance sport that requires one to swim, bike, and run. We'd set off sometime around nine, before it got too muggy, and finished just before noon. Gary suggested that we get a bite to eat, and we found ourselves sitting at a neighborhood burger joint.

After lunch, Gary invited me to his house. We sat in the back yard, resting our tired bodies and working on a six-pack of beer. Later that afternoon, he drove me home. I walked across the front lawn carrying my sneakers in one hand and a partially finished beer in the other. I finished the beer and threw the can in the bushes.

Inside, my father lay passed out on the living room couch in a t-shirt and boxers. There was a half empty bottle of Johnny Walker Red on the carpet next to him on strewn sheets of the daily newspaper. I walked over to a love seat across from him and sat down. It felt so good to sit in that love seat and rest, but my mind was not at rest. The longer I sat there, the more my mind raced, and that "Why?" question appeared yet again.

"Why were we not able to talk about our feelings?"

"Why did we have so much hatred in us?"

"Why did we hurt each other so?"

"Why?"

I don't know how long I sat there, but at some point I decided to wake him. I was wanting, needing, answers because I couldn't carry the questions on my own anymore. I nudged him. I had to nudge him a couple of times before he stirred.

He sat up and attempted to get his bearings. I waited for what seemed an eternity before I announced that I wanted to talk to him. He looked at me for the longest time and then said, "I have nothing to talk to you about, *hijo de puta, infeliz*."

From that point on, everything unraveled in slow motion. I stood up and told him that he was never going to talk to me like that ever again and that he was never going to speak to me, my mother, or any of us that way again!

By this time he had gotten to his feet. I knew he was sensing my rage. As he was making his way up the steps that led to the second floor landing, he screamed, "Get out of my house or I'll call the police!"

"This is not your house! This is my mother's house!" I screamed back.

My rage had shifted to laughter. Watching him standing there in his underwear I yelled, "Go ahead and call the police. They won't help you."

I walked toward him. He ran up the steps to his bedroom. Rather than follow, I went into the kitchen and searched for a knife. I found one—the right one—and made my way up the stairs to his room.

He had locked his bedroom door. I kicked it down. He was on the phone, dialing the police. A look of fright and panic greeted me as he held the phone receiver. I made my way over to him. A struggle ensued. I ripped the phone out of his hand. I grabbed him by the hair and jacked him up against the headboard with one hand as I placed the knife to his throat with the other.

The moment the blade reached his throat he went limp in my hands.

I thought he looked like Gumby, the animated clay character I used to watch on TV as a child. Leaning into him while holding the knife to his throat, I began to cry. Then I repeated the following questions over and over:

"Why couldn't you love me?"

"Why couldn't you love me?"

"Why couldn't you just love me?"

A plea, truth, and desire all combined into one long bottled up wail of pain that spanned years of time and many memories.

Letting go of my father's hair, I stepped back and dropped the knife.

I stood there weeping, feeling utterly lost and abandoned.

In these moments, time stops.

Through my tears, I observed my father's immobile body slumped against the headboard.

I remember it now with wonder, realizing that the man whom I feared most in life was as lost and broken as I was.

It was in this moment—my darkest moment—that a ray of sunlight appeared through the window. It illuminated and enveloped me. Standing there, embraced in its warmth, I became mindful of a *greater* love.

CHAPTER 3

Breaking Down,
Acting Out, Growing Up
and Teaching In

*We found that such adverse childhood experiences
are quite common although typically concealed
and unrecognized; that they still have a profound
effect a half century later, although now transmutated
from psychosocial experience into organic disease;
and that they are the main determinant of the health
and social well-being of the nation.*

~ **VINCENT J. FELITTI, M.D.** ~

It was *greater* love that allowed me to walk downstairs, go to the kitchen phone, and call my mother. She picked up the line. When I heard her say "Hello," the emotion I was trying to contain overwhelmed me.

I couldn't talk. She somehow knew. She asked me to come to her house.

I don't remember the drive over but, when I got there, my mother, sister, grandmother and aunt all did their best to console me. My 6-year-old brother watched. I could see concern on his face. After I'd calmed down, I told them what had happened.

My mother wanted every detail. She wanted to know if my father acted afraid, if he'd cowered, if he'd expressed his fear. "Did he plead for his life?" she asked. She seemed to think that I'd conquered him.

Repeating the experience for her made me feel further deserted and abandoned. That awareness led me to the conclusion that my mother, also, was incapable of loving me.

Days later, I sat alone in a nearly empty apartment. I had a few books on a shelf, and as I scanned the titles I saw that the spine of M. Scott Peck's *The Road Less Traveled* was not in alignment with the other books—it was sticking out as if to get my attention. Having nothing better to do, I opened it and read. In the chapter titled "Love Defined," I came across a line that has stayed with me to this day: "...we are incapable of loving another unless we love ourselves."

In 1982, soon after the incident with my father, I left New Jersey and moved to New York City. I got a job as a caseworker at a homeless shelter across from the Port Authority on 42nd street and rented a room with a bed, a sink, and a toilet in Alphabet City on the lower east side. I also wanted to explore acting, so I went through the trade publications and found an acting teacher who'd left the "Neighborhood Playhouse School of the Theatre" and set up his own acting studio.

What was it that inspired my desire to become an actor? It was a memory from 1983. My father had taken my family and me to the Booth Theater on Broadway for my sister's 23rd birthday. We saw David Mamet's "American Buffalo," in which Al Pacino starred as Teach. I was riveted—mesmerized, even—by the intensity on that stage during the play.

Afterwards, I made my parents wait for over an hour just so I could get Al Pacino's signature on my playbill. I was so naïve that I thought I would get to talk to Pacino. Instead, an usher came through the backstage doors where we'd been told to line up. He took our playbills and went back inside. A short while later, the doors flew open and Al Pacino exited and jumped into a waiting black Chevy Blazer, only to disappear into the night. The usher returned the signed playbills to us.

Playbill in hand, many questions left unanswered, I happened to spot James Hayden—the actor who had played the part of Bobby. I walked over and engaged him in a conversation. I asked him to sign my playbill and, as he did, I asked where one might go to learn to do what he did. Hayden pointed up to the sky and said, "This is it."

I looked up and saw only sky.

"New York!" he said. "Get the trade paper called *Back Stage*. Good teachers advertise there. Find one and study."

The next day my mother handed me the newspaper and told me that the actor I had talked to was dead. I remember taking the paper, his picture staring back at me. The caption explained that only hours after receiving a standing ovation for his performance as a junkie, James Hayden had been found dead of a heroin overdose.

So there I was, in New York, studying with Greg Zittel and learning the Meisner Acting Technique. Shortly after completing the two-year program, a core group of students from his classes came together and formed an acting company. Hearing about our endeavor, he decided to join us.

After we'd mounted our first set of plays, egos, creative differences got in the way and we parted company. The breakup was not pleasant, but by then I'd formed a bond with another member of the company, Nora.

My relationship with Nora blossomed into love. Within six months of meeting, we were married in a small Catholic church in Little Italy on October 20, 1990. My brother David was the best man; my little brother played the saxophone; my mother, grandmother, sister, and aunt Carmen cried when I said, "I do."

My father was not in attendance. He and my mother could not be in the same room.

Following the wedding, Nora and I lived in Hell's Kitchen and worked subsistence jobs, pursued acting jobs, put up plays with our theater company, and threw ourselves into the craft of acting. Eventually, after many, many auditions I got a break and landed an off-Broadway part in Eric Overmyer's "Native Speech." The part led me to sign with what was then the Don Buchwald Agency. The agent convinced me to make the move to Los Angeles to audition for film and television roles.

My wife and I packed our bags, rented a trailer, and, with all our possessions and her cat in tow, we drove west, arriving in California on New Year's Eve 1992. We stayed with friends while we looked for a place; they arranged to get us tickets to celebrate the holiday at the Dorothy Chandler Pavilion.

Low on funds, we had not eaten much that day and expected a meal to come with each $50.00 ticket, but it was only a cocktail party. Nora nearly fainted from hunger, so we left right after midnight and made our way to a burger joint in Hollywood. This black tie to burgers evening foreshadowed our next few years together.

Nora supported us with her job as a personal secretary while I pursued film and television work. I went to a lot of auditions and landed jobs here and there but never found real success. The situation taxed our marriage on emotional and financial levels. Between acting jobs I worked as a substitute teacher and enjoyed the experience. My training as an actor made it easy for me to connect with the kids. Sometimes, the connections were memorable.

Miguel was a boy I met during a two-week stint at First Street School in East Los Angeles. He was only nine years old. Three weeks before my arrival, there had been a drive-by shooting in the area.

On the final day of my substitute teaching assignment, as I was leaving the classroom to go home, I noticed Miguel following me. I stopped to speak with him. "What's up, buddy?"

"You going home?"

"Yes, I am."

"You coming back?"

The teacher I'd substituted for had not left any lesson plans, so I had made my own during those two weeks. *Dia de los Muertos* came up after the first week and I'd asked them do a creative writing assignment about it. Miguel's story involved his love for his sister. She was his best friend, always there for him. When he found himself sitting alone at home, perched at the top of the stairs with no one to play with, she would come along and make everything better. His essay described an interaction that happens everyday in neighborhoods all over the country, but Miguel lived in East Los Angeles. His neighborhood was at the intersection of poverty and violence and his essay referenced the drive-by shooting. Two rival gangs had unleashed warfare near the school's playground during a recess. One of the stray bullets struck and killed Miguel's sister.

The class read their stories aloud. When Miguel read his, the children laughed—out of nervousness, not cruelty.

That afternoon, I asked Miguel to stay after class so that we could have a talk. "Do you miss your sister?" I asked.

"Yeah, but sometimes she comes and plays with me."

"Do you have fun?"

"Yeah. She likes to play with her dolls, but that's OK."

I shared with Miguel that I missed my brothers and sister because they lived far away. I told him that he'd written a sad but beautiful tribute to his sister.

When I reached the parking lot on that last day of substitute work, Miguel was still behind me. I went through the metal gate to get into my car. He stood behind the gate, staring at me, his face pressed against the bars.

I lowered my window and said, "Goodbye, little buddy. You take care of yourself, OK?"

"OK," he said.

Out of the parking lot, going up the street, I turned left at the stop sign and drove to the front of the school. I had to stop at a red light. As I waited for the light to change, I saw Miguel standing at the front entrance, still waving goodbye. He had run from the back parking lot to the front of the school—at least three city blocks—and stood there waving at me.

That experience taught me that I could make a difference in the life of a child—in comparison to the events of my own childhood, where few people had gone out of their way to show me some attention and respect.

Miguel, wherever you are now, thanks.

Seven years into our marriage, Nora told me that she felt secure enough to have our child. After that revelation, I took a long-term substitute teaching job at Westminster Avenue Elementary School in Venice, California for a teacher on maternity leave. It became a full time job because the teacher, Risa Okin, decided to stay home with her baby and the principal, Betty Coleman, offered me the job. Westminster Avenue Elementary School became my second home and, a couple of years after I started teaching there, the teachers and Ms. Coleman hosted a baby shower for Nora and me.

Our baby was born on January 5, 1998. The birth filled my heart with a kind of love that up to then I had never known—an all-encompassing, unconditional love. I watched as Nora endured a Cesarean section. When the baby's head became visible I yelled, "It's a boy!"

Everyone laughed because there was no way of knowing that yet.

Then the doctor said, "Congratulations, you have a little girl!" Tears of joy streamed down my face as I kissed Nora and made my way over to wipe off my daughter.

The nurse who let me take over smiled and said, "You don't have to be so gentle! You're not going to break her!"

Knowing what I know now, gentleness *is* a necessary aspect of all parenting. Children may not "break" but they can be "broken" in ways that are not always visible.

For the next eight years, my daughter and I bonded around my teaching schedule. In those days, I woke early, wrote in a journal, got ready to step into the role of a teacher, stopped at my favorite coffee shop, then made my way to class. By four in the afternoon, I'd walk with tiny Emma along the shore of the Pacific Ocean and let the soothing sounds of crashing waves resonate in our ears. When she got older, I'd put her in a trailer attached to my bike to go for rides of various lengths along The Strand—a bicycle path that starts at Will Rogers State Beach and ends 40 miles later in Torrance.

As I was raising my daughter, I was also 'raising' my students. I found it ironic that many of my students lived mere blocks from the beach, but their parents never had the time nor means to take them. So, every Friday I took my first grade students on a walk to the Venice public library where the children's librarian, Rachel, read them stories and helped them select books for the week. After library time, we'd stop at the farmers' market. The beach, library, and Venice's canal neighborhoods provided great adventures and learning opportunities outside of class.

I'd watched as wide-eyed boys and girls ambled among families of ducks, walked behind gaggles of suspicious geese, and I heard the kids screech whenever they caught a sight of the wingspan of an egret. We'd all stop in the center of a wooden bridge over a canal to peer at minnows. The walk back to school was on the Venice Ocean Front Walk, a two-and-a- half-mile, pedestrian-only promenade that features performers, fortune-tellers, artists, and vendors. For many of my students over the years, the Venice boardwalk was the place where their parents worked. It's an important cultural center in the city of Los Angeles—and people whose median incomes hover near poverty levels are its backbone.

In early 2006, Nora and I separated. We agreed to share custody of Emma every other week.

My marriage fell apart for a number of reasons, but I now understand that I lacked the tools to build a strong foundation for the family I'd created. Building a healthy marriage is like building a house—if it has a solid foundation, the structure will last through all kinds of weather. It will endure repairs, updates, and remodels, and it will do a good job of providing shelter for its occupants over the course of generations.

If I had seen what a good marriage relationship looked like, I would not have repeated the same cycle of violence I inherited from my parents. If I'd come from a nurturing, loving environment, I would have become a nurturing, loving, man, husband, and father.

Somehow, I knew this instinctively, even when I was a child, but I did not have the tools, ability or words to help others see this truth.

I was a broken man when I married Nora. My brokenness led to our broken union. I never physically abused my wife because of what I witnessed as a child, but I was verbally and emotionally abusive, and that is just as bad—if not worse. It was Maya Angelou who said, "People will forget what you said. People will forget what you did. But people will never forget how you made them feel."

To cope with my disappointment over the dissolution of my marriage, I worked hard over the next five years to be a good teacher. It was my identity in the hours when Emma was away. My classroom was a safe haven for me, a place of refuge. When fellow teachers asked me to become a union representative, I did. One aspect of the job was ensuring that all teachers had a voice and received due process. Another was navigating the advent of charter schools and their co-location within the public schools that were suffering from declining enrollments. With the help of my fellow teachers, I was able to keep a charter from taking over the public school where we worked.

In addition to my role as a teachers' union representative, I helped found the Westminster Avenue Elementary School Endowment. This was a not-for-profit entity that focused on strengthening ties between parents and the community at large. I served as the endowment's president for several years.

In 2010, I received a nomination, as one of the top 20 percent of the faculty at my school, to become a fellow with the Cotsen Foundation. I went through a rigorous screening and selection process, taught a complete lesson under observation by several other educators from outside the school district, and gave an interview. Once selected, I was given support in learning what the Cotsen Foundation identified as "the art of teaching," and encouragement to immerse myself in an area I wanted to develop and master as a teacher. I chose writing. It paid off in my classroom—my students and I celebrated their written work.

In the fall of 2011, after six weeks of hard and enthusiastic work, my fourth grade students read their poems, stories, or essays before a classroom filled with their parents, the principal, and myself. Student David Martinez recited his poem titled "Hope." Here it is:

> *Hope is something you always want to have in your life.*
> *It's something you want to pass generation to generation.*
> *Hope is good fortune.*
> *Hope is good luck.*
> *Hope is something everyone wants.*
> *It's something that very little people get to have.*
> *Hope, oh, hope, oh you're lucky to have hope.*

The room broke into applause. David walked over to me and shook my hand. He received the same kind of framed plaque I'd made for the other students. This quote from the famous poet, Rainer Maria Rilke, was on the plaque: "Find out the reason that commands you to write; see whether it has spread its roots into the very depth of your heart; confess to yourself you would have to die if you were forbidden to write."

Later that afternoon, I walked into the weekly teacher staff meeting and was confronted by the principal, who told to me to call child protective services and file a child abuse report. Her directive came from another reading that one of my students shared in the classroom event earlier that morning.

Teaching students to write was a joy, and feeling supported in my work was a privilege. Yet when the topic of child abuse came up in my classroom and challenged my responsibility as a teacher, I was unprepared for the way it became a political issue.

The incident that led to my removal from my fourth grade classroom and remanded me to teacher jail involved a student whom I'd taught when she was in first grade, three years earlier. It was clear to me back then that this student had special needs issues, but I was not successful in getting a proper assessment of her abilities and qualifications. By the time she came into my classroom again, with the consent of her parents, I got her classified and supported as a special needs student.

At the writing presentation, when this student read her essay, it made the principal suspect that abuse was going on in her home. The principal asked me to file a report, but based on my gut feeling and knowledge of the family over several years, I did not follow orders. When the principal discovered that I did not make the report, she herself did. After a prolonged investigation, the principal's allegations proved false, and the matter closed after a couple of years.

But I was not innocent until proven guilty.

I suffered consequences when accused of failing to report a suspicion of child abuse, then endured several months of process (write-ups, responses, meetings, back-and-forth paperwork). After traveling to Sacramento to endure a humiliating questioning and review process in front of about 15 to 20 administrative personnel, I received a six-month suspension for failure to file a report. I held on to my teaching credential but could no longer be a teacher. The system sent me to "teacher jail."

I found myself sitting in a partially enclosed cubicle, separated from other teachers by a tall partition. The space where I sat isolated me from the sights and noises of the 25 or so other teacher inmates who also sat in their own cubicles.

We signed in each morning and sat there until the school day ended. These were teachers like me, taken from their classrooms and in teacher jail for a variety of offenses. They read, listened to music, watched movies on smartphones, texted, played Scrabble on Facebook, knitted, wrote, meditated, slept—all while waiting for their cases to be addressed. A couple of the teachers had been in this jail for over two years.

I was fortunate because I asked for and received a year's leave to work for an education reform organization instead of staying in teacher jail. But that job would not start for a month and a half, so for six weeks, every weekday morning, I was required to show up in District 3 on the west side of Los Angeles to "do time."

My experience in teacher jail reinforced for me how broken the public education systems are and the ways in which they serve to traumatize both teachers and students. Teacher jail re-traumatized me. It was painful—it triggered in me the powerlessness I felt when I was a child in a home where domestic violence occurred.

Think about it: I was kicked out of the classroom and removed from the students I loved to teach! It was my career, my world. I had to take my things and report to a holding center until further notice. Charges against me were alleged. I had to sit there, Monday through Friday, waiting for the process to unfold. Hearings were held, appeals were made; then more hearings, more appeals. The process went on and on. Each and every day was the same as the next.

Report and sign in.

Go to my assigned cubicle.

Take my scheduled, union-contracted recess and lunch breaks.

Do my time.

Miss my students.

Wonder who was minding them.

Having time on my hands, I decided to interview teacher-prisoners who were willing to talk with me. A physical education teacher I sat next to had been there for over nine months. She told me that she was somewhat content to sit there and do time because she was set to retire at the end of the year. She had been a teacher for 29 years and spoke of the changes she'd observed, telling me "These kids now a days, they have no respect. Things aren't like when I started."

She got emotional because having to be in teacher jail made her feel ashamed. "The only people who know are my husband and my kids. I can't tell anyone. It's so incredibly embarrassing because people automatically make assumptions. We are all in here for different reasons, various reasons, but when people hear you are in teacher jail they automatically think you're a pedophile. All I did was stop a girl from coming into the gym after class had started. She was over 15 minutes late and wanted to go to her locker. When I stopped her she tried to push past me, so I blocked her way, and when she pushed I protected myself and pushed her back."

Neither person was physically injured, but the incident rose to the level of punishment for the teacher while the student remained in school. The problem between this teacher and student is common in classrooms and schools everywhere. It is one thing to move away from "zero tolerance" to "compassion in the face of injustice," but a lack of understanding about the need for compassion and its correct application leads to implementing poorly vetted policies and programs that have an inappropriate and long-lasting impact on everyone involved. Teachers and students need effective tools for conflict resolution. The current system of firing a teacher is more cost effective than properly training and supporting them. If more schools and teachers were trauma informed, restorative justice programs could take hold and create better learning environments everywhere.

Another teacher who'd been in the jail for 10 months told me that his investigation had ended and he was to go back to school. He called the principal of the school to inform him of his return, wanting to let him know, and asking him if there was anything he needed to do. The principal said, "I know what you did and you know what you did, and I don't want you back here."

This teacher choked up as he said, "I'm not going to lie. It's been hard. I'm the sole breadwinner. My wife is permanently disabled and my kids are still in college. I've had some moments that I thought they would be better off without me. I've thought about it, I won't lie— thought about killing myself. I feel for everybody here. I'm happy to be getting out, but I feel bad for everybody in here."

While teacher jail may seem like an injustice, many of the teachers who find themselves there may not belong in a classroom with children. Perhaps their skills and demeanor would be better in some other occupation. So how did they get into teaching in the first place?

It's one of the questions I asked myself when in teacher jail.

How did I get to be a teacher?

Did the traumas I suffered in childhood and in my early adult years affect my ability to teach and to make decisions such as the one I made that locked me away?

How many other teachers suffer the effects of ACEs?

How many teachers are seeking to experience healing from the effects of ACEs they suffered?

I also came up with so many other questions about the education system:

How might institutions charged with the welfare of children and their education find a more reasonable method of managing inappropriate behaviors?

Is it a good idea to have teacher jails?

How might administrators better measure the culture, the workplace, and classroom climates in schools to make sure all systems and structures are running in a positive, efficient way?

If school systems are in the business of education, how much prevention, intervention and punishment are also part of this culture?

The education system is supposed to support humanity in positive ways, yet I experienced how it's possible to re-traumatize both teachers and students. It was during my stint in teacher jail that I had time to think about this—and also to see examples of it in others.

I believe that if you learn to "live everything now," as Rainer Maria Rilke advised, there are no coincidences. A couple of weeks into being in teacher jail, I crossed paths with two former students, now young men. After not having seen them in years, I saw both in the same week.

The first encounter took place at Bay Cities Italian Deli in Santa Monica. I walked in, picked a number, and waited for service. The place was always packed. After a while, I heard "Number 95." Before I placed my order I heard the same voice say, "Mr. Encinas?"

"Excuse me?"

"Mr. E! You don't remember me. I'm Edwin. Edwin Jimenez. You were my teacher in third grade!"

I was shocked. This was unexpected. Edwin left the counter to go into the kitchen area. He came back with his father and the three of us made a plan to meet for coffee the next afternoon at an outdoor patio at the Santa Monica Main Library.

Edwin's Story

Edwin met me with his father, mother, and brother, Jonathan, who is a year older than Edwin and was also one of my third grade students. Edwin told me about an incident that occurred during his senior year, which involved his high school counselor at Hamilton High School: "I would ask him," Edwin said, "'Mr. N., can you help me? Can you tell me what I got to do to graduate?' His answer was always, 'Listen, just do your best and you'll be fine.' Mr. N. said that every year—he told me that through 10th and 11th and 12th grade.

"At the end of 11th grade I told my mom, 'Mom, I just need two more classes to finish and I'm done. I can graduate.' Over the summer, I called Mr. N. and said, 'So, I'm graduating next year, right?' He says, 'Oh, no. You need 20 extra credits.' I was so mad! You know, he waits to tell me senior year that you have so many credits. I could have done some over the summer! I was ready to give up, but I promised my mother I was going to graduate!

"So I went to him halfway through senior year, having finished ten credits. I said, 'Tell me what do I have to take to finish?' He asks me, 'Why do you come to me after school? Why don't you come during school?' I say, 'Because you never have time to see me during school!' While I'm standing there the phone rings and he looks at me and looks at the phone. He picks up the phone.

"I got so mad I just literally blacked out. I walked out. My ex-girlfriend was there. She saw me hit the wall six times.

"Mr. N walks out and says, 'What you doing?' I just looked at him.

"So, all those extra credits I needed, I made them up myself. I was taking all the classes I messed up in my first two years. The only time I ever felt relieved that I was going to graduate was when they told me that I was going to graduate, but even then I was worried that they'd tell me 'oh no you messed up five more credits so you can't graduate.' Not even until I got my cap and gown did I believe I was going to graduate."

When Edwin finished, Jonathan spoke. "This is how I see it," he said. "Most teachers don't really care about their students. They just go in and teach what they got to teach. They see you as another kid. Some teachers like you and oh, yeah, my last teacher at the skill center cared that I learned, cared that I graduated. Mr. Encinas, you saw us like, 'These kids have potential—if someone shows them how to do it they can come out on top.'

"I still remember a story you told when I was in third grade. You told us one day that in the morning on the way to school you had seen one of your students and he made a sign to you like 'Do you want to buy drugs?' and how you were disappointed about it. That's one of the reasons I remember that story, and I was like 'I don't want be that guy selling drugs to one of my teachers.' I would probably feel like I let you down. I remember every time I would think about doing something like that, selling, or something like that, I would think about that story you told us."

My second encounter with a former student came about on Friday of that same week. After swim team practice one evening, my then 12-year-old daughter and I decided to get a bite to eat at a new restaurant that had just opened a couple of blocks from Westminster Avenue Elementary. After the waiter took our order, a young man in a chef's outfit walked out of the kitchen, came to our table and asked, "What you doing here, Mr. E.?"

It was Giovanni, a student from one of my fifth grade classes, now in his early 20s. I'd watched him grow up in the neighborhood—me on my bike and him on his skateboard. "Gio, are you staying out of trouble?" I'd ask. "Gio, you doing well in school?"

He told me that he had a 3-year-old daughter; he and his wife had separated. I invited him to bring his daughter to my house for brunch the next Sunday.

Giovanni's Story

Giovanni grew up in the Fairfax area and lived there until his father got sick and his mom had to be the breadwinner. "She got a job in Venice on the boardwalk selling stuff, but she had to take three buses to get there from Fairfax. After she made us food for the day and we got dressed, a lady from the apartment complex we lived in came over to watch my little brothers, Niko and Saul. My older brother Rickie and I would walk with Mikey to school. On weekends we stayed alone because my father was hospitalized and our mom worked weekends. She'd lock the door behind her and we'd watch television all day. Sometimes she didn't get home till nine at night."

Before his father died of AIDS, Giovanni's mother took her boys to see him in the hospital. "When the neighbors found out he had AIDs, they put paper bags of dog shit on our front door. We eventually had to leave because they wouldn't stop, they made us leave 'cause they, I don't know, they maybe thought we would give AIDS to them. That's how we ended up in Venice. We lived in Venice in a homeless shelter for a while, and that's when I got into your class."

The stories of Edwin, Jonathan, and Giovanni are testaments about how ill equipped schools are to deal with the myriad of adverse experiences that children from all ethnic and socioeconomic levels bring into classrooms. Equipping teachers with the tools to provide social and emotional well being to these children should be a priority.

The short time I spent in teacher jail was frustrating. I was forced to sign an agreement stating that I would not be in contact with anyone at the school. I could not submit lesson plans or engage with teachers, pupils, parents or staff. If I had done so, I would have faced serious repercussions. Some days were easier than others, but I went through a myriad of emotions and feelings. Most of the time, my feelings were negative: hopelessness and despair, gloom and depression, and anger and rage mixed with powerlessness.

Days with those kinds of feelings, throughout my life, had been more the norm than the exception. In fact they were so familiar to me that I'd worn them like a second coat—so often that I was not even aware that I was always wearing that real but unseen garment. While locked up in teacher jail, I felt the weight of that coat woven of negative energy every day.

I've found that it is easy for one who has never experienced or been exposed to Adverse Childhood Experiences to get the wrong impression of how those times of trauma impacts someone such as myself. When I've told my life story to people, they see me as the 'other,' and I suspect that they feel emotions such as sentiment, pity, or disdain.

What I also understand is that those feelings about (or judgments of) me do nothing to erase the problem. They serve to exacerbate it by inferring that Adverse Childhood Experiences happen to some poor 'other' person.

The facts are that *everyone* experiences some form of trauma in life. The people who suffer multiple childhood traumas face a hard fight for survival, an uphill climb towards the happiness, joy, ease, love, and freedom in their emotions. Those people who score high numbers on the ACE assessment tool deserve compassion, not pity. They deserve to know that harm done to them in childhood was not their fault.

They deserve to know that healing is possible, and that it is an ongoing process. It was my intention in writing this book to gather stories and resources in one place to shine a light on trauma and on the desire for relief from the effects of trauma, the effects of the memories trauma leaves behind, ways to engage healing, the effects of healing, and to show what healing from the pain of Adverse Childhood Experiences feels and looks like.

CHAPTER 4

Fellowship at Aspen Institute

*To think is easy. To act is hard. But the hardest thing
in the world is to act in accordance with your thinking.*
~ JOHANN WOLFGANG VON GOETHE ~

Before my stint in teacher jail, I was granted a year's leave to
work for education reform activist Steve Barr, the founder of
the Green Dot Charter School organization. About three months
into that job, I received an opportunity to apply for a fellowship for
teachers through the Aspen Institute. I felt it was an honor to apply.

As stated on its website, "The Aspen Institute is an educational
and policy studies organization based in Washington, D.C. Its mission
is to foster leadership based on enduring values and to provide a
nonpartisan venue for dealing with critical issues." The Institute's
two-year fellowship for teachers fosters values-based leadership and
encourages individuals to reflect on the ideals and ideas that define
a good society.

It took a couple of months to go through the rigorous process,
but when I learned that I would be one of 20 fellows out of over 600
applicants, the honor I'd felt earlier came back to me in a new way.
This was in late 2011, and I was a member of the inaugural class of
"Teacher Leaders."

A total of 23 people (20 fellows and three moderators) came
together in Aspen, Colorado, for the first time on February 22, 2012

to participate in the Socratic method of instruction to establish our community of learners. Each of us brought varied points of view and experiences into the space. Compassion and empathy were traits modeled by all participants and, for the first time in my life, I experienced a safe, high-quality learning environment. The experience changed—in a powerful way—how I perceive the world. It also aroused my desire for self-efficacy and mastery.

Two particular writings among the many that we read, reflected on, and discussed, had a profound influence on me and inspired me to act. One item was Ursula Le Guin's short story "The Ones Who Walk Away from Omelas," from her book, *The Wind's Twelve Quarters: Short Stories.* The other was "The Allegory of the Cave," better known as "Plato's Cave," a short story in Plato's *Republic*.

Le Guin introduced me to the conflict-free land of plenty named Omelas, a place where joyous existence was solely dependent on the continued neglect of one hungry, damaged, unloved, and filthy child who was chained in a basement. Some of the people in the story could not abide the bargain—even to be forever happy—so they left Omelas, never to return. Le Guin's story spoke to the deepest part of myself. It troubled me and I still agonize over it. I understood I had once been that child, having lived in a basement of my own making. The day I read that story, it also felt as if a mustard seed of faith was planted in my heart.

A bit later, my reading of "Plato's Cave" provided nutrients for growth. In that story, Plato has Socrates describe a gathering of people who've been chained to the wall of a cave all of their lives. These prisoners, facing a blank wall, watch shadows cast on the wall by things that pass in front of the light from a fire. The prisoners assign names to the shadows, but the shadows are as close as the prisoners ever get to a view of everyone else's reality.

Through the voice of Socrates, Plato explains how the philosopher is like a prisoner freed from the cave who comes to understand that the shadows on the wall don't represent the truth of reality. The philosopher perceives the true form of reality rather than the mere shadows—the shapes seen by the prisoners—beyond the facts of the shadows, the objects, and the fire. This story allowed me to grasp that everyone has the ability to transcend the perception of chains that bind and limit. Everyone has the ability to travel into the light of a new reality—the kind that requires every physical sense and many nonphysical 'senses.'

The Aspen Fellowship experience served as a catalyst that provided me with food for thought and the desire to engage in action. Those two stories took me back into my own perception of the darkness of the basement, and in the cave, but this time it was different. Those around me in Aspen held space for, and validated, me. My colleagues opened their hearts and shared with me their strength. They gave me encouragement. They listened to and appreciated my experiences with the darkness of domestic abuse. They allowed for a space to exist that led me to re-examine my life and discover my truth. The Aspen experience and the friendships forged there facilitated and illuminated my sense of purpose.

To express the gratitude I had for the group in Aspen, I learned to be good at listening to the life stories of others. Carrie and Tia were in

Aspen with me in 2011. Their stories are important to share because their lives and their stories shaped my own.

The readings and discussions we had while in Aspen often left me feeling drained. During breaks, I sought solace and rejuvenation by going for solitary walks on the many nature trails in the woods. On one such walk the sight of my fellow classmate, Carrie Bakken, startled me. She also sought peace in solitude. On the banks of a brook, we enjoyed a conversation. I felt both admiration and a deep kinship with her. My memory of that conversation always brings to mind the words of Spanish poet Antonio Machado:

> *Wanderer, your footsteps are*
> *the road and nothing more;*
> *wanderer, there is no road,*
> *the road is made by walking.*

Carrie's Story

Born the youngest of three, Carrie remembers a happy and good childhood in St. Paul, Minnesota. Her dad was a law professor and her mom was a Lutheran minister. When Carrie turned 14, life got more complex when her parents' marriage came to an end and they separated—her mom moved out at the same time her sister went away to college. A year later, the parents divorced.

Although Carrie stayed mainly with her dad, she had a close relationship with her mom. She said, "I stayed at mom's apartment one or two nights per week. Because I was busy with friends, schoolwork, and sports, I felt like we spent a lot of time together." Her relationship with her dad changed—he was always at work, so Carrie and her brother went from having a very strong structure with safe boundaries to experiencing a great deal of freedom. They didn't have any curfews or rules.

With her mother's absence in the home, Carrie experienced a loss of what she calls "a spiritual place." Having a Lutheran minister for a mom at a time when it was unheard of that a woman would hold that position gave the church a powerful role in the lives of Carrie's family members. As the marriage came to an end, Carrie's mom left the church because she "couldn't take another minute of the resistance she encountered while advocating new rules for women." Carrie says that the religious system against which her mom was battling was not going to be inclusive of women as leaders, nor forward thinking. The intransigence and narrow-mindedness of the male-dominated institution was just too much... her mom was fed up with what it meant to be a woman in this society.

Carrie said, "Parents are very important role models for a teenager. They have a tremendous impact on how their child views the world, so when the parents question their lives, the teen is forced to question theirs, too." In her young life, Carrie was subjected to rules like going to church every Sunday; she heard about other people's needs, and was taught the ability to do good works to meet those needs. She was taken to homeless shelters to donate items and to soup kitchens to volunteer. She learned about suffering and its contexts. Then, all of a sudden, she was on her own to figure things out because all that structure went away.

An imbalance happened due to Carrie's loss of boundaries, stability and safety, and of all that was familiar. It left a void. In order to fill the void, Carrie became a self-destructive partier. From the age of 15 through the end of her college education, Carrie was the most self-destructive of her three siblings.

While in college, Carrie questioned the value of the choices she was making and realized that she wanted her life to be different. She stopped using alcohol and other substances; being a partier wasn't who she was as a person. She refocused and got back on track, went to law school, and earned a degree in 1998.

But she never took a bar exam.

Carrie met her husband while in college. "He graduated right after we met but our courtship continued and we lived together for over nine years before getting married in 2000." Her husband was a partier who used mind-altering substances up until the birth of their first child, a son. Becoming a father was the event that forced him to take stock, confront his addiction, and find help to maintain his long-term sobriety. He now runs the Peers Enjoying A Sober Education (P.E.A.S.E.) Academy in Minneapolis. It's the oldest continually operated high school in the U.S. for teens recovering from addiction.

One summer, Carrie worked for P.E.A.S.E. and it was a turning point in her life. "I was so uninterested in practicing law that I didn't even take the bar exam. But while in law school, I worked as a law clerk in juvenile justice for the county and that experience, and working with my husband, made me decide that I would much rather be a teacher. So following law school, I worked at an alternative school teaching middle school students. Three years later, in 2001, I joined a team of teachers to start Avalon, a charter school."

Carrie, Gretchen Sage-Martison, Nora Whalen, and a group of like-minded teachers founded the Avalon School in Saint Paul. It is teacher-led and students learn through self-directed, project-based study. Being a teacher-led school, Avalon offers its faculty a professional environment—even when that means doing janitorial chores. Right from the start, teachers held class, did administrative tasks, developed curriculum, negotiated for space, built the budget, recruited students, and even mopped floors. The goal was to run the school as a cooperative. The entire team made decisions as a consensus.

Avalon School's model is a safe and nurturing environment—one that makes it easy to retain teachers. Over the course of seven years, the retention rate was between 95 and 100 percent (per year). This high teacher retention means the teachers build relationships with each other, their students, and families. Because they are not constantly hiring and mentoring new staff, they also continue to improve their learning programs year-to-year.

Carrie said, "This stability allows us to build on our strengths and let go of practices that are not working. I think we do a better job engaging community resources than many other schools because there isn't as much red tape to go through to build the partnership. We can create programs with nonprofits, such as the St. Paul Parks and the county library. Some partnerships have lasted a decade; some have come and gone. It depends on student interest and follow-through. We've changed our schedules over the years, added the middle school, changed teacher roles, and stayed flexible—we are always adapting and changing to meet student needs."

Stability at Avalon is key. Many students come to Avalon with one or more of the following issues: persistent truancy, significant deficits in class credit, substance abuse, and/or homelessness. Over 50 percent of Avalon's students have a diagnosed disability. Avalon is an inclusive, empathetic, and caring environment in which all children can thrive. "We are a safe community for LGBT students and have several transgender students. We have many families with parents who are in same-sex partnerships. I don't have the statistics, but we have a reputation for being inclusive to LGBT students and families. We just built an all-gender bathroom to meet the needs of our transgender students."

Avalon School has a framework for governance that helps students acquire positive learning skills and attitudes. In 2014, 99 percent of students surveyed said that they felt safe at Avalon.

Entrusted with 24 students for their entire high school career, Carrie is responsible for shepherding them from ninth grade through to graduation. Carrie understands that in order to be effective, she must constantly reflect on how best to support them in their journey. She understands that the work requires her to engage in a great deal of self-care in order to be fully present, to be self-reflective, to leave her ego behind and her heart open to stay in a strong willingness to grow. It is clear that Carrie believes her work requires her staff, students and their families to share information, to communicate well and to share in the intellectual and spiritual growth of her students. She teaches in a manner that respects and cares for the souls of her students and responds to their uniqueness. She loves them.

Carrie has two children of her own. Her goal is to raise them to be "socially conscious" because of the traditional Scandinavian values she learned as a child. Both her parents were Norwegian. She told me they taught her a "socialistic model where one is taught to do good, not because someone is watching you or is going to judge you at the end, but because doing good is the point." Another very strong Scandinavian value she practices is that "the goal in life is not to outdo others or to shine, but to help others and to be humble in the process."

Yet, Carrie says that she is "not religious;" she does not attend church. Her belief is that life is full of mystery and very special. Being good to others is expected. In her job as an educator, she supports her students and strives to do what is best for them.

Tia Martinez, Keith Berwick, and Kim Smith were the moderators of the two-year Aspen Teacher Leader Fellowship I attended. Of those three people, I got to know Tia best. She works as a social justice consultant.

Martinez collected degrees from Harvard (history), Berkeley (public policy), and Stanford (law). For over 25 years, her careers involved social work, policy analysis, strategy, and management, and covered issues ranging from HIV/AIDS to immigration, education reform, drug abuse, homelessness, disconnected youth (the school-to-prison path), transforming pain to hope to relief in the lives of boys and men of color, and affordable housing.

Tia's life story deserves a documentary but here it is—most of it—in her own words.

Tia's Story

"My parents were hippies. I was born in 1968, a couple of weeks before Nixon was elected. We were living in San Francisco. My dad's family came from New Mexico but moved to San Francisco when he was a young boy. My mom was from a town outside of Boston called Malden.

"As a kid, from the age of 2, I didn't feel comfortable in girls' clothes or being referred to as a girl. I didn't want to be referred to as a boy either. I said I would prefer 'mouse' or 'bear' or some other thing that wasn't gendered in my little kid's mind. My mother was an ultra feminine woman, an extrovert, and beautiful. She wanted to have a kid like herself, and I don't know if it was in reaction to her or just who I was (or some mix of the two), but I was the exact opposite. I was introverted, shy, and didn't feel like a beautiful girl.

"My mom's mother left her father for another man when she was about 12 and her sister was five; both girls went to live with their dad which was pretty unprecedented in the 1950s. I think her upbringing was pretty rough. My mom had me when she was 24 and she hadn't really had the opportunity to heal. She didn't know how to regulate herself or care for little children. She was raised with an ethic that any family member could say anything and it would all be forgiven.

So there was a lot of fighting in her family and then in ours. We would say some really horrible things to each other, and create a lot of chaos and anger.

"My mom didn't have a model for how to be a mom. From a very young age, she and I fought; a lot of screaming and yelling, fights over me getting dressed because I didn't want to put on girls' clothes; just wanted to stay in my pajamas. I remember intense fighting and a kind of fear. It wasn't that I felt she didn't love me—she did love me—it was just very complicated.

"My dad was quiet, more introverted. He was a construction worker and his nickname on the work site was Gentle Ben. I was really close to my dad and he was really good to me. I wanted to be just like him. My mom also had a lot empathy for others—I got empathy from both of them."

Tia grew up a small town in northern California called Eureka, in Humboldt County. For many years, Eureka was a prosperous logging town, but by the late 1970s, the timber industry was dying and its residents (mostly working class Caucasians and Native Americans) suffered.

Her brother, Danny, was two years younger and very extro-verted, just like their mom, but boy-gendered. He wanted to ride motorcycles and play football but he had a harder time in school than Tia. He was hyperactive, had trouble sitting down, and was always getting in trouble. Tia remembers feeling that he was her mother's favorite and recalls her saying, " I love him more because the world loves him less."

About herself, Tia says, "I was always quiet and cerebral. It was very easy for me to be with adults but I was extremely shy and it was hard for me to connect with other kids. I was afraid that they hated me. My mom said things like, 'you don't have any friends,' and, 'why can't you be more like your brother?' Our parents were trying to figure out who they were and what life was about, seeing themselves as non-conformists, and we were left to feel like afterthoughts, supporting players. Left to our own devices, we endured a lot of chaos and unpredictability.

"When I first started school and kindergarten I was terrified. Once, I escaped and ran home. I'd hide under my desk because I was in a constant state of high alert."

Then an amazing teacher, Mrs. Hartman, came into Tia's life for first and second grade. Tia says, "She must have been in her mid-to-late 50s then. She was such a good teacher, so kind. From that point on, I took to school. I got love from this incredibly skilled, loving older woman. I felt that even though I was picked on by kids and teased a lot, I had this one thing. I was good in school and I loved the love I got from Mrs. Hartman.

"School became the thing that I could do to help me deal with the chaos in my life, the difficult relationship with my mom, and grownups busy doing their own things. So I studied. I did well in school and that became part of my identity. The more I studied, the better I did and the more love I got."

Tia's sister Emily was born when she was 11 and a new chapter of Tia's life began. "The whole time my mom was pregnant with her, I was sure the baby was going to die. My whole life I had been wired for disaster, to expect terrible things to happen. The baby didn't die and Emily changed my life. I felt like I had a person who looked up to me, needed me," Tia said.

"My memory was of having this person I believed in. I could take care of her and I loved her and was loved by her. Emily killed herself when she was 25, but before that happened I used to say that my life started when she was born.

"A couple years after Emily was born, we moved to Marin County and things got worse. I was in a new school, poorly dressed, awkward, nerdy, funny looking. I was just that kid who others picked on and

I remember how mean they were. It was a very brutal time at home, as well.

"My father was struggling with his brother, a heavy drinker, who we later learned was schizophrenic and, later on, with the death of his father. We lived in little cabins with no running water and no heat in a mostly Caucasian, wealthy environment. I was a teenager and it was clear to me that I was gay, which created more problems with my mother. I think she thought it was her fault because she had brought me up around her lesbian friends. But my dad was always so supportive. I remember him telling me to never let anyone make you feel less because of who you are.

"A couple years later, after my grandfather passed away, my dad started to use crack cocaine. This was like 1986 or 1987. Emily was around the age of 6. At that point I embraced the role of being the protector of my little sister and at the same time I also got this chance to help my mom—to gain her approval and love. I was the one who'd call the hospitals and jails when my father disappeared, while my mom was frozen, asking over and over again, 'Do you think he's dead?' I got a chance to be somebody.

"Emily would call me her hero. I felt a sense of agency and power. I saw myself as competent and capable. She was just like my own kid. I could be her hero, and that was profound, especially because I felt inadequate and neurotic and crazy in so many other parts of my life. For the most part, I didn't know how to have relationships that weren't crazy and violent. When I was Emily's protector I was never crazy, never violent. I was steady and loving and true."

Tia said that, apart from Emily, the things that saved her were her academic gifts. "It probably was the thing that carried me through. When I look at the resiliency literature, I'm able to see that it was my academic skill and how I parlayed that into relationships that allowed me to continue. That skill also got me into Harvard, Berkeley, and

Stanford. The gulf between my life and the lives of the other kids going to these schools was pretty big and I certainly didn't feel like I belonged there. But I found a couple of friends that shared my experiences and they helped me through."

At this same time, during the late 1980s and early 1990s, three other things were happening around Tia that influenced her life's direction: the HIV/AIDS epidemic, a rise in street homelessness having to do with deinstitutionalization of the mentally ill, and widespread use of illegal drugs. "All of these served in influencing my decision about what to do—what I felt I was on this Earth to do—to carry out my strong sense of justice and injustice that I had since birth."

With only the benefit of her Catholic grandmother's influence, Tia started to attend mass every Sunday at her community's parish, Holy Redeemer. "I really didn't know anything about being Catholic, I just used to watch my grandmother say the rosary, and hear her say the 'Hail Mary,' the 'Our Father.' She'd bless me with holy water, but that was enough for me, and when the pain became unbearable I sought solace in prayer in my local parish. This was an amazing parish, right in the middle of the Castro district, during the height of the AIDS epidemic. Eventually it became this amazing place under two priests, Father Tony McGuire and then Father Zachary Shore."

Tia told me what she saw happen in the midst of the HIV/AIDS epidemic. Gay men with the disease (or who were in grief over losing their loved ones to it) came back to the church. Father Zachary welcomed them and the parish was reborn. Many of the new parishioners got thrown out of their homes with parents who followed the Catholic traditions. Tia expressed surprise that father Zachary was not kicked out of the church for ministering to the men who were dying. She said, "It was everything the church should be. I think that the HIV epidemic, homelessness, and the crack epidemic mirrored my internal suffering and my family's suffering."

Tia got a job at the AIDS office at the Department of Public Health and went to work on a research study addressing youth living in the street economy, selling drugs and sex. That job led to a lot of work with young gay men. "It lasted for about seven years and led to me seeing the relationship between drug addiction and mental health. Every young man who was having unsafe sex, using drugs like speed, heroin, crack...." Tia paused at this memory.

"When I would talk with them as part of my job and listen to their stories, I reflected on my own life as well as their lives. I saw a need is to reframe any addiction as a health issue, to have a medical response in the same way that HIV was a health crisis—not a moral crisis."

During the time she was interviewing kids on the street for her job, Clare showed up and became the love of Tia's life. "She was British, punk, maybe 22 with a stand-up blue Mohawk. I found Clare to be a wonderful mix of messiness and academic brilliance."

Clare was a Fulbright scholar from Essex by way of Leeds—a street kid and a professor all in the same person. Tia recruited her to work on a project for homeless kids while Clare was on her Fulbright scholarship in public health at UC Berkeley studying the HIV epidemic.

Tia and Clare worked together for two years and have been together as partners ever since. "She has been an amazing rock in my life," Tia says, "and she was also very close to Emily, who met her when she was 12. My sister loved Clare."

Early in her relationship with Clare, Tia's best friend and room-mate, Matthew, committed suicide. Clare saw her through the pain of losing Matthew.

Ten years later, when Emily took her own life, Clare was with Tia through that darkness. Tia was flattened and overwhelmed with guilt. She felt that everything she'd been able to create meaning out of in her life was gone. "I was shattered. I still kept going to church but I just wanted to die, just wanted to die. I was dismissive of everything and a deep hopelessness and cynicism set in.

"Someone recently asked me about when the turning point was, when did I see hope again. I remember...and it was such a little thing. Clare and I had been invited to a benefit that our local bartender was putting on for dogs in Thailand. She went to Thailand every year and was concerned about the suffering of stray dogs in that country.

"My kneejerk reaction was to dismiss it and criticize it. Damn privileged San Franciscans and their dogs! They care more about animals than people! They care more about stray dogs here than thousands of homeless on our streets—more about stray dogs in Thailand than the poverty and suffering of the humans there.

"I was also deeply depressed and hadn't really gone to anything celebratory in the past year and a half since Emily's death. For some reason we went. And something happened there that shifted things. Here I was in a bar with an open courtyard and all these queer folk were there with their dogs. And they loved their dogs, they deeply loved their dogs...and they loved these dogs they had never met in Thailand.

"It hit me that they cared about something bigger than themselves, something more than the specific comfort they got from their pet. They cared not just for their dog, but all dogs. I was overcome with their love for something outside of themselves. I was touched by their connection and how they treasured these living creatures. Something in me broke. I realized what matters is to love like that. To care for someone, something, anything—that that feeling for another was sacred. And that was my turning point. I began to get better; not immediately, it was an enormous struggle. But I began to heal."

Now Tia wants to help other people understand their suffering, to work on issues that matter to her and to the world. She believes that "underneath everything that is transformative is relationship. It is the deep interconnection that people have forgotten. People have forgotten how connected they are; they only know how sacred they are. The only thing anyone leaves this world with is the indelible marks made by relationships with others. That mark can be ugly or it can be beautiful. I just know that relationship matters, love matters."

The friendships I forged with Carrie and Tia continue to this day, as does the one I have with Tom Loper. Tom was the deputy director (now managing director) of the Aspen Action Forum. In general, he is the grease that allows the wheels of the Action Forum to keep rolling forward; he is also committed to being a positive role model for gay youth. He believes that any person with commitment, passion, and desire can make positive changes in the world.

My first conversation with Tom was at an Aspen Fellows dinner in Brentwood, California a few weeks before my second bicycle trip. I shared the purpose of my trip with him and he shared his story with me. It was then that we agreed to stay in touch with one another. His personal story is remarkable for the compassion shown to his family by people within the Catholic Church, even though this religion teaches that homosexual acts are violations of divine and natural law.

What follows is the story that Tom shared with me after my second ride, while I was in the process of writing this book. It contains wisdom, grounded in love, that informs the rest of the stories collected here. After all, one of the purposes of our gathering at the Aspen Institute was to ask the question, "If love is present at Aspen, how do we see it manifest in the world?"

Tom's Story

Tom enjoyed a very comfortable upbringing in small town of Wilbraham, Massachusetts, during the late 1980s and early 1990s. He attended public schools, earned good grades, and enjoyed being a popular extrovert, holding the role of class president all four years of high school. Tom felt that he could be gay but didn't have any positive role models of gay people to track. At the time, the HIV epidemic was in full swing, and there were many stigmas associated with homosexuality. Tom wanted to avoid stigma so he chose to live in the closet.

The struggle with his identity led to a period of depression that began in middle school and lasted throughout high school, despite his outgoing personality. Now he recognizes that such depression is common in gay youths. He says, "There is an indirect trauma that manifests itself and is different for every person who is closeted; it's due to having to hide something about the self due to shame and uncertainty that other people will neither accept nor embrace who they are."

During our conversation, I shared with Tom an African tale about a farmer who was raising chickens. Among the chickens was a strange looking one that was doing the same as all the other chickens—pecking the dirt, searching for food. A visitor came to the farm, observed the odd bird, and said to the farmer, "That's not a chicken. It's an eagle! May I take him from you?"

The farmer thought the man was crazy. He shrugged his shoulders and said, "Fine. Take it away."

The man took the eagle. Before dawn the next morning, the man climbed a tall mountain while holding onto the bird. When he arrived at the top, he held the bird up to the early, soft yellow light rays and said, "Fly like the eagle you are!" The bird extended its strong and beautiful wings and flew towards the bright light of the rising sun.

I then asked Tom when it was that he embraced the truth of himself. He told me that people like his high school art teacher took him aside and discussed his feeling that Tom could be gay. She told him that if he found out he was gay he could come to her for support. There were people who saw him as gay, but it wasn't until college, when he met and dated a man of Mexican descent, that he realized the truth.

For the first time, Tom felt that it was natural for him to be attracted to another man, and he wasn't trying to be someone else. However, he says that only three people knew that he was in something much more than just friendship and this went on for about a year.

Just after Tom had pulled off two all-nighters to finish his midterms, he left at 11 p.m. to drive Route 495 to visit his boyfriend. His was one of five cars involved in an accident. None of the drivers or passengers suffered injuries, but Tom's parents wondered what he was doing at midnight on Highway 495. He gave them an excuse.

Later that night, while walking back to his apartment in Washington D.C., Tom broke down in tears on the side of the road as he walked by the National Cathedral. In that moment, Tom "made a decision that I either have to start admitting who I am to people and stop lying or suicide was definitely on the table. So I went into my apartment building, found my friends Mike and Heather, and told them I was gay. They were so supportive of me. They were there for me when I needed them. And, I am grateful to be here today."

Tom's next step was to tell his parents. He'd known people who'd come out and who didn't tell their parents for fear of losing emotional, familial, and financial support. "These people either dropped out of school, took on massive loans, or paid for their lives with credit cards. So I began by telling friends in order build a strong network of support before going home.

"On the Thanksgiving holiday, I told them. I began with my mom. She and I went shopping for the upcoming Thanksgiving dinner and I told her on the way home. She had a hard time processing. She couldn't eat lunch. She said that she always thought she'd see me in church at the altar, waiting for my bride. That image died for her.

"She called my dad. He came home from work and I talked with him. He asked if I was happy. He asked if I was depressed. My parents knew I'd suffered from depression, but they couldn't figure out why. I said, 'I'm happy and I'm not depressed.' That was enough for him. My dad then called my sister, who led operations for my dad's factory. She told him that she was too busy to come home, but my dad demanded that she leave the office, and she did.

"When she saw me in the kitchen, she said, 'OK, so you either got a girl pregnant, you're sick with something, or you're gay. Which of the three?'

"I said, 'I'm gay.'

"She said, 'that's totally fine with me. I love you, and Dad, I'm going back to the office now."

Tom's mom went to church that afternoon. She was still having a difficult time with the announcement. "I had been an altar boy at that church from ages 7 to 18. The priest came to dinner with our family once or twice a month. We viewed him more as an uncle than as a figurehead of the church. He was my mom's best friend, next to my dad."

Tom explained that a nun, Sister Mary, greeted Tom's mom, who was crying, and this kind sister got Father Joe out of a meeting. The two of them sat with Mrs. Loper and worked to calm her anguish. They asked her what was wrong and she said something like, 'Tommy just came home and said he is gay.'

What happened next is an example of the way in which everyone wants to be treated. The two clerics reassured Tom's mother by saying the equivalent of this: 'If Tom's saying he is gay, it means he wants people to know about the way he loves another person, and that is what the world needs right now—more love.'

Tom followed up with them and told me what happened. "I saw them a couple of days later and they were very sweet to me; they offered me love instead of judgment."

As the holiday progressed, Tom's extended family arrived, other siblings came home, aunts and uncles arrived…and he told all of them that he was gay. They were all very supportive.

Years later, Tom met and fell in love with his husband, Dirk. He said, "I was brought up Catholic but am now non-religious. I am spiritual and faithful, but don't read or know if I even believe in the Bible. When Dirk and I decided to marry we had to address how we would carry out the ceremony when one of us didn't want the Bible to be a part of it. My parents got involved and said they felt Father Joe should be a part of it. So I went to the church and asked. He said, 'Tommy, I would love to be a part of it.' And he was.

"There were fifteen of us at the courthouse. Father Joe was one of them. The next day at the wedding reception, we had another small ceremony and Father Joe said, 'Yesterday Dirk and Tommy got married at the courthouse and I was able to join them. And in recognition of their union, I want to offer them a special blessing.' And he did."

Tom feels that all people have the right to be whoever they are and to have the freedom and opportunity to express their truths. He does not want society to look at differences and to segregate us and reduce benefits and protections for people who most need them. He said, "I have been in a position where for the first three years of our marriage we did not have full marriage benefits. That was the first time in my life I wasn't an equal citizen of the United States. It frustrated me more than anything else, and it also made me realize how lucky I was in my upbringing and how people need to fight, to demand equal rights and protections for everyone. And the people in power need to become involved in that fight. My experience has made me more empathetic for everyone. It has made me understand and relate to people of different backgrounds and the injustices they face. I'm really grateful that I'm gay because it's made me a stronger person, a more caring person, and a brave person."

Tommy told me that he felt like he had walked away from the community that raised him, as in the story "Walking Away from Omelas." He decided to confront his own "Omelas." When he and Dirk sold their home in Washington, D.C., they returned to Wilbraham. They lived with Tom's parents for about two months before they moved to Boston.

In the summer of 2013, at the first Aspen Action Forum, Tom decided to reach out to gay kids in his community. "It was my action pledge, a small pledge. So I emailed the vice principal of my high school and let him know I was back in town. I asked if there were any gay kids at the school who could use a supportive model of a gay man—someone out and proud about it. If there were, I told him I would be happy to be there for them."

Within a couple hours, Tom got a response inviting him to visit. The high school administrators put together a meeting with 20 kids who came to meet with Tom and another alumnae. "We started by sharing our experience and then talked about where we are now. It was incredible—one of the best afternoons I've ever had! The kids shared that they did not feel discriminated against, but they still had some issues. They told me about how the varsity football captain gave a talk to the whole student body asking everyone to accept the gay students at the school. I was blown away by that story because that is not what I had grown up with."

In his role as managing director of the Resnick Aspen Action Forum, Tom said that he felt fortunate to interact with over 2,200 Fellows in 50 countries. "I have never once felt a need to hide who I am. I want to be and think I am a positive gay role model or influence who believes that everyone has a personal story about knowing themselves. I try to inspire the Fellows to take that first action—to be bold and even audacious—to challenge the status quo and to ask, 'Why?' I work toward creating that safe space in which leaders who are pushing society forward can feel loved and supported and part of a community of equals."

Friedrich Nietzsche expressed best what I felt when I learned Carrie's, Tia's, and Tom's stories: "He who has a why to live can bear almost any how." The gratitude I have for Carrie, Tia, Tom, and all other Aspen Fellows is deep. My selection as an Aspen Teacher Leader Fellow in 2011 changed my life and illuminated a new path forward for me.

Keith Berwick was one of three who moderated our Aspen Teacher Leadership cohort. He is the founder and executive director of the Henry Crown Fellowship Program. There is a chair named in honor of his leadership at the Aspen Institute. After I sent him a draft of this book, he sent a note asking how I felt love was expressed in my Aspen experience. My answer is that I found love in the stories of Tia, Carrie and Tom. Those three people, plus moderator Kim Smith and Keith himself strengthened me with their examples of love. They loved me, and, helped me to blossom.

That path of knowledge was about to widen. At Aspen, I learned new ways to look at childhood trauma (my own and others'), and I wanted to keep learning about the science behind it. When I learned about the ACE study—in 2013—my path widened.

CHAPTER 5

The Road Rises Again

*None of us go into our spiritual maturity of our
own accord or by totally free choice. We are led by
mystery…. Maybe we should call this book* Tips for
the Road, *a sort of roadside assistance program.*

~ RICHARD ROHR ~

(FROM HIS BOOK *FALLING UPWARD*)

Continuing my avid quest to collect knowledge related to childhood
trauma, I drove from Los Angeles to Modesto on October 7,
2013 to attend Stanislaus County's 14th Annual Family Domestic
Violence Conference. The conference featured an all day workshop
with Bruce D. Perry, M.D., Ph.D., senior fellow of The Child Trauma
Academy in Houston, a renowned child psychiatrist and researcher
in children's mental health and the neurosciences. I'd just finished
reading two books by Dr. Perry (with Maia Szalavitz): *Born for Love:
Why Empathy is Essential—and Endangered* (2010) and *The Boy Who
Was Raised As A Dog: What Traumatized Children Can Teach Us
About Loss, Love and Healing* (2007).

Listening to this passionate and empathic man articulate the
extraordinary and vital importance of healthy, loving relationships,
especially in childhood, confirmed and strengthened my resolve
to become part of the solution. In the notes I took while listening
to him appear these important truths: "We are born wired to be

interconnected and need each other to survive," and "Violence is not genetic. It is learned."

I watched the women at my table nod in agreement when he said, "What is learned can be unlearned." I was intrigued, excited, and heartened to hear that the brain has plasticity—it is capable of healing itself! The amazing human brain can make and redesign changes in neural pathways and synapses due to changes in behavior and environment. It is never too late to change, shape, and mold the brain. My heart filled with hope to hear Dr. Perry confirm what I felt I knew deep within, but until then could not verbalize: "Human beings are wired for empathy, not violence."

Dr. Perry presented unquestionable, indisputable proof that repeated exposure to domestic violence has a severe and negative impact on brain development. The experiences of threat and exposure to domestic violence produce a state of fear that literally shuts down the systems at the top of the brain that are involved in thinking.

When, as a child, you have the misfortune of watching your father beat your mother, it forever changes you. If you experience repetitive exposure to violence, it gives rise to long-term problems in your life... unless you desire and are willing to engage in healing.

Children externalize their feelings by exhibiting aggression, rule-violation, and acting out, or they internalize their feelings, and doing so causes anxiety, depression, moodiness. These patterns, as well as their consequences, continue into adulthood. One of the hardest things to come to terms with for traumatized children *who are now adults* is the fact that many who experienced violence in the home and other early traumas are predisposed to engaging in violent behavior and passing on abuse.

A child who witnesses violence may also sustain impairments to cognitive functioning that lead to difficulty in school and challenges in negotiating appropriate social relationships. I experienced this myself.

Adults want to deny that the violence they experienced in child-hood—and also imposed on their own children—has had the adverse effect of causing them and their children to live with depression, inflammatory anger, low self-esteem, and to be more inclined to abuse substances in order to self-medicate and feel some semblance of relief. For many years, there was no scientific connection to early trauma and adult health.

While I was at that table listening to Dr. Perry's presentation, my heart filled with emotion. Some sort of light washed over me and filled me with insights into myself, into my behaviors, and into the choices I'd made. I knew that something entirely different was possible now with respect to how we, and I, as human beings can deal with social issues such as violence, poverty, addictions, abuse, homelessness, and mental health. Society and I must rethink and revise for the better, the raising and educating of children.

As I thought about this, I realized that there is also a need to change the trauma and abuse inflicted on individuals who are in the juvenile justice and prison systems. These institutions compound the traumas they experienced as innocent children.

This information bears repeating because it has been held back for so long. Childhood traumas, such as witnessing domestic violence, experiencing sexual abuse, and other forms of household dysfunc-tion are related to and have a direct relationship with individual health conditions and social problems. It is time to embrace these problems and start asking the right questions. Solutions are possible through dialogue, in partnership with funding, and with foresight so the goal of relief from childhood traumas is accomplished and so that future traumas get attention in order to keep them minimal and to neutralize them when they happen.

Perhaps there will always be trauma—wherever there are humans, traumas happen. We as a species can accept this and do nothing.

Or we can choose a path of healing for the self and watch as it opens up paths of healing for others.

During one of the breaks, I worked up the courage to take my copies of Dr. Perry's books to him and ask him to sign them. We talked. He signed the books. But he kept calling me John! When I corrected him, he said that my voice and demeanor reminded him of his brother, John. I laughed, thanked him for his autograph, and verbalized an idea that his talk had inspired in me.

In our conversation, I declared my intention to ride a bicycle across the country to shine a light on the effects of childhood trauma because he had made me understand that it was the most pervasive challenge of our time. I felt that the impact of ACEs on youth and adults in our communities, our society, and our world had to be taken in hand—and with heart—on the road, in a personal way, for others and for myself. Dr. Perry laughed and told me it was a noble cause and a great endeavor to pursue.

He wished me well.

I spent the six-hour drive back to Los Angeles thinking about the quest to which I'd just committed.

The first time I crossed the country on a bicycle, I was in my early twenties. I was searching for purpose and adventure—and a way to ease the pain in my heart.

This time, I was 56 years old! But life had again informed my purpose. No longer a young man, I had a beautiful 16-year-old daughter to raise and support. I also felt a sense of calling. It was greater than I was. Since returning from the Aspen Fellowship in 2011, I'd been on a spiritual quest that I felt destined to fulfill. I'd searched for the tools and the information that would help me rescue Omelas's child in the basement and enable me to lead people out of Plato's cave.

The bicycle was my tool of choice. My mission was to collect stories, share the word about trauma's impact and to live to write about my experiences in this book.

As soon as I got home from the conference in Modesto, I sent a journalist named Jane Stevens an email about my inspiration to act. I included my phone number, a brief synopsis of my personal story, and shared a line or two about wanting to do something about Adverse Childhood Experiences I'd learned about, particularly domestic violence. I asked if she would be willing to speak with me.

A few days later, I received a very gracious reply. Jane thanked me for sharing my story, expressed her willingness to talk, and gave me her telephone number and a good time to call. I was nervous and full of uncertainty when I dialed the number.

Upon hearing her voice, I launched into a manic overview of the past two years of my life. I spoke of how I'd searched for anything and everything that would increase my knowledge and understanding of what happens to children who live through Adverse Childhood Experiences. I spoke of the workshops I'd attended, books, magazines, and articles I'd read, and how I had devoured anything and everything I could get my hands and eyes on—studying and reading the work of neuroscientists and doctors such as Bruce Perry, Bessel van der Kolk, and Daniel Siegel...to name a few. Finally, I told Jane how, after reading two of the many articles she'd written about students on the website she developed and dedicated to ACES, I'd been inspired to visit Principal Martinez at La Grand and Principal Higa at Cherokee to see their work for myself.

Then I told Jane about my idea of going across the country on my bicycle to gather stories of Adverse Childhood Experiences to highlight the fact most people experienced some type of trauma as a child. I told her how I thought that sharing these stories would create a demand for new policy or policies that focus on providing trauma informed care as a foundation for practice in all areas of social programming, but especially for children.

In my mind, I was thinking of all the current teachers and inmates in teacher jail who'd experienced trauma during their childhoods, and how it was continuing to inform their work as adults in charge of children, as well as those in need of nurturing in the criminal justice system.

When I finally stopped talking, there was a long silence on the other end of the line.

Jane's silence triggered my personal insecurities and made my heart sink.

Then, to my great relief, I heard Jane laugh. She shared that she had been listening to every word I'd said. She was just waiting for me to give her a chance to speak.

Jane said she thought that my bicycle trip was a great goal and as I talked she suggested ideas for what else I could do. She said I should start a blog and, as I interviewed people along the way, I could post the stories I gathered on the site she created: www.ACEsconnection.com. At the time, the ACEs Connection site had about 3,000 members throughout the country to whom I could reach out to while on the trip. I thought I could meet with them and get a story from each.

Jane encouraged me to pursue my vision and told me that she would be happy to help me achieve my goal in any way. That call with Jane made my day. Her compassion, enthusiasm, and support supplied me with the courage I'd looked for and needed.

So with faith, hope, a goal, and a bicycle, I did the work of putting together all the basic requirements necessary to undertake the cross-country trip: gathering camping equipment, proper clothing, shoes and gear, extra tubes and spare tires, and weather defense items like rain ponchos, hats and, sunscreen lotion. My first ride took me across the central United States but this time I wanted to ride through the Southern states, through places I'd never travelled such as Texas, Mississippi, Louisiana, Alabama....

I contacted Adventure Cycling because of the bike maps they publish that I'd used so many years ago. When I told them about my trip, they became sponsors and provided me (free of charge) with all the maps that I needed to go from Southern California, across the South, and then up to Philadelphia. I also dropped my bike off for service and to be equipped with racks for the panniers I needed to carry supplies.

Now I had to decide on a starting point for the journey.

The idea came to contact principal Javier Martinez and inform him about my plan to ride across the country and ask him if he would be open to having me make Le Grand in Merced be the starting point. Javier told me that he was honored and that the timing was perfect because around the time that I was looking to depart they would be having their second restorative justice conference and over 300 kids from area schools would be in attendance. He said that we could work it out for me to be part of the event—that maybe some of the kids and he and Andre Griggs, the school counselor, could accompany me for the first 10 miles.

That conversation brought to mind my visit to Cherokee Point Elementary School in San Diego, so after saying goodbye to Javier, I called principal Higa. We talked about the tentative dates that I would be coming through Southern California and he invited me to participate in their annual Compassion Day Celebration and talk with the children about why I was riding across the United States.

As I was planning the trip, I remembered an article I'd read on the ACEs Connection website by Louise Godbold titled, "The trauma of domestic violence: reality v. the classroom," (Nov. 25, 2013). Godbold was the co-interim executive director of Echo Parenting & Education in Los Angeles when she wrote the article. It was about second-guessing herself regarding the handling of a situation where abuse—and re-traumatization by police—had or might have occurred with a young girl she knew.

I spoke with Louise to inform her about my upcoming journey. That conversation led to me attending a conference titled, "Changing the Paradigm: Trauma and the Developing Child" and later enrolling in one of their 10-week parenting classes, where I developed a close relationship with the staff of Echo and its founder, Ruth Beaglehole. During the conference, Ruth asked, "What action are you willing to take to make this world nonviolent?" and "What are you willing to do so that all children grow up safe?"

She also stated, "The time for action is now. We must take action right now!"

Her words reminded me of those spoken by Martin Luther King, Jr.: "Faith is taking the first step even when you don't see the whole staircase." My relationship with Echo Parenting and the powerful women I'd met there fueled my drive and determination. I asked Louise if she would be interested in raising money through social media to support me on the bicycle journey.

"Absolutely," she replied.

And then, at the end of March 2014, I attended a conference at the California Endowment called "Everyday Courage." Robert K. Ross, M.D., the director of the California Endowment gave the keynote speech. His message was that humanity is facing an epidemic of childhood trauma.

He cited studies to show that two out of every three children in America experience some form of trauma. At least one in five are exposed to multiple traumas, such as: physical, emotional and/ or sexual abuse; seeing alcohol and/or drug abuse in their home; being related to an incarcerated or on-probation person; living with a household member who is chronically depressed, mentally ill, institutionalized, or suicidal; experiencing violence in their neighborhood, school or home.

Dr. Ross spoke of the scientific research that shows traumatic stress literally blocks brains, bodies, and personalities from developing in a healthy way.

He also shared some good news stating that well-timed interventions in schools, neighborhoods, and health settings can help people heal. He said, "Children need trusting relationships with adults and each other. They need to be taught how to manage their emotions when scared and overwhelmed." He informed us that each one of us is endowed with the "everyday courage" to meet those needs. Discovering your courage is necessary.

A few days after hearing Dr. Ross speak, I had lunch with Katya Fels Smith, and Audrey D. Jordan. Katya is the founder and CEO of Full Frame Initiative. Katya and Audrey, a dear friend of mine, and I spoke about domestic violence, poverty and trauma and its impact on children, families, and communities. They introduced me to Full Frame Initiative's Five Domains of Wellbeing: social connectedness, stability, safety, mastery, and meaningful access to relevant resources. See www.fullframeinitiative.org.

Reflecting on Dr. Ross's talk, I see that having the Five Domains of Wellbeing enables anyone to have "everyday courage."

CHAPTER 6

Packing and Unpacking:
The ACE Information

Hurt people hurt people, I've frequently observed.
Sacred Wounds [a book by Teresa Pasquale]
shows us how to honor our hurts so that we
become healing people healing people.
~ **RICHARD ROHR, OFM** ~

After I'd planned and prepared for the trip, I realized that I'd also packed my mind with information to share with people I'd meet along the ride. This chapter contains that narrative.

ACE. It stands for Adverse Childhood Experience in the context of this book, but in the past, it had other definitions that are curious. The term, perhaps originally from the Greek word, eis, meaning "one" or "as one" (it was the name of a Roman coin made of copper), was brought into common use in Old French in the 1300s. The word "ace" as used in English in the early 1500s referred to the side of the die with one dot. Later it jumped to new meanings for a playing card, a wartime airplane pilot, and the point scored in tennis.

One dot on the die, a low number, was a metaphor for bad luck, but the ace in cards is usually of high value. The phrase, "ace in the hole," was first used in 1904 in the game of poker to mean a "concealed advantage." Students in the 1950s began to use "ace" to mean excellent test scores or high grades: "Terry aced that exam!"

Are there any "concealed advantages" or "good scores" inside the ACEs of Adverse Childhood Experiences?

To answer this question for yourself, know your ACE score, and be willing to remember and understand your own life's history—whether or not it includes the trauma that results from abuse, lack, disappointment, or even abject horror.

Your ACE score is where your story begins.

Take the ACE assessment online at http://www.acestudy.org/ace_score. It is available in English, French, German, Icelandic, Norwegian, Spanish and Swedish.

The Story of the ACE Study

The story of how the ACE Study came into being is worth knowing. It began with a medical doctor named Vincent J. Felitti.

The son of a pediatrician, Felitti was born in New York. He had a significant personal experience with medicine at the age of 10, just before a tonsillectomy. At that time, ether was the common anesthetic—the smell of which was horrible. When the nurse anesthetist saw him wince, she whispered advice: "If you don't like the smell, hold your breath." He thought the nurse was his friend, so he followed her instructions and when he could no longer hold his breath, the large inhalation that followed was ether. The experience made him feel betrayed—and almost drove him later to become an anesthesiologist.

Felitti graduated from Dartmouth College and then attended the University of Minnesota and Johns Hopkins Medical School. He interned and did most of his residency at Baltimore City Hospitals, with a final year at the University of Maryland Hospital. He served as a captain in the U.S. Army Medical Corps, was post surgeon at the Pine Bluff Arsenal in Arkansas, and then joined Kaiser Permanente in the late 1960s as an internist with a specialty in infectious diseases. Later he founded and chaired their Department of Preventive Medicine in San Diego.

It was an honor, he says, to work in preventive medicine because he had always wanted to provide in-depth medical evaluation of patients so that doctors routinely would have comprehensive information on which to base their treatment. Before any treatment took place, patients who came into his department filled out an in-depth medical history questionnaire at home. He found that large amounts of relevant medical information could be easily and inexpensively obtained by this approach—often adding significantly to understanding of a patient's condition.

In this department of preventive medicine, at peak 58,000 adults came through each year for comprehensive medical evaluation, and that volume made clear the need to create certain medical risk abatement programs. The risk to health of being overweight was obvious, but the unexpected and counterintuitive findings in the resulting Weight Program are what led to the Adverse Childhood Experiences (ACE) Study.

At the time, Felitti thought that being overweight was "just an annoying problem to be gotten rid of," and he set up a program using the then new technique of Supplemented Absolute Fasting (SAF), in which patients consumed no food or caloric beverages for prolonged periods of time. A special supplement—Optifast°, made by Sandoz Pharmaceuticals—was essential; it contained certain electrolytes, amino acids and vitamins. A person on the SAF program for one year would reliably lose about 300 pounds (unless he or she cheated). Many of his patients lost significant amounts of weight.

These extraordinary initial successes led Felitti to think this was a solution to the obesity problem. However, it soon became obvious that there was a high drop out rate, basically limited to patients who were successfully losing weight. Felitti was perplexed. The dropout rate was 50 percent.

He then tracked down the dropouts and began asking questions— without knowing what to ask! He started by asking their birth weight, weight in first grade, at puberty, etc. He asked about incidents in their lives. One day, he happened to ask a woman how much she weighed when she first became sexually active.

"Forty pounds," she said. "It was with my father."

From that moment on, he asked all the obesity patients if they'd ever experienced sexual abuse during childhood. Over 180 interviews later, he'd heard affirmative answers from slightly over half of the dropouts. He then asked five colleagues to interview the next 100 dropouts; they confirmed that a majority of the 'successful' dropouts acknowledged sexual abuse when asked.

Other kinds of adverse experiences during childhood were uncovered in these interviews. The findings progressively suggested that overeating might often be a coping mechanism for the depression, anxiety, and fear resulting from various forms of childhood abuse. Felitti deduced that these patients commonly were overweight because of traumatic life experiences, particularly during childhood and adolescence.

Presenting these findings at a major obesity conference in 1990, Felitti's chance meeting with David Williamson, Ph.D., an epidemiologist with the CDC, led to Williamson's comment to him, "If what you are saying is true, it's got enormous importance for the nation as well as the practice of medicine."

Dr. Williamson then introduced Robert Anda, M.D. to Dr. Felitti... and it was a good match. Anda graduated from Rush Medical College and became an internist before completing a fellowship in preventive medicine at the University of Wisconsin along with his master's degree in epidemiology. Then accepted into the Epidemic Intelligence Service at the CDC, Dr. Anda conducted research studies on behavioral health, disease surveillance, mental health, cardiovascular disease, and origins of risk behaviors.

Anda and Felitti became partners in the design of a major survey of childhood trauma in 17,337 adult members from the Kaiser Permanente Medical Care Program in San Diego. About half of the volunteers were female; 74.8 percent were Caucasian; the average age was 57; 74 percent had attended college and almost all had good jobs with healthcare benefits.

The participants answered questions about 10 types of childhood trauma that had been repeatedly uncovered in Felitti's weight program by detailed medical histories:

- Recurrent physical abuse

- Recurrent emotional abuse

- Sexual abuse

- An alcohol and/or drug abuser in the household

- A household member absent due to incarceration

- A chronically depressed, mentally ill, or suicidal household member

- Domestic violence

- Both biological parents not in the household throughout the first 18 years of life

- Emotional neglect

- Physical neglect

Based on the data from detailed self-reports done as part of the ACE Study, Drs. Felitti and Anda discovered that more than two-thirds of the participants experienced at least one category of adverse childhood experience when growing up; over two-fifths had a history of at least two categories of these experiences. One in nine had experienced five or more categories.

They also were able to determine that the higher the number of "yes" answers for the ACE categories, the greater the chance a person would engage in high-risk coping behaviors (smoking, alcohol and drug abuse, promiscuity, overeating/severe obesity, and violence) in adulthood. They also discovered that the number of ACEs had a proportionate dose-response relationship with ill health: depression, heart disease, cancer, chronic lung disease, liver disease, many auto-immune diseases, and a significantly shortened life span. For example, experiencing at least four categories of ACEs was associated with a seven-fold increase in subsequent alcoholism. An ACE score above six was associated with a 30-fold increase in attempted suicide.

The demographic of the people involved in the ACE study is important. Most were Caucasian adults with jobs and good health-care benefits. If a clearly middle-class population who are financially stable had such personal difficulties coping in life, what is the case for individuals in other demographics who live with social disadvantage, poverty, or violence?

The ACE Study achieved international recognition by the World Health Organization, the CDC, and numerous state and local governments in the United States. Felitti says, "I still marvel at how this all came about by accident; it was because of annoyance with patients who were fleeing the threat of their 'success' in terms of weight loss. It took a long time, but we came to uncover a major public health paradox."

The paradox is that many difficult public and individual health problems are really unconsciously attempted solutions to gain relief from unrecognized problems that often occurred many decades ago. For generations, "nice" people did not ask nor talk about abuse and trauma experienced or witnessed by children, though it is those things that are at the root of much illness suffered by humans around the world today.

Your ACE Score and What it Means for Healing

So, what is your ACE score?

I wrote that your ACE score is where your story begins.

But this number is only part of your story.

It is not enough to acknowledge the traumas and the disappointments you experienced while you were a child, or to know your ACE score.

You must believe in your own power to heal.

You must envision what the process of healing feels like.

You must be unafraid to experience emotional freedom that comes with healing.

Healing from childhood trauma is personal.

Healing is a process that keeps happening.

There is no end to healing, but there is relief!

As a child, you are "disappointed" in yourself when you experience trauma. A young, developing brain is wired to believe that the child's being is at fault for the trauma because of his or her inherent belief and biological need for caregivers to love it. A child believes that caregivers are to be trusted—even when the caregivers act in ways that are rooted in emotions other than love.

It is this kind of deep disappointment that leads to the emotional state of depression in the developing brain. And depression leads to behaviors that reinforce it by causing even more personal harm.

Childhood trauma wounds show up as anger issues, low self-esteem, and in the neediness that results from ill health. For example, think of a child who witnessed a weekend of domestic violence and wakes up on Monday morning with a legitimate headache that stems from the fact that the child feels they cannot face the social navigation expected of them at school.

Think of a similar experience in your own life. *Everybody has at least one.*

There are many ways to heal the damage of trauma experienced in childhood—some are medical-psychiatric, some are faith-based, some are philosophical. Sometimes, the things or events that open a body, mind, heart and spirit to healing, defy medical, scientific, philosophical explanations.

For some people, turning to faith-based, or "faith related" organizations (and the leaders within them such as a minister, priest, pastor, nun, sister, lama, rinpoche, sensei, guru, imam, elder, or a member of the laity within a church organization or 12-step program, etc.) is a first step in understanding emotional pain and working through it toward the relief of healing. Religious leaders who are or become trauma informed will best serve their followers, congregants and fellow worshipers.

I believe it is time that all people discuss the values in any faith practice, or religion, with honesty, and talk about it in the ways they experience these truths. Some of this honesty and truth may lead to hurt feelings or disappointments, but I believe that if your own faith or religion did—or did not—work for you in some way or in some situation, it's right to be truthful about it when telling your story.

From my perspective, religion's job is to teach and guide people on a path of discovery towards the idea of "true self." Religion is not a worthiness contest of belonging to the 'right' group, practicing the 'right' rituals, or believing the 'right' things. The Jesus I've come to know was a healer and a teacher who brought a message of positive transformation, not punishment or shame, for humanity.

My mission in writing this book is to create a platform wide enough to support any method of healing that will resonate for any person, especially those with high ACE and low resiliency scores. I believe that alternative methods of healing emotional pain do not conflict with any spiritual practices or religion as long as the modality supports the best and highest good of the individual, gives relief from pain, and supports the process of healing.

This is what healing is all about.

In her poem "Stirrings," from *Psalms of a Laywoman*, Edwina Gateley describes a series of moments that we all experience in our own personal way: "There is a strange, untouchable, unseeable thing in me. It hungers, grasps, strains for something I do not know, far beyond...."

For me, her words best convey my understanding of the mystery that is God. These words give purpose to the descents and ascents, the sorrows and joys, the beauty and cruelty, and all the moments in between that one encounters on the road, the journey. The poetry characterizes the longing and faith that lives inside, has guided, and will continue to guide the truth of my own spiritual existence.

On a personal note, here are some understandings and experiences I felt or witnessed that speak of truth for me and who I am as a human being:

- The moment my father's father struck his mother—my grandmother

- The moment my father struck my mother—my daughter's grandmother

- The moment I read about the child in the basement in the story "The Ones Who Walk Away from Omelas"

- The moment that an unseen force—God—planted a seed in me and illuminated my path away from the shadows in the cave

- The moment I recognized that I had to leave my "Omelas" to someday return with tools of change

- The moment I knelt in Jackson, Alabama, as pastor Chad laid his hands on my shoulder and prayed over me as I professed Jesus Christ as my Lord and Savior

All those moments are still alive in my memory, for they gave me the understanding that all lives are affected by the choices others make, and the choices you and I make affect others. Some great energy holds us all together inextricably and only together will we overcome. These moments are also charged with a deep hunger to act, to be a healer, to live a life of value—as many of the people I have written about in this book are and have been doing.

For example, minister Dave Lockeridge of ACE Overcomers uses a platform for healing supported by faith in Christ, although he has also developed a "nonfaith" version to teach kids in public schools how to deal with repressed anger from ACEs.

Therapeutic counseling sessions with a psychologist allow a person to talk about their suffering. Expert therapists who are trained in neuroscience, such as Diane Poole Heller, Ph.D. and Louis Cozolino, Ph.D., employ methods where patients use the power of imagination and the wisdom of attachment theory to transform negative memories from life experiences into ones that empower them to create new memories that enable greater happiness and well being. Psychotherapy involves therapeutic conversation and psychiatrists (medical doctors) consider possible drug use when medical science identifies chemical imbalances in the brain and there is need for a physical method of treatment and correction.

Many healing modalities are available; some are outside the practice of Western medicine. Because this book is about finding ways to heal from ACEs, and because I believe there are so many ways to heal, this book contains a list of resources.

The Resilience Factor

For healing to start, set in and continue, you must be given a belief in the power of your own strength, your survival skills, your means of coping with how it feels to heal—and most importantly—your capacity for resilience.

Resilience as a factor in your quality of life after enduring ACEs was not part of the original study. It was the year 2006 when a resilience questionnaire was developed by early childhood service providers, pediatricians, psychologists, and health advocates of Southern Kennebec Healthy Start in Augusta, Maine. Two psychologists, Mark Rains, Ph.D. and Kate McLinn, Ph.D., came up with 14 statements that allow people to evaluate their resilience. The resilience assessment and score model follows the ACE Study. That first resilience questionnaire was updated in 2013.

After reading about the ACEs study on www.acestoohigh.com, I took the ACE survey and scored a six. I also took the resiliency survey (http://acestoohigh.com/got-your-ace-score/) and scored very high. Having a high resiliency score in addition to a high ACE score helps a person understand the way they've mitigated the problems that adverse experiences created.

The ability to have resilience is crucial to everyone's wellbeing. I experienced domestic violence between an alcoholic and violent father and a traumatized mother, and I suffered physical and verbal abuse that resulted in depression. But people such as my grandmother Raquel and grandfather Medardo were vital in my life. These two people, as well as others throughout my life who nurtured me and treated me with love, built into me the resilience that allowed me to survive.

If you have a high ACE score and a low resiliency score, I urge you to undertake a program of healing that includes building your vision of what it means and what it feels like to become emotionally free to express your love—first for yourself, then for others.

In your own healing, you contribute to the healing of others.

On the first cross-country bicycle trip, I had no idea of who I was except that I was hurt. I was lost. My idea of God was that He was going to find and save me. I was having a conversation with Him and myself on that first ride—talking the talk, but not walking the walk—or in my case, cycling the bicycle.

In the time that passed between the first and second cross-country bicycle trips, I learned how to talk the talk, walk the walk, and cycle the bicycle into territory with a message made of my own growth and understanding.

CHAPTER 7

The Wheels of Wisdom: Journey 2.0

All that is gold does not glitter,
not all those who wander are lost.

~ **J. R. R. TOLKIEN** ~

On Friday April 18, 2014, at 6:30 in the morning, I placed my equipment and bicycle in the trunk of a rented car and arrived in Merced County six hours later. The front office staff at Le Grand High School greeted me when I walked in and walked me over to greet principal Martinez. He showed me the room where my bicycle and traveling gear would be stored during my participation in Le Grand's Second Annual Restorative Justice League Conference.

We drove over to Le Grand American Legion Hall where counselors, mentors, and kids were waiting, and walked in just in time to catch program coordinator Andre Griggs and youth engagement coordinator Jerome Rasberry, Jr. lead a cheer. After a very loud and boisterous session, principal Martinez excused himself and left. I walked around the hall as Andre and Jerome got everyone prepared for the conference. There was a full agenda: ice breaker exercises, forming peacemaker teams, creating 20-second commercials, and reviewing written respect agreements. The next day, 200 middle and high school students from the area would attend the conference.

During lunch I sat and talked with Rebecca and Crystal, graduates of Le Grand who were there as mentees. Each wanted to give their time because they had participated in the Restorative Justice program and received so much in return. Now parents themselves, Rebecca and Crystal wanted to make a difference in these young peoples' lives, to share the skills they'd learned, and help the youth understand that they are not alone.

Rebecca and Crystal each had totally different life experiences and stories but have been friends for over 20 years and share a special bond. Part of their bond stems from a mutual desire to be there for others the way others where there for them. They believe everyone needs healthy connections, to be loved and to be free to feel love given to them.

After lunch, I was introduced to four youth leaders: Rudy, Gaby, Edith, and Tony. For the rest of the afternoon I worked with them on writing their stories. Later that evening, when our work was completed and the students felt confident and ready for our presentation, I left them and went off to have dinner with Dave Lockridge—a connection I made through Jane Stevens.

Dave's Story

A Baptist minister, Dave holds degrees in biblical studies from Pacific Coast Baptist Bible College and psychology from Liberty University. He also has a certificate to be an anger management facilitator. During our meal, a few important moments in our conversation stuck with me.

Dave told me that he grew up in one of the boroughs of New York and recalled a memory from his childhood. In his house, along with his parents and siblings, lived his elderly grandmother. In the house next door there lived a Jewish family who had their grandfather residing with them.

One night after everyone had gone to bed, Dave and his family woke to the sound of frantic knocking at the front door. His father opened the door to meet the panicked daughter of the elderly man who lived next door. She explained that her father had fallen out of bed and they couldn't get him up. Dave's father didn't hesitate and went right over. David, then 6-years-old, followed.

When they arrived in the bedroom they found the elderly man on the floor. David's father gently picked him up and carried him toward his bed. The grandfather began to cry. Thinking he was hurting him, David's father asked the man if he was all right.

The man responded by saying, "I never thought the day would come when one of you would ever help one of us." The grandfather was a Holocaust survivor. David's father's compassion and empathy had overwhelmed him.

David took that lesson in love, compassion, and empathy shown by his father in that moment and made it his life's work. He applies what he's learned through his studies of theology and psychology and ministers to people in need through ACE Overcomers—a 501(c)(3) nonprofit he created. (See www.aceovercomers.com and/or www.aceovercomers.org.)

Through his work he combines the knowledge shared by people such as Dr. Vincent Felitti and Dr. Bruce Perry with the study and application of scripture.

I find David's work to be important and exciting because faith-based organizations are on the front lines when it comes to dealing with people impacted by trauma. If these organizations can get their clergy to follow David's lead, they can have a monumental and tremendous impact on society.

Within any faith-based organization, there is the potential to reach out to and start a healing process for millions of people who are seeking to become better people in so many ways. The potentials exist in:

+ Emotional relief of suffering

+ A place and a community in which to seek a better understanding of what is seen and unseen in life, death, and even beyond

+ Allowing the development of a capacity to have faith in God, a Higher Power, Universe, Energy (whatever word they use to mean a wisdom and purpose greater and beyond themselves)

+ By problem solving and beauty-celebrating done in community

+ The merging of 'spirit' with science

This is the merge that takes place when an individual seeks to heal damage done to their soul in order to bring their body, mind, and spirit into both alignment and agreement.

The next day, a Saturday, the Restorative Justice League Conference continued. Rudy Gonzalez, age 19, was a panel speaker.

Rudy's Story

Microphone in hand, Rudy stood in front of over 200 students and shared the story of how he came home from school one day to be greeted by both parents. They told him that they'd decided to divorce. He was 10 years old at the time—short, chubby, and a victim of bullies. "My rolls had rolls," he said.

He spoke of how he is now involved in numerous young men's leadership programs. His appearance was physically fit (no more "rolls"). Rudy credited Le Grand High School and programs like Restorative Justice for teaching him to be himself; to be resilient; and most importantly, to care about others in his community and to teach, encourage, and help other young people find their true potential.

A young lady I'd met the day of my arrival at Le Grand, Gaby Lopez, spoke next. Even from our brief meeting, I knew that it took a lot of courage for her to stand with a microphone in front of hundreds of peers.

Gaby's Story

She cleared her throat and said, "I used to be shy and would always keep things to myself because I was afraid to speak."

Now overcome with emotion, she paused.

The youth in the audience kept quiet until a girl asked Gaby if she needed a hug. Gaby nodded. The girl walked up to her and they hugged. Then a boy came down from the bleachers, made his way over to them and also gave Gaby a hug. As he made his way back into the bleachers Gaby said, "That was my little brother and I love him."

Bolstered by that show of love, Gaby said that she wanted everyone to know that the work she'd done through Restorative Justice training helped her learn how to be herself, how to express her feelings and not keep them bottled up. "I used to be a person who, if I had an opinion, I would stay quiet because I thought it might be the wrong thing to say. But now I have a voice! I'm not afraid to be standing up here—something I would have never been able to do before—and I'm up here to let all of you know that it is important to have a voice, to never be afraid to speak up and to always have the courage to express how or what you feel."

The next speaker, Edith, got up from the table, hugged Gaby and took the microphone.

Edith's Story

"I want to tell you that I was like many of you and would always keep things to myself," she said. "I remember that I was about 10 years old and I didn't like going home after school because my parents worked and I had to go to my aunts' and uncles' houses after school. They were always fighting. When it got real bad I would take my cousin, their son, who was 7-years-old, and go outside because I didn't want him to see that. It affected me a lot and I couldn't concentrate and do my homework.

"I also had a problem at home because my father drank. He didn't drink beer; he drank vodka. When I was 11, I went to the hospital to see him and when I walked in he looked at me and said, 'I'm sorry.'

"'I don't want you to be sorry,' I said. 'I want you to promise me that you'll stop drinking.'"

Edith continued: "From that day on he never drank again. I'm a daddy's girl—have always been one, and I'm happy he stopped. He has diabetes, he lost an eye, but he is alive and doesn't drink and I love him. Like Gaby, I was part of the First Restorative Justice League program here at Le Grand last year. I'm back for the second annual conference as a youth leader because I want to be a role model for you younger kids. I learned so many things in this program and it's also helped me in college at Fresno State. I am studying nursing with a minor in criminology."

Antonio Ramirez, "Tony," was the last panelist and final speaker.

Tony's Story

Tony shared that he felt he didn't have parents who offered him love, guidance, and support. When he was in eighth grade, his parents separated. Tony's freshman year of high school was really hard for him—a real low point in his life—so much so that he contemplated hurting himself. He said, "I used to have a negative perspective on my life back then, but now I know that life is how I choose to react to it."

He spoke about growing up in a very "macho culture and family," where people did not let their feelings be known. "It was really tough to be myself in that world," he said.

At the age of 16, Tony got up the courage to go to his father and hug him. "His face was priceless when I hugged him and told him I loved him." Tony explained that his father's generation was "strict macho," and explained further, "Just like me, no one had ever hugged him in his childhood!"

In his senior year of high school, Tony became very active in the Advancement Via Individual Determination (AVID) Program, joined Movimiento Estudiantil Chicano de Aztlán (MEChA) and attended Young Democrat meetings at Merced College. It was during that time that he also got involved with the Restorative Justice program and started to see that he was living a lie.

"I am who I am. God made me this way," he said.

He got an invitation to attend the Born This Way Foundation event featuring Lady Gaga in Los Angeles. The mission of Born This Way Foundation states: "Born This Way Foundation is committed to supporting the wellness of young people and empowering them to create a kinder and braver world. We achieve this by shining a light on real people, quality research, and authentic partnerships." (www. bornthisway.foundation/about-the-foundation/)

It was then when Tony realized that he—and everyone else— came into this world to be happy with who they truly are. He told everyone in attendance that they should always be proud to be who they are, then to share that happiness. "Make a difference in some-one's life," he said.

As each of these young heroes spoke, all audience members listened intently. Looking at them, I could feel the collective emotions of empathy and compassion resonating through the building.

When it was my turn to speak, I thanked the students on the panel and told them why I was making the bicycle journey. When I finished speaking, the five of us were presented with T-shirts that had the words "You Are a Hero" emblazoned on the back.

As I stood next to the four youth leaders, I understood how they personified the true meaning of "everyday courage." It filled me with hope. Seeing the effect that the interventions made possible by the Restorative Justice program were having at Le Grand (supported in part by California Endowment's Healthy Communities funding) validated the belief that early interventions do work. And in order to work, interventions must contain empathy, compassion, and love in the hearts and minds of youth, adults, and all community members.

At 2 p.m. it was time for me to get my bicycle on the road. I only had four to five hours of daylight ahead. My plan was to ride at least 50 miles. I went back to the room where my bike and gear were stored. Once there, I changed clothes, put on gear, and made sure that everything I had brought was secured and ready to go.

I made my way back to the front of the auditorium. Students had assembled to give us a send off. Javier Martinez and Andre Griggs were ready to ride with me for the first 10 miles. I watched them adjust their helmets and smiled. My heart was filled with gratitude.

Le Grand to Madera, California

Then, we put the pedal to the metal. With a roar from the crowd cheering us on, we rode off into the sunset. After we had gone a mile or two I slowed to a more moderate pace, chuckling to myself, because I was aware that for these two men their ride was no picnic. We rode on in silence, stopping only once to help Andre adjust his bike seat. Their selflessness and generosity I knew would stay with me throughout the ride.

Each man shared with me a bit of his life's story. As I rode with them, I thought about what they'd told me.

Javier's Story

Javier Martinez immigrated to the United States from Mexico at the age of 15 with his parents and attended La Grand High School. While a student there, he was told that he would never be anything but a field worker, like his parents. Enter a civics and economics teacher named Mr. Wallace in Javier's senior year.

Mr. Wallace took Javier under his wing and asked him what he wanted to do with his life, a question that no one had ever asked him before, and for which he had no answer. So he sent Javier to a guidance counselor who suggested fieldwork or possibly welding.

After that meeting, Javier reported back to Mr. Wallace who again posed the question. When Javier answered, "welding," Wallace asked another question.

"Javier, have you thought about going to college?"

Receiving no response, Mr. Wallace asked Javier to meet with him after school, and the two filled out college and financial aid applications. Because one person cared about Javier, he is where he is today—making a difference in the lives of many students.

Andre's Story

Andre grew up in Oregon. His father was addicted to alcohol, but not abusive. The neighborhood he lived in was an area of gang violence. His mother placed him in the school's music program and he remembers having to hide his musical instrument on his walks home so he wouldn't get beat up. Music turned out to be a key in his life—it opened many doors through travel in Europe before college.

The first in his family to go to and graduate from college, Andre's degree led him to a job in juvenile justice as a corrections officer. He married a teacher who sensed his talent and desire to help children and encouraged him to pursue a career that allowed him to work with kids, something he feels that he was born to do.

Ten miles later, having reached the edge of town, we stopped, dismounted, and said our goodbyes. As I pedaled off, I glanced back briefly to catch a glimpse of them making their long way back to the kids and their school.

I rode another 35 miles before I treated myself to a room in a small motel on the outskirts of the town of Madera. I was not physically tired, but the emotions of the day were flooding through my being.

Madera to Cholame, California

After a good night of sleep, I left the motel and made my way onto California 41 with the intent of making it to Paso Robles by evening.

It was not to be.

I had overestimated my fitness for the climbs that I would be making as I made my way through the Sierra Nevada mountain range.

That night around 8:30, having ridden for the past hour in semi-darkness I endeavored to complete a grueling climb that I had been on for the past four hours. Large 18-wheelers went rumbling by me. I saw a light in the distance and kept going.

The light turned out to be emanating from a restaurant called the Jack Ranch Café in the small town of Cholame. I arrived and knocked on the door. I asked for food but learned the restaurant had closed for the day. "Would you like some pie?" they asked.

"That would be great!"

"Do you want vanilla ice cream on your pie?"

"Sure!"

The apple pie a la mode was great. I asked if I could pitch my tent in the back of the restaurant. They told me they had no problem with it but to watch out for rattlesnakes because one had come into their office yesterday. They recommended that I pitch it on the grass next to "the memorial," where the grass was soft.

I lugged my tired body and bike to the side of the restaurant over to the grassy area, set up camp, and passed out. No snakes!

The next day, voices from a family of Japanese tourists woke me. I got dressed and left the tent to find out that the memorial I had slept next to was in honor of James Dean. Seita Ohnishi, a Japanese real estate mogul, commissioned the memorial in 1977. The location of the car crash site where Dean died at age 24 was about a mile away, at the intersection of Highways 41 and 46. Born in Indiana, Dean considered Santa Monica his hometown. His mother—with whom he was very close—died when he was 9. A Methodist minister from whom he sought spiritual counsel may have sexually abused Dean. It was determined that the car crash was Dean's fault; he'd been going at a rate of speed too fast to prevent the collision.

After packing for the day's ride, I went into the Jack Ranch Café and had a much needed, delicious breakfast. Chris, a waitress, inquired about the ride and I shared with her information about ACEs. At some point in our conversation she confided in me that she had a daughter with special needs and that it broke her heart to know that there are children who live in homes where they are not safe, nurtured and loved.

When I asked for the check, Chris said, "Breakfast is on the house."

Cholame to Paso Robles to Pismo Beach, California

I rode the 23 miles to Paso Robles, had lunch and then got back on the bike and arrived in Atascadero by late afternoon—14 miles later. The next day, I reached Pismo (30 miles) and decided to camp on the beach for two days because the weather was gorgeous and I had over 10 days to make the 173 mile trip to Santa Monica for the next ACE-awareness raising event.

Oscar de la Torre, Executive Director of the Pico Youth Center, ACE's supporter and friend collaborated with me to create the event. We titled the event "Trauma, Transformation and Triumph" and hoped to convene a gathering of youth advocates, educators, and students on Saturday, April 26, from 2 to 4 p.m. at Virginia Avenue Park's Thelma Terry Center in Santa Monica. The program included presentations from young adults who overcame severe trauma in their lives but were now thriving. I was ready to present a PowerPoint talk to highlight the effects of ACEs on children and youth.

After some rest on the beach, I was back on the bicycle, averaging about 50 miles a day. I enjoyed peddling along the beautiful California coast, savoring the sun and shore, the wind at my back.

On a Sunday morning near Oxnard, I got my first flat tire.

Fifteen minutes later I got a second flat tire.

Lucky for me, it happened just as I was approaching A Street in downtown Oxnard, where the town square is located. Across the plaza I spotted a Starbucks and walked my bike over. Parking the bike at an empty outside table I got out my tools and materials for changing the tire. As I removed the rear tire, I made eye contact with a woman sitting at a table nearby. I initiated a conversation and she responded. Her name was Linda and, as I worked to fix the flat, we talked.

Linda's Story

She was born and grew up in Santa Monica, the town I'd called home for over 20 years. We spoke about that city's landmarks such as the Pioneer Bakery on Rose where you can get delicious fresh bread daily and how the smell of bread baking permeates the neighborhood. The bakery had been sold; high-end condominiums sprung up to replace it. Linda informed me that the area where I taught on Abbot Kinney Boulevard in Venice was farmland when she was a child. She asked me if I knew of St. Clement Church on 3rd Street—the one she'd attended as a child. "That was a long time ago," she said.

Linda was homeless and had been for some time.

Time passed as I repaired the tire. I asked her if I could get some ice cream for us to share. She asked for sherbet instead because of diabetes. I walked across the way and bought two cones while she watched my things. When I handed her the cone she said that I was one of her angels.

I commented that it was good of her to watch out for her health and she said, "I choose to live."

We spoke a lot about religion and angels. Linda told me that she was able to see angels right there at the Starbucks. I thought nothing of it and the conversation continued as she shared about her life and how she survived on the streets.

At one point two men walked over and one handed her a brown lunch paper bag, saying that his friend standing next to him wanted her to have it. As they walked away she identified them to me as some of her angels. She opened the bag and pulled out some granola bars and an orange and, with a smile on her face, said, "I'm going to eat well tonight."

Shortly after the men had left, a woman came up, hugged Linda, and informed her that she had found her a place where she could stay for a week. The free space was available the next day. I introduced myself to this woman, Darlene Elaine Miller. She told me that she was an advocate for the homeless through a program at her church. When Darlene left, Linda identified her as another one of her angels.

The talk of angels started to make sense to me.

On April 26th prior to the afternoon event scheduled at the Thelma Terry building, I sat drinking my morning coffee, eating the warm muffins and listening to speakers at an invitation-only gathering sponsored by the Rand Corporation promoting the release of the second annual City of Santa Monica 2014 Youth Well Being Report Card. City Hall staffers built the report card with data from Santa Monica's youth to evaluate their school achievement, physical health, social skills, and mental health.

The first report card of this kind came out in 2013. The idea behind it came about after a young man, John Zawahri, went on a shooting rampage in Santa Monica that killed five people before police gunned him down on the campus of Santa Monica College. The incident, although tragic, made some people pay attention.

An article I'd read, written by one of his preschool teachers (now a teacher at Santa Monica College), revealed that 20 years ago, when John had been her preschool student, he was timid and quiet. She wrote that this man had grown up with domestic violence. On one occasion, his mother contacted the teacher to tell her that when the husband threatened her and her sons with a knife, she'd sought help through the school's administrators. The administrators referred her to a battered women's shelter, where she and her children had found refuge.

Shortly after the shooting incident, city officials looked at the idea of well being in childhood.

In attendance at the Rand gathering were dignitaries, politicians, social service providers, educators, school administrators, a smattering of community activists and even some parents. Attendees heard that, according to data, more than 87 percent of Santa Monica kindergarteners were proficient in literacy. More than 92 percent of Asian and white Santa Monica kindergarteners were proficient at reading compared to 77 percent of Latino kindergarteners and 70 percent of African American kindergarteners. That was the good news.

They also heard some bad news. In this fairly affluent city by the sea, there still existed pockets of people living in poverty. The report card showed that literacy was worse among those low-income and minority kindergarteners, and that the gap widened by third grade as reading scores dropped across the board.

In third grade, only 67.7 percent of Santa Monica students were proficient in language arts. Nearly 80 percent of Caucasian and 87 percent of Asian students were proficient in language arts but proficiency dropped to 53 percent for African American third graders and 43 percent for Latino third graders.

Another troubling aspect of the data in the report card was that a quarter of middle school aged children reported feeling unsafe at school. Four in 10 seventh through ninth graders reported that they'd been harassed at school. Slightly more students than in 2012 said they'd felt hopelessness or extreme sadness recently (26.3 percent). As many as a third of high school juniors reported binge drinking in the past month, and 17 percent of high school students reported having suicidal thoughts.

The rate of child abuse and teen pregnancy was up slightly in Santa Monica. The number of family households on food stamps was also higher than in the prior year.

Disadvantage and trauma in childhood affect the body. About a quarter of incoming Santa Monica kindergarteners were not on track in physical development—most likely due to lack of nutrition. Boys from one of the areas where poverty still exists, the Pico neighborhood, were more likely to be physically vulnerable, according to the report.

Later that day, as I sat next to Oscar in the Thelma Terry building, the morning's experience was still fresh on my mind. I worked to be present and listen as people shared their perspectives on how to create a better community.

As the young men and women from the Pico neighborhood shared their stories, I saw human beings attached to the percentages, bar graphs, statistics and numbers. In that moment I was aware of what was missing from the experience I'd had in the morning at Rand. The power of the personal story, people's stories.

Are people becoming that disconnected from one other?

It is only by the grace of God that some people are thriving in this society. In order to deal with those who remain unhealed, society reduces them to data—these souls become just bits of information that translate into forms that are more palatable and more convenient to process.

Michele Castillo, one of the young people who spoke in the Thelma Terry building that afternoon, shined a light on my quest. I beheld her open heart as she shared her story in public for the first time, and I realized that my job, from this point on, was to be a witness for people who need one—people who wish to reveal their traumas as a way in to healing.

Michelle's Story

Michelle, in her mid-20s, had already witnessed an inordinate quantity of violence and loss. Born in the Pico neighborhood, Michelle was the youngest of four children—two sisters and a brother. She said, "My dad, my uncles, and their friends, who are the fathers of many of my friends, worked at a neighborhood factory down the street from Cloverfield Park in Santa Monica. When I was still very young, the factory closed down and my father, my uncles, and many others lost their jobs. Up until then, my father had been the family breadwinner; I think losing his job and his lack of ability to find another job caused him to start drinking. Not like he didn't drink before that, because he did. We would see my dad and uncles drink all the time. I think it's a cultural thing that was part of his life and the life of many of the men I knew in the community, but when he lost his job he really started drinking and it became an everyday thing. Eventually he became an alcoholic."

With the loss of her father's job and the fact that her mother was a stay-at-home mom who didn't work (due to cultural traditions about women and mothers), the family was forced to depend on food stamps and government assistance to make ends meet. "Not having a job, my dad spent most days drinking at Cloverfield Park. I think the fact that my dad wasn't around and drinking so much and because of other things too, two of my siblings got involved in gangs. When I was 5 years old, my sister (then 13) was shot; a bullet went through her chest and out her shoulder. She survived. From age 15 to 18 she did time at a juvenile correctional center in Ventura.

"My brother, who is five years older than her, was already in prison by the time my sister got sent away. Our oldest sister hung out with gang members but never joined. At 16, she came home one day and told my parents that she was pregnant. My father didn't deal with the news very well; she's like him and has the same personality and they were constantly fighting. My parents were having a hard enough time feeding us and couldn't really provide for another baby so my sister moved out and went to live with her daughter's father. I don't really remember her being around that much when I was a kid. She had a life of her own."

One day, Michelle's dad did not return home from the park. "We're not sure what really happened, but we think he either fell or got into a fight at the park that night." She recalled her mom getting a call from the police the next morning. The officers found him unconscious and totally soaked, on the grass under the sprinklers, with a bad cut on his head. The paramedics took him to the hospital. "I remember my mother taking me to visit him everyday that summer," Michelle told me. "My dad never came out of the coma. They kept him in the hospital for a month and then they moved him to a hospice, where he passed away from pneumonia and cirrhosis of the liver a month later. I never got to talk to him."

She reminisced about the park being like a second home. The Pico Youth Center provided healthy relationships and activities for Michelle. "All I had to do was jump the fence and I was in Cloverdale Park. My dad knew all the homeless men that lived in the park. He would walk by with me and they would say, 'Who's that little girl with you?'

"He'd tell them, 'my daughter.'

"'That's not your daughter,' they'd say.

"'Tell him you're my daughter, mi hija,' he'd tell me. My dad died the summer before I began eighth grade at John Adams Middle School. On the first day of school that year, I had to do a writing assignment about what I did during my summer vacation."

By age 11, Michelle had experienced the loss of her father and had seen the denial of a request by her brother, in prison, to attend the funeral. Her eldest sister was living with the father of their daughter, and the sister in detention in Ventura returned only a couple of weeks before their father's funeral. "Most of the people that I knew and grew up with got involved in gangs; many of them were and are still my friends. And even though I never joined a gang, throughout middle school I was pretty angry. I got into fights and then kicked out of or suspended from school. If it hadn't been for one person, Marie Everett, I don't know what my life would be like now. My family didn't know better and, as a result, never cared what grades I brought home.

"But our assistant principal, Ms. Everett, she did care. Every time

I'd get into a fight I would have to face her. And I was always afraid because I didn't want to disappoint her. Every single time she would take me into her office, sit me down, and tell me that I could do better. She would say, 'Michelle you're going to be somebody someday!' Ms. Everett believed in me. She pushed me to be better. She made sure I focused on my schoolwork. I was in honors English in high school because of her. She never gave up on me."

While in high school, Michelle applied herself and used another very important resource of support: the Pico Youth Center's after school program. "I felt like the people there knew my story. Mentors like Jaime Cruz and Oscar De La Torre had grown up in my community and they could relate to me. They made me feel like they cared. I never thought of going to college but they were always on me, telling me that I should. One of the caseworkers at the center helped me fill out my college applications. I would have never been able to get through all the paper work without his help."

With the help of caring people in her life, Michelle did better in high school than in middle school, but her struggles continued because the Pico neighborhood and the environment in which she was growing up didn't mirror her growth.

In 2005 when she was still at Santa Monica High School, Michelle went to a dance party. "A group of us had been at an event at the Pico Youth Center and somebody said that there was a party at the Moose Lodge on Ocean Park Avenue in Santa Monica. So with my boyfriend and two of our friends, Jonathan and Hector, we decided to go. We didn't know anything was going to happen; we got there and everything was normal. We saw people we knew and decided to sit and hang out with them.

I think we'd been there for about an hour or two and the music the DJ was playing was really loud. No one reacted to the first couple of bullets, but when the DJ stopped playing all of a sudden, it was like everything went into slow motion. You know, I'd never heard so many bullets being fired. Ever! It just kept on going and going and all I could think of was that I was going to die! My mind was, like, racing…I thought of my mom…what would happen to her…what would my mom do if I died? From under the table, all I could see was the shoes of one of the guys I knew, the shoes he always wore, Reebok classics. I thought, 'I think they shot Jonathan!' I looked at him after the shooting stopped, and I found out that Jonathan was dead. They shot him like sixteen times."

Despite the trauma she experienced, due to her perseverance and resilience Michelle gained admission to Mount Saint Mary's University and was doing well. Through her freshman and sophomore year at school, she was able to flourish and grow. But she couldn't completely escape the violence she'd lived through as a child.

During her junior year in college, her brother (now out of prison) was hanging out with a suspected gang member. Due to the gang injunction laws in place in Santa Monica, the police often raided Michelle's home looking for him. She told me: "When police come to your house it's not a nice scene at all. They usually come at five in the morning when you are completely asleep, completely vulnerable. It was my sister, mom, niece, and myself living in the house. They came three times within a week, broke down the door and windows. My mom has high blood pressure and diabetes. Our anxiety levels were through the roof. I haven't gone to war but I would describe it like war. An army of police with weapons comes in screaming; you are not able to speak or move. It was after that I began to experience panic attacks."

Michelle and her family got an eviction notice because of all the police raids and searches. Michelle remembers having to take an exam the day her family got the eviction notice. She had to work up the courage to go to her professor, let him know about the eviction, and ask for an extension. "I remember telling my professor and him saying, 'Michelle, you're one of my best students. Do what you have to do and we will work it out.'"

The panic attacks became more common for Michelle. The last semester of her senior year she experienced moments where she felt she couldn't breathe. She thought she had asthma. It was shortly after her graduation from Mount Saint Mary's that Michelle had the first of several really scary post-traumatic stress episode. "I was sitting down somewhere and all of a sudden I felt like I needed to get up because I was really scared, the adrenaline was flowing. I felt the same feelings as when the police broke down and came in through my window. I couldn't make it stop and the feelings of panic lasted for over an hour."

At this point Michelle, her mom, and sister were in a one-bedroom apartment in East Los Angeles. Shortly after Michelle's hour-long panic episode, they moved to a larger place in Lynwood. It was in Lynwood that the panic attacks became so intense that she couldn't function. "I couldn't go out, couldn't be on the bus. I moved into the living room because I couldn't sleep alone in my room. I didn't want to leave the house."

When she did leave the house, Michelle was crying.

She was uninsured, so finding help for her mental health status was not easy. Yet Michelle pursued numerous avenues and finally found a drop-in clinic in Culver City. She says the individuals there were dealing with severe mental health needs, and when she went to register for help, the psychiatrist was not available; no one would be able to see her for at least eight hours. She was not encouraged to stay, but she did. After eight hours, Michelle saw a psychiatrist and received a referral for mental health care and a prescription for anti-anxiety medication. The medication helped, but she had to be proactive in order to continue to receive it. This entailed going to a number of clinics and each time going through the process from scratch.

Michelle was determined to get well. She was also thinking about and planning for graduate school and the pursuit of a master's in social work degree. When I met her, she was in her second year at the University of Southern California, bringing about her dream of getting that degree.

I asked her what she planned to do with it.

"Having gone through my journey," she said, "I feel that there are many changes that need to be made in the system. Whether it's mental illness, or getting evicted, or growing up in a gang neighborhood, it's so hard to get help. Right now it's like you go to one door and they tell you 'we can help you with this.' If you need other services they tell you that they can't help. So you have to go from door to door. And then the doors are shut in front of you. For those who go through trauma, it just seems so overwhelming that people just give up.

"Also, the systems that are supposed to help people actually hurt them. For example, my brother who went astray at a really young age—he was a little boy. When he did get out of prison, he wasn't the same. He was hardened, a whole different person. The system made him hardcore. So when I'm done I want to create change and want to help other human beings who are going through what I did. I want to continue helping to take care of my mom and somehow change the system for the better.

"When I think back, all my mentors were always men. I feel that young women need more women as mentors and I feel a responsibility to fill that role.

"I'm going to focus on mental health and try to influence change at the macro level. Fortunately for us and for our communities, there are also many loving, caring, amazing people and organizations that are making a positive difference in peoples' lives. The word resiliency comes up a lot when I engage in trauma informed conversations and people tell me, 'Michelle, you are so resilient!' To me resilience is more than a concept. It's a doing, a way of being! It comes about through having a safe, stable nurturing relationship with a caregiver. It comes through a connection—a healthy connection can help ensure that people like myself overcome the violence and toxic stress experienced in our lives and our neighborhoods. I've come this far and know I'll make it."

Pismo Beach to San Diego, California

The morning of April 27, I set off once again. Five days later, after another uneventful and lovely ride along the California coast, I arrived at Cherokee Point Elementary in San Diego's City Heights on Friday, May 2 at 2:30 p.m.

I pulled into the parking lot to find principal Godwin Higa unloading eight huge pallets of food. The food delivery was the result of a relationship that principal Higa had forged with the city government. Cherokee was designated as a site where, every other Friday, 4,000 pounds of donated fruits and vegetables get distributed to the community. The distribution of food is only one of the things that this amazing man has been able to accomplish during his tenure at Cherokee.

Under Higa's leadership, the school has held events such as the Food 4 Kids Program–75 Backpacks in 2010-2011. This program provided students free food in a backpack every Friday for their use over the weekend.

In 2013, he started a pre-kindergarten student assessment team that is now on campus to assist parents with children with disabilities. He teamed up with the Copley YMCA to offer swimming lessons. Through the parent education department of the school, domestic violence awareness training, and other legal and health services are offered to parents. Classes on topics like immigration rights and how to prepare for a college education are also available. Higa also developed a close relationship with mid-city precinct captain D. Nisleit, of the San Diego Police Department. Through this partnership the

school participates in monthly curfew sweeps where they can identify community members' needs and provide access to community
services when necessary.

When he saw me, Higa stopped unloading the crates of produce.
After a greeting, he took me into the auditorium to meet nearly 100
students. These kids had stayed after school with their parents and
several visitors who were members of the ACEs Connection website
from around Southern California. I wheeled my bike to the front of
the auditorium. The students were standing and clapping; I saw the
stage lined with many drawings of me on my bicycle. Principal Higa
and Dana Brown had worked with the kids the whole week before
my arrival to provide such a welcome.

The kids sat down as I was introduced and we engaged in a
conversation about why I was doing what I was doing. I wanted to
emphasize how every individual has the power to change the world
for the better—just as their principal and all the adults in their lives
were doing for them.

Higa told me the story of how he came to be the principal at
Cherokee Point Elementary.

Godwin's Story

Of Japanese American ancestry, Godwin was born and raised
on the island of Oahu as the eldest son of a family of six, one brother,
four older sisters. In Japanese culture before World War II, men were
masters of the family. Wives and children had to obey the men; upon
a father's death, the first son of a family was expected to take over
the role of leader and he inherited all family properties. As first son,
Godwin's family treated him like a prince. Anytime something bad

befell him, his sisters took the blame. To this day, he feels guilty about what they endured because of him.

When he was 3 years old, Godwin witnessed his father take a plate of food from his mother, smash it against the wall, then walk out the door and out of his life forever. He recalls feeling sadness and relief, but the departure compelled the family to move to his mother's parents' home. The mother's family came together to build a two-bedroom house for Godwin's family on their 300-hog farm and banana plantation. From the age of six, Godwin's job was to get up in the early morning to feed and care for the hogs. This period of his life was his best ever; during that time his mother and father divorced.

Godwin's mother was 42 when she died—he was 15. It was only then that he learned how his mother had struggled to keep her family together, worked three jobs, and searched for the discounted food at the back of the supermarket to make ends meet. To honor her, Higa promised himself that he would always help others in need.

His path led him toward education and he's been improving the lives of students since 1995. By helping his students process their trauma, Godwin's selflessness for them also helps him cope and heal. Their mutual and reciprocal understanding creates relationships in which both individuals benefit. His students see him modeling compassion, listening skills, and finding thoughtful, reasoned, heart-centered solutions for their problems.

Godwin creates conditions conducive to the process of healing by running a trauma-informed campus as principal of Cherokee Point Elementary School. This community educates students where the median family income is $25,000 a year. All of the children are under Title 1—they receive free meals at breakfast and lunch. The part of San Diego where Cherokee is located also has the highest rates of domestic violence, gang activity, and drug abuse in the city.

Godwin developed a relationship with the city, the community, the school's staff, and the children in his care as part of his life of service. Cherokee Point is a safe place where restorative justice and practices are more than words; they are actions where the health and wellness of students are the number one priority. He has imbued Cherokee Point Elementary with the same work ethic that he developed from working on the hog farm in his younger years with his family. As a result, the people who participate in school-sponsored programs do not talk about the importance of community/school engagement—they live it! They understand that actions are stronger than words and children learn through what they see.

Later that evening, I chose to stay at a motel. After my talk with the kids, Dana Brown convinced me to stay an extra day in order to participate in the school's annual Compassion Day. This is an event that the school hosts for the entire City Heights community to learn about compassionate care for all human beings.

Dana is involved in a great deal of work that keeps the heart of Cherokee Elementary school beating. Among the many, many, things she does, including working with students and running a youth leadership program, she is a critical and integral part of advancing Cherokee's model of community service. Dana shares her passion for social justice with youth by providing them with the skills to become leaders on issues that matter to them, skills that will be useful to them for the rest of their lives. She is a living example of someone who understands social betterment and lives a life of service. Through her work, she is engaging future generations in the development of a more equitable and inclusive society and creating a generation of change agents who will one day become civic leaders. Her legacy will be a generation of 'heart based' and compassionate leaders who will develop, enrich, improve, and enhance the communities in which they live.

Dana picked me up the next day and drove me back to Cherokee Point Elementary where I had left my bike. During the ride we spoke about a shared deep belief: we are here for a reason and the greatest happiness is to live a life of purpose. We also talked about how there is so much more to life than the acquisition of things and that true happiness is achieved through connection with others. "Once you learn to love yourself," she said, "you are able to love and give of yourself to others and, in doing so, you get so much in return."

All the speakers at Compassion Day restated versions of those beliefs. For example, a fifth grade student read her essay on the topic of compassion: "Having compassion is caring, understanding, and helping others. It is knowing a person and not judging, but helping that person with what they need."

Another speaker, a young engineering student from San Diego State University, spoke about Islamic faith; love is embedded in it. The word "Islam" has its root in the Arabic language, from the word salema, meaning peace. This young woman also shared a story about the prophet Muhammad. Her story stayed with me for days after I left San Diego—see if it has meaning for you:

A woman put garbage in a basket and threw it on the prophet Muhammad when he passed by. Much to the woman's disappointment, he did not say anything and continued on his way. She did the same the following day thinking, "Maybe this time I will be able to annoy him." But he was too gentle to shout at a woman. She did this day after day.

One day, the holy prophet Muhammad did not find the woman to be on the roof of her house with the basket. This worried him, because he thought something must have happened to her. So he knocked at the door.

"Who is it?" asked a feeble voice.

"Muhammad bin Abdullah," was the reply. "May I come in?"

The woman was afraid. She thought, "I am sick, and too weak to fight or talk back. Muhammad has come to take revenge for what I have been doing to him." But he'd asked permission to enter her house in such a gentle voice that she allowed him in.

Muhammad entered the house and told her that not finding her on the roof had worried him and he thus wanted to inquire about her health. On finding out how ill she was, he asked if she needed any help. She asked for some water. He gave her some and prayed for her health while she quenched her thirst.

This made her feel very guilty for being so cruel to him in the past and she apologized for her mean behavior. He forgave her and came to her house everyday to clean it, to feed her, and to pray for her until she was on her feet again.

As I left the Compassion Day event, I saw compassion in action. Principal Higa and Dana were distributing food to those in need. I said goodbye to each of them and as I was riding away, I heard Dana calling out, "May you feel the hordes of angels surrounding you, James."

.

CHAPTER 8

More Roads, More Stories

You are not a human being in search of
a spiritual experience. You are a spiritual being
immersed in a human experience.

~ PIERRE TEILHARD DE CHARDIN, S.J. ~

Heading east toward Arizona I worked to hold the heat at bay by thinking about the ocean I'd just left behind. The soothing sounds of crashing waves resonating in my ears, the feeling of the soft sand beneath my feet, the breath of salty air.

These sensory experiences were easy for me to summon because of my years of teaching elementary school students. My most memorable times were when we'd walk on field trips to the beach.

San Diego to Blythe, California

Thoughts of past students mixed with ocean landscape memories came to mind as I cycled across the desert. Many of the students I taught were undocumented immigrants. For much of their lives they'd lived with Adverse Childhood Experiences. I hoped I'd made a positive difference in their lives. As the bicycle's wheels spun around and around, my mind spun thoughts and prayers for all students, especially ones like Giovanni, Jonathan, and Edwin. It's amazing to me how much teachers don't know about the lives of students who walk through their classroom doors.

On May 7, I arrived in Blythe, a town on the California-Arizona border near the lower Colorado River. After five nights of camping, I decided to treat myself to a warm meal, soft bed, and long shower. As I cycled into the parking lot of a small motel I watched a young woman who was watering plants. She put down the hose, turned off the water, and asked if I needed a room.

I said I did, locked the bike to a post, and followed her inside. We chatted as I checked in and noted her nametag. Stephanie told me she was a little nervous. The owners of the motel were away on vacation and she'd been trusted to run the place in their absence. She had been working at the motel for nine months; it was the very first time the owners had ever chosen to go away and not close down. She didn't want to make any mistakes.

I told her she was doing a great job.

She thanked me and asked me what I was doing riding through the desert and heat.

I told her about my journey and why I was doing what I was doing.

"I could tell you some stories!" she said. "In fact, I'm writing a book."

"Would you be willing to share your story with me?"

She hesitated then said she was busy but that when she took her break she'd see if we could talk. Handing me keys, she led me outside and pointed in the direction of my room.

Stephanie returned to the task of watering the garden. Reaching the room and unlocking the door, I turned to pull my bike inside and couldn't help but stand for a while in wonder at the sense of joy that seemed to be emanating from this young woman, lovingly tending to the flowers.

An hour or two later, I approached the office with a bag in each hand and asked Stephanie if the motel had a washer and dryer available for guests to use.

She said they did and walked me over to the room. While unlocking the machines she said, "Your laundry cost is on the house."

That evening, after repacking my cleaned and dried gear, I took a hot bath in Epsom salts and, after getting into bed, I decided that in the morning I would again ask Stephanie if she would be willing to share her story.

Stephanie's Story

Stephanie was 6 when she was introduced to her stepfather for the first time. "He swatted me the first day I met him because I didn't say hello. He said it was disrespectful. I had never been hit before. My mom would never—my mom was the type who would take us roller-skating even though she worked two jobs, always found time to do something with us. Until she met him. It was drastic the way she changed. We went from number one to number last," Stephanie said.

"My mom worked two jobs so he became our babysitter. My job before he came into our lives was to get my little sisters and myself in the bath because I loved helping my mom out in that way. It was my job, but now he thinks he can come in and do it…and it escalated…."

Stephanie told me that from that point on, from the ages of 6 to 16, he sexually molested and raped her and two of the three of her sisters. "A kid knows when it's wrong but they don't know all the time how to speak out and say it's wrong; at that time I didn't know how. I was taught it was wrong by my mom but when it was happening to me I thought, 'Oh my God how do I say something?' I was scared and ashamed."

At this point in our conversation Stephanie's youngest sister, now in her 20s, walked in with her beautiful 13-month-old baby boy. They had come by for a visit. She spoke to her sister concerning what we were doing and I asked her if we should continue at a later time. She said, "No, my sister's my best friend and has experienced it herself."

She told her sister what we had been talking about and continued without missing a beat. She said that this sister never let her stepfather do anything sexual to her but he "abused her physically and mentally."

The sister said, "Yeah, my sisters taught me how to defend myself. I was a fighter. I was physically a fighter!"

"She took a chunk out his mouth," said Stephanie as she laughed.

Stephanie shared that once he started the sexual abuse, she never again had a safe moment in her life. She lived her life in fear and wished he would die on the way home. She "prayed hard" and even had hatred towards God because she couldn't understand why God would let this happen. "Once we heard his truck coming down the road we didn't know what to do," she said. "We never knew what was going to happen depending on his attitude when he got home."

I asked them why no one got involved or attempted to end the abuse. They both replied that no one knew and that they were afraid to tell anyone.

"He owned his own business in town and was a well-known person. Behind closed doors, a person can be totally different, and that's what he is," Stephanie said. "When he was out there working, he was 'super family guy,' 'super dad'—whatever you want to call him. Later down the line, when he was arrested, no one could believe it. It happened when I turned 16 and I spoke to someone in social services. They came in, investigated, and told my mom she had a week to get us out of the house or they would take us from her. My mother did move us, while blaming me for everything, because of his arrest. He's now in prison."

The impact of the sexual abuse on Stephanie's life created her path; many abused children follow a similar path. If you have a high ACE score, you get it. If your ACE score is low, paths like Stephanie's might be difficult to understand.

As Dr. Felitti said, "We see people's problems when what we are really seeing is their solutions." He means that the problems they display are the results of choices they've made to find relief. The choices aren't always good ones; in fact, most often they are unwise and lead to more problems.

For example, Stephanie used methamphetamine when she was 12; she'd graduated to heroin use by age 15. A year later, she got pregnant. When I met her, Stephanie's son was 10 and her daughter was 3—both were born addicted to drugs. Her children were living with Stephanie's family members, whom she described as "caring and loving."

For a moment, I was distracted from the conversation by the loving interaction that Stephanie's sister was having with her baby. The sight compelled me to ask how one could teach others not to do what had been done to her.

Stephanie answered: "Everybody has a story and until you figure out, or they figure out what it is that makes them the way that they are…until they learn that to be sincere, loving, giving, and caring is the way to be…because if you are that way it really comes back to you. Until that happens, then there is no changing anybody." She tells me that she turned into a "cold, cold person," because of what happened to her. "I'd say whatever to get whatever. I was dead inside."

Counselors? Stephanie saw many, but there was one counselor she met at a rehab whose name was Christine. Christine stood out. "She was one of those people who you know cares…made me feel that she really cared. When I told her that I would die for my kids, she said, 'Why would you want to die for your kids when you can start living for your kids? You know that's what they want! They don't want you to die, to be gone! They want you to live, so why not start living?'

That message hit home with Stephanie. It touched her soul.

Stephanie was 12 months sober and drug-free the day I met her. She shared that she'd reconnected with God. Through her church she'd found the strength within to go to schools, talk to kids, and let them know that what happened to her shouldn't be happening to them. She tells them that if it is, they should not be afraid or ashamed to tell someone; that there are people who care. They are not alone.

Stephanie smiled when she told me how great it makes her feel to have earned the trust to run the motel, to be able to go to schools and tell her story, to ask kids questions like, 'If you had one wish what would it be?" and to see them open up to her. "It's awesome. It's awesome to know that good things that you do and say have an effect on people."

Blythe, California to Phoenix, Arizona

The route I'd planned took me through Phoenix and about a week before my arrival I'd contacted Kimberly Flack, a former teacher and now the general manager of PBS's Eight Educational Outreach. In April 2013 Flack and her staff organized an ACE summit hosted by Arizona State University and Eight Arizona.

Even though I was on the road, my daily routine included reading information on the ACEs Connection website, and I'd read an article that detailed the creation of the ACE (Adverse Childhood Experiences) Consortium by social worker Marcia Stanton through Phoenix Children's Hospital. And that's how I found Ms. Flack.

The ACE Consortium is a group of individuals representing organizations that have made it their mission to strengthen Arizona's families and communities. The consortium includes partners such as Phoenix Children's Hospital; Southwest Human Development; Arizona Department of Economic Security; East Valley Child Crisis Center; Arizona Association for Supportive Child Care; Northland

Family Help Center; Prevent Child Abuse Arizona; and, Valley of the Sun Arizona Association for the Education of Young Children.

Kim agreed to meet with me in her office in the Edward R. Murrow building at Arizona State University. She introduced me to two of her staff, Colleen O'Donnell Pierce (public relations) and Sam Becker (special projects coordinator).

I listened as Kim described the nature of their work. In partnership with PBS and Arizona State University, they aimed to serve as a trusted, independent catalyst for educational improvement by supporting educators and students in the classroom, and families at home, by creating and connecting them with relevant and engaging, quality content. They do this work through the power of noncommercial television, internet, radio, other media outlets, outreach activities, and, a variety of community-based initiatives.

One of the keynote speakers at the summit in April 2013 was one of the founders of the ACE Study, Vincent Felitti, M.D. He supported the fact that children are unable to learn unless they feel safe. Because of her teaching experience, Kim grasped the reality that educators are on the front lines; her mission was to spread information about the ACE survey to educators. One of the ways they do this is through a "Train the Trainer" program that has added to the professional development of many educators in the city of Phoenix and the surrounding counties.

Sam shared information about "The Darkness to Light Curriculum," created through a Strong Families Build Strong Communities grant from the Steele Foundation. He said that the curriculum is in use throughout the state. One of the topics addressed in the curriculum is emotional health and creating safe environments.

"People are hungry for this information," said Kim. One factor that supports Kim's statement comes from the response they had from a show they've been producing on PBS called "Ask an Expert."

The show has a panel of experts discuss topics such as sex trafficking, child abuse, sexual abuse, substance abuse, and suicide, to name a few.

Colleen mentioned that they've done the show several times. People called in to ask questions such as, "I'm addicted, so what do I do?" and "I think this is going on in my family. What do I do?" and "I just want to talk to someone! With whom can I talk?" The show has gotten the highest number of viewers they have ever had. It's even made the Nielson Ratings. They determined that the volume of calls was lower than the large numbers of people who were watching. "From what we know about the impact of ACE in our communities, I wonder how many people watching would have called if the denial and silence that persists in our communities didn't exist," Colleen said.

Sam introduced me to his father, Mark Becker, the associate director of the program. Mark had been a teacher but now worked at Eight Arizona (PBS) running the "Train the Trainer" programs. Mark, an avid bike rider, made sure I had plenty of water and some protein bars. Then he walked me to the freight elevator, a much more convenient way to get my bike out of the building, and went down with me to help point me in the right direction.

Biking now toward the east, I wondered how much good would happen if all the PBS affiliates throughout the country were inspired to do the kind of work Flack and her team were doing and had done.

Phoenix to Apache Junction, Arizona

Later that evening I sat in a small motel room outside of Apache Junction, Arizona, contemplating the upcoming ride across New Mexico. The ride through Arizona, given my age and level of fitness, was going well enough, but the spring's heat in these desert lands was taking a big toll.

The next morning, I gave in to the heat wave after I'd come up with zero points of contact with anyone in New Mexico who was putting ACE information to work. I decided to trade two wheels for four, rented a car and drove across New Mexico. I planned to resume the bicycle ride once I got to Texas.

I knew that New Mexico was a state much in need of ACE information and I felt regret that I had to drive through it without being able to meet people who'd connected to the study. On my first bicycle ride, it was in Tucumcari (in the northeastern part of the state) where a truck ran over me and I suffered a minor injury and needed repairs for the bike.

Was the fact that I wanted to drive across New Mexico this time a connection to the trauma I suffered near Tucumcari when I was younger? Is this an example of how the body remembers trauma?

Apache Junction, Arizona to Ingram, Texas

Ten hours later, after driving nearly nonstop, I arrived in central Texas. In the town of Kernville I returned the car, got back on the bicycle, and rode about six miles to the town of Ingram. There, I found a campground and reconnected with the southern tier route I'd mapped out on the maps from Adventure Cycling.

Never having travelled through this part of the country before, I became aware of the beauty of central Texas. Over the next two days, the ride took me through a landscape of rolling hills and lakes, much of it along the path of the Pedernales River.

Ingram to Austin, Texas

It was a little over 100 miles to Austin from Ingram. After riding less than 50 miles I made the decision to stay and camp at Pedernales Falls State Park. It's about 40 miles outside of Austin, and I was in no hurry. The next ACE meeting I'd arranged through Jane Stevens was going to be in a couple of days. She gave me the contact information for a Texas ACE Connections member, George Patrin, M.D. of San Antonio. He'd agreed to drive from San Antonio to meet me in Austin.

Now in Austin, I stopped at a sidewalk juice bar and told the owner (who made a beverage for me) that I was looking for a reasonable place to sleep. She directed me to the Firehouse Hostel in downtown Austin.

At the hostel, I spoke to a young lady at the front desk who told me that a bed in a four-person room had just become available on the second floor and offered to let me store my bike in the laundry room. I booked the room, took the elevator to the second floor, locked the bike to a metal pipe in the laundry room, and schlepped my gear to my room.

I settled in and called George. He offered to meet for breakfast the next morning.

George's Story

Early the next day, George picked me up and took me to an International House of Pancakes. After we sat down in the booth, George put on a red clown nose! It's what he's been doing since meeting and traveling with Patch Adams, M.D. and 32 clowns (from all nations) to Russia in 2012.

"There's power in the nose," he said with a grin. "Everyone should put on a clown nose every once in awhile because it helps to remind you to get over yourself and to remember that you are in service to those who depend on you." He pulled another clown nose out of his pocket and gave it to me. He said it would come in handy on my trip and told me that every time he puts on the nose, people drop their guard, brighten up, and go beyond judgment to actually engage and connect.

When the waiter came to greet us, his response to the nose emphasized George's point. With both of us wearing red noses, the waiter reacted with surprise and laughter and treated us as if we were friends instead of customers.

George told me that early in his career as a medical student—after he'd been a paramedic and experienced coming to the aid of people in their homes—he'd had a unique, life- altering experience.

It was during the beginning of the AIDS epidemic when not much was known about AIDS or how it was transmitted. There was a great deal of fear surrounding the disease. One day, George was working in a hospital and came upon an AIDS patient. The man asked for help—he wanted to sit, and in order to do so needed someone to pick him up and put him in an upright position. George felt somewhat afraid, but he picked up the man and moved him. During the act, their faces touched cheek-to-cheek as George wrapped his arms around the man and moved him to a sitting position.

George filled with emotion as he shared his memory of that moment. It was that moment when he woke up to the fact that above everything else, a doctor needs to feel empathy and act with compassion.

Having finished medical school at the University of Minnesota, George got his pediatric board certification at Madigan Army Medical Center, and got a master's degree in healthcare administration from Army-Baylor. He went on to work as a pediatrician, then in healthcare administration, focusing on patient-centered, family-focused health. He retired from the U.S. Army after 23-plus years as a pediatrician, battalion surgeon, and patient and family advocate.

George helped a lot of people over the course of his career. But someone he was not able to help, and who has put him on the path he is currently on, was his youngest son. On April 7, 2009, Andrew Patrin, a sensitive and creative young man, committed suicide.

Of course, he struggled with the questions of how could it have happened and why. He believes that it shouldn't have happened to Andrew and that it doesn't need to happen for other people. George believes that suicide is preventable and, due to his history in the military, George is on a mission to end suicide by veterans. He created an organization named the Serendipity Alliance that assists veterans with Post-traumatic Stress Disorder (PTSD) to get the help they need to keep living.

"It hasn't been easy to fix a broken system," George told me.

George feels he's been "batting zero" in getting veterans access to effective resources for their mental and emotional health. Despite the passion he feels for his mission, and his knowledge of both military and civilian systems, George struggles with the fact that people in power positions who should be accountable are not. Many of the veterans he's worked with since Andrew's death were not able to get more than mediocre healthcare, especially when they went in and asked for help before they decided they couldn't go on living. George remained convinced that these former soldiers, men and women, did indeed want to keep living—only they wanted to live without the pain of betrayals, losses, grief, and other memories of lifetime events tainted with trauma.

After breakfast, George drove me back to the hostel as dark rain clouds appeared on the horizon. Although George braved the weather and drove back to San Antonio, I decided to wait out the rain. I sat in the common area of the hostel and made use of free Wi-Fi, while enjoying a cup of tea.

I scrolled through the statistics on veterans and suicide:

- Every 65 minutes a military veteran commits suicide

- Every day 22 military veterans commit suicide and 31 percent of that number are veterans aged 49 and younger

- Nearly 1,000 veterans attempt to take their own lives every month (more than one attempt every 30 minutes)

- The Veterans Crisis Line has answered more than 890,000 calls and made more than 30,000 life-saving rescues since its launch in 2007

- The number of active duty suicides in 2012 surpassed the number of American troops killed in Afghanistan and the number who died in transportation accidents in 2012

- More soldiers in U.S. uniforms have died from suicide than have been killed in Afghanistan since 2001

- At least 20 percent of Iraq and Afghanistan veterans have PTSD and/or depression

The rain lasted for a couple of days in Austin. On the third day, I took advantage of a break in the clouds and left the city. I made my way eastward, following a great bike path alongside the Colorado River.

Austin to La Grange, Texas

That day's ride took me through the town of Bastrop where I stopped for lunch before pushing on to La Grange. The weather was taking a turn for the worse, so I searched a map for places to stay. The Colorado Landing RV Park was a recommendation, and it was only five miles away. I called and got a reservation. I also got there and checked in before the rain did.

As I was setting up camp, the owner of the park came by and told me that the skies were going to open up and my little tent would probably wash away. He said I was welcome to stay overnight in the community center. There was a couch I could sleep on in there.

I ended up staying in that community center for three days. The skies did open up to deliver a hammering rain. The owners were extraordinary in the way they allowed me to feel at home; a true shelter from the storm. I was grateful for the attention and hospitality as well as a few days' rest to build resiliency for the road ahead.

La Grange to Beaumont, Texas

In Beaumont, I was supposed to meet with a couple of ACEs Connection members: Antoinette and Sheila. Both worked with returning veterans at the Beaumont Veterans Administration Outpatient Clinic. I'd called them a couple of times to make arrangements, but upon my arrival they apologized. Both had family issues arise; neither of them was able to meet with me.

So, I spent the night in Beaumont with the intention to leave Texas. I put the pedal to the metal, and pressed on to cross the state line into Louisiana.

Beaumont, Texas into Louisiana

Louisiana was everything I imagined it would be: the people, the landscapes, and the Cajun and Creole cuisine. I met up with traditional soul food such as smothered pork chops, candied yams, hot cornbread, fried chicken, collard greens, black-eyed peas, red beans and rice, gumbo, jambalaya, po'boys and more. I've always enjoyed savory and delicious cooking and this was indeed food for my soul.

Pedaling across this land, I felt a kinship and familiarity. Louisiana seemed similar to my birthplace in Bolivia. Enjoying the atmosphere in small towns and having a few otherworldly experiences were part of my travels through Lafayette, Baton Rouge, Hammond, and Covington. For some reason that remains a mystery, I felt a profound link to the past—a history that I still cannot explain but certainly felt in my heart.

I spent a great deal of my time while on the bicycle (much like the first time I rode across the country) conversing with God. What changed on this second trip is that these talks involved the concept of faith. Sometimes I talked about my faith but more often I wondered about that of others. My faith in God at this point in my life was not in question. The truth is that I was riding alone on a bicycle at the age of 56, sometimes for 40 or 50 miles before coming upon another living soul. I had faith!

My faith in God kept me pedaling, kept me company, and kept me safe. But this time I was more present and therefore more conscious that other people—through their actions—were showing me that there existed something or someone greater than us, that every single soul is here for a reason, and that a life of service to others is the greatest life that one can aspire to live.

I became a witness to the other people who relied on their faith to guide them through good times and bad, to keep them company and be their only solace when times got tough. I watched their faith unfold before me, beheld grace in action, and came into contact with stories that stood as testaments to God's part in every life.

For example, a preacher, R. C. Linton, Sr., came along as I was struggling through a patch of bad road and gave me a lift in his pickup truck. On that ride, we spoke about ACEs and how one's faith can help build resilience and enable recovery.

R. C.'s Story

The preacher shared that he had gone to Vietnam at the age of 19. He thought he was a man, but came to learn that he was just a boy thrown into something that he still struggles to understand. R. C. came home after being injured when the truck he was driving was bombed. He'd survived the attack, but was haunted by the fact that his best friend, who'd been sitting next to him, did not. The Veterans Administration helped with his physical needs, but at that time, PTSD was not yet a 'thing' and there was no appropriate mental health support. He lost himself in alcohol and drugs for years.

One day a preacher came into his life and told R. C. that he owed it to the memory of his friend to get himself together; that he had a responsibility to live not just for himself but also for the friend who died. Touched by the way in which this man reached out to him (and also offered assistance with quitting the addictions), he began attending church. Eventually he became a preacher and followed in that man's footsteps by ministering to other people's spiritual needs, helping as best as he could to be useful and put people on the right path.

After saying goodbye to R. C., and as I was crossing one of the many bridges along the Louisiana bayou, I spotted a family on the docks below. Compelled by something I can't explain, I turned the bike around and decided to stop and visit with the young couple in their mid-20s.

Erin and Darryl's Story

Erin and Darryl lost their son, Ayden, age 3, in a drowning accident. The loss was devastating, but their love of God, and prayer, allowed them to overcome grief and filled them with compassion for others.

Their loss forced them to confront the fact that few services existed in their community for people who suffer the loss of a child. They knew they had to take action. In what I consider an act of selflessness, and to honor their son, they created Ayden's Foundation of Hope. On the day I happened to be riding by on that bridge, they where holding the third annual fishing tournament fundraiser for Ayden's Foundation. The money raised was to assist other couples dealing with the loss of a child or who had a child suffering from a life-threatening illness.

When I learned their story, I remembered close friends of mine Scott William and his wife Catherine. After the birth of their son Shane Alexander, the baby was diagnosed with spinal muscular atrophy, a genetic disorder afflicting one in 10,000 children. Shane lived only two weeks. Shane's life and death caused his parents, family and friends to reach farther than ever before when they created Shane's Inspiration (www.shanesinspiration.org). Ayden and Shane were catalysts to show how tragedy may be transformed by love.

Faith is what Erin and Darryl leaned on when tragedy struck; faith carried them through and then spread to create something beautiful out of something so painful and tragic.

Darryl's mom made me a ham and cheese sandwich, and I was invited to the crawfish boil that they had planned for when the tournament participants returned, but I had miles to go before the stop I'd planned. I thanked them and pushed on while thoughts of their faith filled my body, head and heart.

The experience Erin and Darryl provided was in direct contrast to times during my ride when God did not seem to be present anywhere except within my being. One day, I saw a man who was spread out, face down, under a bridge overpass; a young woman hunched over, sleeping against the wall of a dilapidated building; a young couple sitting in a truck while she cowered from a man who screamed curses and vile epithets at her—his face mere inches away from hers; a woman with young children at her side holding a sign that read "Lost my job help me feed my kids."

Bayou Country to Hammond, Louisiana

I had stopped and was resting at Hidden Oaks campground in Hammond, Louisiana. When I was about to leave, I was invited to share a cup of coffee with three women in their 50s. The experiences they shared with me were lost in time and memory—until they met me.

As I listened I remembered something Dr. Felitti said: "ACEs go unrecognized because for many of us, our adverse childhood experiences are lost in time, protected by shame, secrecy, and social taboos."

The Stories of Nina, Melinda and Chris

Their names are changed here to protect their privacy but their stories are relevant and common. Nina owned the campground; Melinda and Chris were employees. The three were all women of faith; warriors who'd braved many battles, and developed friendships, camaraderie, and a special kind of sisterhood.

Raised by two alcoholic and abusive parents, Nina said, "They never gave me nothing." When her dad returned from Vietnam, he threw Nina out of the home, choosing his sister's family over her. At age 14, Nina was alone, living on her own in an apartment. She was pregnant with her first child by 16, got involved with drugs, but at some point found God and the strength to quit. Around that time, she met the man who would become her husband and co-owner of the campground. They raised seven kids. One of her sons committed suicide in 2008. She was matter of fact when she talked about the suicide—and even as we talked, Melinda had to remind her of the year of his death.

Melinda was not much for speaking. But I got her to tell me about the sexual abuse and beatings that occurred throughout her childhood.

Nina then spoke for her and said that Melinda ended up marrying a biker who beat her half to death and that she was nearly dead when she arrived at the camp. Melinda joined the sisterhood of Nina and Chris. After building some strength, she realized she'd had enough. With the help of her new friends, Melinda left the biker and chose to live at the camp and work with Nina for the next 10 years. It was clear that it took a great deal for Melinda to speak her truth. I could see that she was full of emotion. That fact did not escape Nina either. As Nina told Melinda's story, she placed her hand on the woman's shoulder.

Chris was the most verbal of the three women. She was born in Oregon but said she'd "been all over the country." She moved to Louisiana to care for her son's baby because the son was serving time in the Army, stationed in Kuwait. We laughed when Chris said, "If and when I die, I don't want to be buried here! I want to be buried in Connecticut."

Without missing a beat, Chris told us that the reason she travelled so much in her childhood was because her father was a Baptist minister. He kept moving them from place to place—and he was abusive beyond words to her, her mother, and her brother. He once beat them with such force that he nearly killed them. The state had to step in and rescue them. The father was schizophrenic and sent to an institution. While he was locked up, Chris's mother taught herself to drive using the tractor in the barn, got some money, a car, and moved with Chris and her brother to Connecticut. Her father got out and found his family, but by that time Chris was away at boarding school.

A woman coach employed at the boarding school got Chris to play basketball, baseball, and volleyball. Through sports, Chris found her power. Looking at us she paused for a moment and then said, "Mrs. Agee cared about me and changed my life."

Magical moments passed as these three women, connected by chance and faith, opened little doors into their lives and shared forgotten moments.

Mainly, I got to witness Nina's great sense of humor and large heart.

I was amazed when I found during the course of our conversations that she had been in the hospital two weeks earlier. She'd passed out while suffering a heart attack. Yet while we chatted, I'd been watching her work. She was lifting large cases of soft drinks that had just been delivered to the campground.

I jumped up to help her saying, "You shouldn't be lifting those!"

Nina waved me away saying, "Son, I'm not done living and I ain't gonna slow down 'til God comes to take me."

Hammond to Covington, Louisiana

When riding long distances on a bicycle, a person gets into a rhythm. This was mine: I put my head down, pedaled forward and focused on the road ahead, often missing the landscape that surrounded me. Now I was doing just that, with my thoughts focused on getting to Mississippi, less than a day's trip away.

But serendipity knocked and I got out of that rhythm.

Something took me out of the reverie and rhythm of my two wheels on the road and made me look up. I saw a sign that read, "Florida Parishes Juvenile Detention Center." I stopped, turned around, drove through the parking lot to the front of the building where the sign was hanging, laid my bike on a nearby bench, and pushed the speaker button.

The guard on the other side wanted to know how she could help me.

I replied, "I would like to speak to one of the supervisors."

She told me to hold on and, a few minutes later, the metal doors clicked open and a young man came out.

Steve introduced himself and asked me what he could do for me.

I gave him some details about the reason for my journey and asked if he would be willing to speak with me about the facility and the work he was doing there.

He said he could give me a couple of minutes and invited me inside. I said I wanted to lock my bike and he said, "No need. We have cameras everywhere. No one will touch your bike."

We went through the metal detectors and sat down in what was like a visitor waiting room. I took off my helmet and told Steve about my purpose, and in doing so I happened to mention Dr. Vincent Felitti and the ACE Study. Everything changed! Next thing I knew I was sitting in a conference room with Steve and the executive director of the Detention Center, Tom Jarlock.

Conversation began in earnest. Actually, it was not really a conversation but a lesson for me in leadership, courage, vision, and faith. I don't know what to call it—providence? Coincidence? Fate? Perhaps you'll have a word for it after you read the story.

It turned out that Tom and Steve had been to Chicago to hear Dr. Felitti speak. They each got the opportunity to spend time with him, ask questions, and gather information. "The ACE study confirmed a lot of what we experience and know already," said Tom.

The Florida Parishes Juvenile Detention Center houses kids who have many risk factors and very few protective factors. Tom said that it's no surprise they get caught up in criminal behavior. These young boys and girls come from dysfunctional and broken homes; many of the girls in the center are victims of sexual abuse. From Tom's perspective—a viewpoint supported by the ACE Study results—these boys and girls get involved in criminal behavior as a coping mechanism. Tom repeated Dr. Felitti's insightful quote: "We see people's problems when what we are really seeing is their solutions."

Tom's Story

Tom was born in 1963 and grew up in Michigan. He has three siblings. He said he experienced "a childhood that was not so remarkable for the period that I grew up in." After elementary school he attended a rural high school located just outside of Midland. His parents divorced when he was 12. When his father was no longer in the home, the atmosphere changed.

As Tom entered adolescence, there was much less structure and discipline than there had been. There were many parties at his house, hosted by adults. He was thrust into a world he knew he was not ready for, a world that children should not be exposed to at that age. He witnessed substance abuse and the chaos that ensued. "I was not protected from these events and I was prematurely exposed to these adult behaviors," he said.

As a child of divorce, Tom experienced what it's like to only have one parent. His mother made sure that Tom and his three siblings had nothing to do with their father, convincing them that he was a reprobate. She reinforced that notion to the point where none of them wanted to speak with their father. "I understand the concept of parental alienation and how divorce can rob a child of access to both parents," Tom told me. The divorce became one of the traumatic events in his life that colored his perspective. "Not having a relationship with my father during my early adult years...I would say, looking back over those years...I felt less than complete."

Yet Tom was able to build resilience while enduring emotional pain. He adopted exercise as a coping mechanism; sports and exercise became a great outlet for him in his teens. Now in his 50s, Tom sets goals related to physical fitness. "I do my best to mix it up and include different types of activity. I have done years of bicycling, some different running events, some mountain climbing and hiking events, and other events in my community." Tom also added journaling and music to his coping mechanism toolbox. He said, "I find great relief from journaling and some solace in playing the guitar."

In 1982, Tom graduated from high school and entered the United States Marine Corps. Four years of honorable service there was one of the significant events in Tom's life. He said that it was where he "grew up, learned about cultural diversity, and understood what it meant to lead by being immersed with the highest caliber of men." He is able to apply what he learned in the Marines to his work at the detention center.

The work of Dale Carnegie also had an impact on Tom's life journey. (Dale Carnegie built an empire based on his belief in the possibility that you can change someone else's behavior when you change your own behavior first. Carnegie is the author of a pamphlet titled *The Golden Book,* published in 1936.) Tom enrolled in the course "after a failure at work and it changed the way I thought of and spoke to people. He said, "I practice the principles I learned from Dale Carnegie with every interaction and I have taught these principles for over 20 years. Even my daughters apply these principles in their normal conversations."

After 28 years of not speaking with his father, Tom reconnected with him. This permitted the release of a heavy burden that he carried, and allowed for vital healing to come about. Tom told me that he was now able to see his relationship with his father as a protective factor and a source of wisdom and support in times of need. This was a positive in his life. Due to his parents' divorce Tom is empathetic to the fact that marriage endings exact a toll on families across the world, and he strongly identifies with them. "I'm especially sensitive now to the destruction that adults can apply to their own children in the process of struggling to be free of a marriage they no longer desire to be in. It saddens me to see how indifferent adults can be to their own children while in the fog of divorce."

Tom acknowledged that his experience gave him a greater insight and made him more compassionate to the struggles that children endure at the hands of their parents.

In 1994, Tom became the program director for the North American Family Institute, Inc. (NAFI) in DeFuniak Springs, Florida. The NAFI is a 40-bed residential program designated as a "serious or habitual offender program," and it was the first of its kind in Florida.

After five years, Tom received a promotion to regional director of NAFI. He supervised nearly 200 residential beds at several facilities in Florida.

Then Tom joined the Florida Juvenile Justice Provider's Association as a regional board member and became its president in 2002. His priority was to challenge the tactics that the juvenile justice system mandated for defiant and combative youth. The policy was nicknamed "Use of Force." The association advocated that kids in custody be handled with more humane tactics, foregoing the "pain compliance techniques" and "joint manipulation" mandated by the department.

In 2004 Tom was selected by the Florida Parishes Juvenile Justice Commission to become the executive director of the Florida Parish Juvenile Detention Center. After taking the helm, Tom was mindful of the need to examine the detention center's operations. He asked questions such as: Why do we do that? Why must it done that way? Can it be done differently? He took a values concept taught by the Marine Corps, "a belief in excellence," as a call to change the culture of the center.

Tom discovered that the answers to his questions were not in Louisiana at the time. "It wasn't done differently anywhere in Louisiana, so I started asking outside the state," said Tom. "We found a place that was doing it differently when we went to Chicago to visit the DuPage Detention Center." The National Juvenile Detention Association recognized that center as a model program. There, all the residents participate in an intense program geared to reduce their risk of recidivism. The concepts of restorative justice form the basis for effective interventions now done with juveniles.

Tom said, "We brought those principles home after spending a week up there learning their processes. Over a period of 18 months we implemented the cognitive behavioral interventions model." Over the next two years, the center lost 90 percent of its staff. Many of them couldn't make the transition from the authoritarian to the caregiver model. "They could not go from being guards to what they are now—more like shepherds. We treat kids by asking, 'Are we removing dignity from them or are we caring for them?'"

For example, in 2004 the center didn't have shower curtains—the kids showered under supervision. Now they have shower curtains because, according to Tom, "We shouldn't be looking at kids who are naked. How do kids feel when they are seen naked? They feel awful. They're unsure about their bodies, they're experiencing a lot of change, and they're in an institution. Should they ever be seen naked? Our perspective is no! That is a huge dignity removal, so we don't do that anymore. And we don't do strip searches for random events. We do them only if and when we have probable cause. We are very careful in how we train people to speak to kids. We don't use derogatory terms. We don't curse at kids. We don't strike them. We don't use chemical agents on kids. We are very cautious about every interaction and our main focus is letting them keep their dignity. We do a lot of training on de-escalation of kids; therefore, we are very patient.

"Some people see that as coddling. We see that as giving kids ample opportunity to express themselves, which gives us the opportunity to resolve things without using force." The numbers explain everything. In 2004, Tom said there was "a full, hands-on violent restraint of a kid every day" that involved handcuffs or pepper spray. "Now that happens maybe once a month."

No one asked Tom to make the Florida Parishes Juvenile Detention Center a model, but because in the past 10 years he focused on what he and his staff could do to provide the best in this industry to provide the best services for kids who required assistance, it is a model program. "It's not been easy," Tom said. "While making these changes, the judges were saying, 'Well, we don't like that!' For example, every kid would have their head shaved when they came in. Judges seemed to like that! I said, 'I don't feel good about that. Why do we do that? Why don't we offer kids regular haircuts?'"

One day, a judge called Tom and said, "Look, I want this kid's head shaved."

"Your honor, put that in their order and I'll go ahead and shave this kid's head."

Later, Tom got this message: "The order's coming."

He replied, "Great. I'm waiting to see it."

The order came and it said, "Youth shall have hair cut."

By 2005, the Florida Parishes Juvenile Detention Center had the reputation of being too soft.

Tom responded by giving a stuffed animal to kids during their intake. He explained, "You got a 14-year-old, 15-year-old kid, maybe a girl, first time away from home in jail, an institutional environment, how does it feel? Feels awful! Feels awful. Did they do something bad? They did something that warranted them being detained. Does that mean we treat them like a criminal or thug? They're a kid! They're a recoverable resource that we want to help recover!"

Tom's aim is to train all employees to preserve the dignity of the kids who live at the center. He looks to finding the right people to employ—people who have an interest in doing things that don't require chest-banging machismo or an "I'm going to go in there and kick some ass" kind of mentality. Tom believes he's made a significant impact on the lives he's touched—those of his employees and the resident kids.

"We want kids to leave here feeling better than when they came in," Tom said. "We want them to be reinforced as human beings, to leave here thinking, 'I got detained, but these people cared for me while I was here. They didn't stomp on my chest. They didn't feed me bad food. They didn't taunt me for whatever reason—my sexual orientation, the crime they alleged I'd committed. They didn't taunt me because I'm poor and came in only having one shoe. They didn't taunt me because I live in a certain area. They respected me!'"

Together with the staff Tom said that he's been able to preserve the purity in this model for juvenile detention. He described it as "a pure soup that people can taste. If the right team comes together, it can be done in other places. A doable thing. Somebody can do it if they have the will and desire!"

Tom has been able to be caring and open with the human beings in his charge because he recognized that he was not much different from them. "We have all been children and we have all suffered some adverse childhood events. Everyone has a story to tell—and yearns to tell it. It is a pleasure to have someone engage at a level where they feel comfortable relating their life story to another human. It is a Carnegie principle to get other people speaking about themselves. I find it humbling to be in the presence of someone sharing his or her ACEs with me. Seeing their vulnerability helps me understand that we are all so very much alike even though the experiences we have had in our past may differ." Tom is able to share his own experiences with others knowing that it helps them understand that we are in fact, suffering or recovering from suffering, or watching others in our lives suffer or recover from suffering. He also believes, and likes to point out to folks, that some suffering in our lives is quite optional.

Similar to the message of de Chardin's quote for this chapter, Tom says, "I believe that we are souls locked in robes of temporary flesh. My belief that all of us are responding to our desire to become complete gives me the ability to see people who are in transition from where they have been to where they want to be. We all need help along the way. I have received a tremendous amount of assistance in my journey to become and evolve. I believe we are created in the image of our Creator. I am able to love and care for other human beings because I know they too are on a journey. I am grateful to be in the path of many souls in robes of flesh who are traveling through very difficult times. I have always believed that

I could be a resource to help those around me, that I can improve myself and therefore improve the care of those in my charge. So by becoming better and improving myself I can help the lives of those that I have contact with."

I saw that Tom's optimism was fed by grace. He counts many positive experiences in life. At the top of Tom's list of positive experiences is being a parent to his daughters.

"I believe that positive interactions with others—making an investment in their lives—is what will help them grow. And it helps me grow," he said as we ended the meeting.

Covington, Louisiana to Pass Christian, Mississippi

Leaving Covington, and Louisiana, I followed the beautiful Tammany Trace Bike Trail and crossed into Mississippi. Then I bicycled onto the Mississippi Coastal Heritage Trail, a border-to-border trail that traverses the Bay Bridge into Harrison County and makes its way along the coast through the towns of Pass Christian, Long Beach, Gulfport, Biloxi, across the Ocean Springs Bridge into Gautier, past Pascagoula through Moss Point and into Alabama.

Making my way along Mississippi's coast I witnessed the power and fury of Mother Nature because the route I traveled followed Hurricane Katrina's path in 2005. Eight years later, I saw many structural signs of damage and ruin along the road, although many of the buildings and homes demolished were rebuilt—especially in the affluent areas.

My planned routes sometimes veered away from commonly travelled areas. I liked cycling through areas and communities off the beaten path. During one such stretch I saw block after block of boarded up homes. This was a blighted area where the streets were still littered with piles of debris and wreckage. Turning a corner,

I had to stop at the sight of a small group of young African American kids, around ages 7 or 8. They were riding their bikes over wooden planks they'd fashioned into a ramp. One of the boys hit the ramp at a bad angle and went flying off of his bike. He cried out on landing and I started to go over but stopped. I got wary looks from his friends. He seemed to be OK and I sensed that the kids didn't want or need my help. So I got back on my bike and continued on.

Less than ten minutes later I was riding past a gated community of manicured lawns and luxury homes. Questions filled my head.

Economic inequality isn't a theoretical concept. It is alive and thriving. This inequality took root. It is growing. The rich get richer and the poor get poorer. I saw the visual proof up close and in person while travelling through these towns. The truth of economic inequality led me to moral questions about society.

What are the common interests that unify us today?

Do common interests exist in our cities, towns, or neighborhoods?

Are there now two Americas?

Are we bordering on the threshold of the world of people-as-self-interested-animals as envisioned by the British philosopher, Thomas Hobbes?

Martin Luther King, Jr. said, "We no longer live by God's law but rather by man's law."

What I see while on this bicycle, on the side roads as well as the main roads, is that we've created neighborhoods but we continue to fail to create brotherhood.

It was evening when I reached the beach town of Pass Christian. With 60 miles under the bicycle's tires that day, I saw a large sign advertising the Pass Christian RV Park—two miles inland. At that point, my cell phone had almost no charge left. Tired, hungry and losing daylight, I decided to go for it and said a prayer that my phone wouldn't die before I arrived.

The further inland I ventured, the thicker and taller the trees grew. Tall trees covered with moss were obstructing light from the setting sun and ominous shadows lay in my path. My imagination ignited.

I was in flight-or-fight mode.

Growing up with domestic violence made me hyper-vigilant. I remembered the tale of the scorpion and the frog as I rode. In that story, a scorpion and a frog meet on the bank of a stream and the scorpion asks the frog to carry him across on its back. The frog asks, "How do I know you won't sting me?"

The scorpion says, "Because if I do, I will die too."

The frog is satisfied, and they set out into the water. Midstream, the scorpion stings the frog. The frog feels the onset of paralysis and starts to sink, knowing they both will drown, but has just enough time to gasp, "Why?"

Replies the scorpion: "It is my nature."

Being on alert is part of my nature. Even when it's not warranted, it takes hold of me. I remember being 11 years old and waking up to the sound of deep, piercing screams. I jumped out of bed. I ran across the hallway and burst through the door of my parents' bedroom. And then, instead of the violence I'd envisioned, I was comforted. I witnessed my father's awkward attempts to soothe my mother, who still wailed and howled. He'd just returned from Bolivia the night before with bad news for her, but was unable to deliver it until that morning. He told me that my mother's father, my grandfather, had passed away. As I closed the door behind me, I wondered if I was relieved that he wasn't hitting her.

Now, with almost no battery power in my phone on a shadowy dirt road, I was on hyper alert, deep in the unfamiliar territory of rural Mississippi. I pushed on, repeating the "Our Father" prayer to myself while at the same time contemplating turning around, tracking my way back to the coast and camping on the beach. A light came toward me from the opposite direction. It caused me to pull to the side of the road and stop. The car turned about 50 yards from where I stood. Gathering courage, I got back on the bike and rode toward where the car turned. To my great relief, the road seemed to be the entrance to the camp.

As I wheeled in, I saw that off to the side two Caucasian men were sitting in beach chairs having beers and cigarettes. I asked them if I was at the Pass Christian RV Campground. They nodded. I told them that I was looking for a place to pitch my tent for the night. They stared at me without giving me an answer.

Finally, one of the men took a long drag on his cigarette, pulled his glasses down over his nose to take a serious look at me, pointed to the man sitting next to him, and said, "The man you need to talk to is sitting right here."

All sorts of scenarios played themselves out in my head— thoughts about how they were judging me. The memory now causes me to feel shame.

The man's name was Dusty. He owned the camp and let me stay there for free. He provided me with the use of a warm RV with a soft bed. He brought me fresh towels, toothpaste, a new toothbrush.

The inhabitants of the RV campground fed me, opened their hearts to me, got to know me—free of judgment—as I got to know them. It made me wonder what the world would be like if everyone could go beyond the surface and take the time to see into each other's souls; to get to know each person that we are fortunate to meet beyond the masks and labels that are imposed.

I was reminded of a passage from the Bible, found in the gospel of Matthew 7:1-5:

Judge not, that you be not judged. For with what judgment you judge, you will be judged; and with the measure you use, it will be measured back to you. And why do you look at the speck in your brother's eye, but do not consider the plank in your own eye? Or how can you say to your brother, 'Let me remove the speck from your eye'; and look, a plank is in your own eye? Hypocrite! First remove the plank from your own eye, and then you will see clearly to remove the speck from your brother's eye.

On my second night at this campground, Dusty visited me. He brought his wife and three daughters. He placed the youngest one atop his shoulders and walked the family over to introduce us. His wife was a public school teacher. Dusty told her that I was a teacher and she'd asked to meet me.

She was eager to share her experiences on the conditions of the school systems in that part of Mississippi. I told her about my teaching style—how I worked to develop relationships with the parents of my students, got to know many of them and, in doing so, knew and understood the children I taught.

I talked with her while Dusty went to pick up supplies for an impromptu barbeque he'd decided to throw. When he returned, we watched as his daughters tackled him with love—they knew he'd brought candy. Camp residents who knew Dusty well brought dishes of food: hush puppies, okra stir-fries, fried green tomatoes, southern fried cabbage, burgers...

That night I was reminded that no matter the skin color, social class or culture, food unites people. Food is cultural expression. Food is history. Food is love.

People transform through the simple act of breaking bread together.

Pass Christian, Mississippi to Mobile, Alabama

When I planned this cycling trip across the southern states, I discovered that Adventure Cycling created a route that honors the Underground Railroad—which was neither a railroad nor underground. It was a network of clandestine routes and safe houses by which the African people, freedom seekers, attempted to escape slavery before and during the Civil War.

The Underground Railroad Bicycle Route starts in Mobile and makes its way north all the way to Owen Sound, Ontario, Canada. Mobile is the starting point because in the 1800s the town was a key port where slaves were unloaded from ships that brought them from Africa. Mobile was one of the busiest ports for the slave trade during the pre-Civil War era.

Riding my bicycle through the southern states to engage people in conversation on the impact of the trauma of adverse childhood experiences, I wanted an opportunity to spread news and learn for myself the ramifications of generations of oppression. People of color suffered and continue to suffer the terrible cost of generational and historical trauma.

The following essay excerpt, written by Frederick Douglass, inspired me:

> For those who bask in the light of privilege in the dominant culture, they take for granted their right to assert themselves and to be acknowledged as 'somebody who matters.' For those who live in the shadowy margins, such as the American poor and/or minorities, they experience the systematic denial of the basic human rights—to live at one's fullest potential, in other words, an outright denial from living a 'dignified life.' Such a denial might cause one to feel 'voiceless and choiceless.' It has been the minority's experience, historically and in the present day, that the right to achieve one's full potential is kept just

*out of reach. Minorities must first fight for survival. Then, if
there is enough energy and hope remaining, they can strive to
utilize vehicles of assimilation or resistance in order to carve a
place for themselves in the world. However, this does not mean
that a full realization of the 'American dream' is even possible.
For every small victory, there remains a bitter aftertaste. In
other words, for every step gained, there is a 'personal or
cultural sacrifice.' Meanwhile, on the journey to freedom, the
individual is plagued with 'ghosts' of the past. These 'haunt-
ings' can appear in the form of individual/family oppression,
knowledge of emotional pain, and physical violence.*

On Sunday May 25, I arrived in Mobile, Alabama, and went to the
center of town where the slave market once stood. I leaned my bicycle
against the wall of an historical building on the corner of Royal and
St. Louis streets.

A large plaque titled "The Slave Market" commemorates the site
with the following words: "After the abolition of international slave
trading in 1808, dealers transported slaves from all over the South
into Mobile. On this site, Africans were sold as chattel to southern
planters through public auction. Between auctions, a three story
holding facility housed the slaves until they were displayed and sold."

Standing in this place of human suffering while reading these words,
a truth Frederick Douglass revealed haunted me. It was in another essay:
"What to the Slave is the Fourth of July?" The thoughts he expressed then
are as true today for many people who live on the margins of poverty and
violence. Douglass's ghost seemed to stand on that corner with me and
ask: "What, to the American slave, is your Fourth of July?"

In Douglass's voice again:

I answer; a day that reveals to him, more than all other days in the year, the gross injustice and cruelty to which he is the constant victim. To him, your celebration is a sham; your boasted liberty, an unholy license; your national greatness, swelling vanity; your sounds of rejoicing are empty and heartless; your denunciation of tyrants, brass fronted impudence; your shouts of liberty and equality, hollow mockery; your prayers and hymns, your sermons and thanksgivings, with all your religious parade and solemnity, are, to Him, mere bombast, fraud, deception, impiety, and hypocrisy-a thin veil to cover up crimes which would disgrace a nation of savages. There is not a nation on the earth guilty of practices more shocking and bloody than are the people of the United States, at this very hour.

For two days I stayed in Mobile. Then I got back to pedaling along the rivers that led north. I sang a song I'd taught some of my fourth grade classes, "Follow the Drinking Gourd." The slaves did not have maps to take them north but they sang directions. Here are the lyrics:

When the sun goes back
and the first quail calls
Follow the drinking gourd
The old man is a-waitin' for
to carry you to freedom
Follow the drinking gourd

Chorus
Follow the drinking gourd,
follow the drinking gourd
For the old man is a-waitin'
to carry you to freedom
Follow the drinking gourd

The riverbed makes a mighty fine road,
Dead trees to show you the way
And it's left foot, peg foot, traveling on
Follow the drinking gourd

The river ends between two hills
Follow the drinking gourd
There's another river on the other side
Follow the drinking gourd

I thought I heard the angels say
Follow the drinking gourd
The stars in the heavens
gonna show you the way
Follow the drinking gourd

Mobile to Grove Hill, Alabama

On May 28, 2014, when I stopped in a small town outside of Jackson for supplies, I learned that Maya Angelou had died. I admired her. The bicycle allowed me to express my grief; as I rode alone I cried over the death of this great woman. Her work, life, and writings influenced and taught people to be authentic—to write or say truth without fear. When I read her autobiography, *I Know Why the Caged Bird Sings*, I felt it was a gift and a lesson in courage. Angelou's valor in sharing with the world her harrowing experience of sexual abuse and rape at the age of 8 opened doors of healing for many. Her sense of herself as that of a bird struggling to escape its cage was her truth. It said, and still says, so much about resisting all forms of oppression. I once watched an interview of her in which she described words as living, breathing beings. Maya Angelou forced us to look at truth embedded in struggle; truth that everyone has an obligation to face, confront, use for change...and to share with others.

As if my grief affected the weather, later that day the skies grew overcast and gloomy. Dark clouds formed. For the next three days, the rain never stopped. I believed that the angels were crying for Maya Angelou.

Rain made the roads difficult. After struggling to stay north along the river, I decided to get off. In Mobile, I'd met a cyclist who liked to ride on U.S. Highway 43 because of the paved shoulders. I located it on the map and saw that it led all the way to Jackson, Alabama, a town 60 miles north of Mobile. It was a good option and it allowed me to reconnect with the Underground Railroad Bike Trail a mile or two east of Jackson.

Little did I know how this detour would change the course of my journey.

About 20 miles into the ride on Highway 43, I felt beaten down by strong headwinds and persistent rain. I saw a sign that said "Grove Hill, 3 miles." I got there after another half hour's worth of pedaling.

Grove Hill, Alabama's population is 1,527. The town offered up an affordable motel, and even better, Maria's Mexican Grill. I checked into the motel, hung my wet clothes, and took a long hot shower. In warm, dry clothes I walked over to the Grill for a hot meal.

The rainy weather kept me in Grove Hill for a couple of days. On Sunday, June 1, I decided to get back on the ride. Early that morning, I packed, walked the bike over to Maria's Mexican Grill, and fueled up on a plate of *huevos rancheros*.

While I was enjoying breakfast, a Caucasian couple and their two young boys came in and sat in the booth directly across from me. I smiled at them. One of the boys was African American and the other was Latino. We began a conversation and I learned that Steve and Patrice lived in Grove Hill. On Sunday mornings they go to Maria's for breakfast after church because their two sons love Mexican food. The oldest boy, 8-years-old, was born in Guatemala; the youngest, aged 4, was born in Mobile.

In my mind, I was thinking about how in 1963 Alabama's governor, George Wallace said, "Segregation now, segregation tomorrow, segregation forever." For me, this family was a sign that Wallace's comment was not true. The family was a sign of change. As I left, we took a photo together in front of the restaurant. A mural with the words *Bienvenidos Amigos* was our backdrop.

Grove Hill to McIntosh, Alabama

I had been cycling on Highway 43 for about three hours when once again I thought of life and its duality—how people move in and out of darkness and light all of our lives. The rain had been holding back, but I saw ominous clouds on the horizon.

Without any warning, I saw a small blue pickup truck shoot out onto the highway from a side rode about a thousand feet ahead of me. Then, sounds of screeching tires, crunching metal and shattered glass permeated the air. A semi-trailer truck in the southbound lane, unable to stop in time, made impact and sent the blue truck tumbling through the air.

I arrived on scene as the semi-truck driver was getting out; he seemed uninjured. But the traffic was backing up and I could hear sirens in the distance. The blue truck was right side up on the side of the road but its driver was not wearing a seat belt. He was laying about 15 feet away. Onlookers, and Good Samaritans, were getting out of their cars. Some Samaritans helped a young woman get out of the truck. Those Samaritans then laid her on a patch of concrete on the median. Her bent leg gave me a feeling it was broken and that she was in shock.

Paramedics arrived and ran to the young man. Another one got out of the cab and tended to the young woman on the median. Bystanders were milling around; questions filled the air. The paramedic told the girl that she might have a broken leg and that the ambulance was on the way. The state police arrived and dealt with the traffic that had backed up.

A woman approached the girl as the girl asked someone to loan her a cell phone. The woman did not have one, but she asked if any other bystanders would loan their phone. I laid my bike down, walked over to the girl and let her use mine. Her hands were shaking when she made the call. I took a few steps back but I still overheard the conversation. In a monotone voice, the girl explained that the accident was bad.

The ambulance arrived as drops of water fell from the dark clouds. I got my phone back and discovered that my back tire was flat. The rain intensified. I walked over to the African American state police officer and asked how far it was to Jackson. "Twenty-five miles," he said in a brusque tone.

"Sorry to bother you, but I just found out I have a flat and was...."

"You see me trying to deal with an accident here."

Then the sky opened up. I retrieved my bike and took it over to a cluster of trees in hope that the overhead leaves would help keep the bike, my gear, and me somewhat dry while I changed the flat. The rain came in torrents; water was pooling, flooding around me. Yet I got the fix done and got back out on the road.

I rode only about a half mile down the road and was relieved when I saw a U.S. post office. I left my bike under a small awning and stepped inside. My clothes were drenched. Although somewhat guarded, a female postal worker offered some paper towels. She also let me bring the bike in and allowed me to use a side room to change into some dry gear. I told her about the terrible accident and she said that accidents were common in the area. A few days before, two people had lost their lives in a head on collision; they were not wearing seat belts. Changing the subject, she asked me what in tarnation I was doing on a bicycle in the rain on Highway 43.

I told her. For the next two hours we talked uninterrupted, with the exception of a single customer who braved the rain to drop off a package.

A Postal Worker's Story

Taking me into her confidence, she said that her first marriage to an officer of the law was destroyed by domestic violence, sexual abuse, suicide, and a terrible judicial system. Based on her experiences (and also on those of the many women she knew), the courts in the county contained judges who were not impartial. She said they had a bias against women; they seemed to side with the man no matter what the situation dictated. It was especially difficult in her case because the abuser was a male cop. Even though she was the one abused, he got full custody of the three children. She endured horrific beatings from this man, then experienced isolation from her family and friends because no one believed that "such a wonderful man" could ever do the things she'd accused him of doing.

After the suspicion of his sexual abuse of his daughters surfaced—and when he was charged—she was able to win back custody of the children. He committed suicide before being brought to trial.

She had given me a lot to think about as I straddled the bicycle to push onward. As the post office disappeared from view, I realized how exhausted I felt. What was I doing alone on a remote road, in the middle of nowhere? Did God know? Was this His plan for me? Will this journey ever end? What happened to the boy who was the accident victim? Did he make it or was he dead?

What was life teaching me?

McIntosh to Jackson, Alabama

As the sun was beginning to set, I arrived in the town of McIntosh, Alabama. After a long, traumatic rain soaked day, I stopped for a map check. As I was removing the map from my front pouch, I watched the front tire go flat. It was the third flat tire of the day. To make matters worse, I was out of spare tubes.

Why?

Why did my tire go flat at this particular moment?

The sound of laughter interrupted the bleak picture I'd painted. I became aware of a house at the end of the long driveway I was standing on. I walked the bike through the puddles and up the driveway. I crossed a patch of rain soaked grass and made my way to the front of the house. Turning a corner, I came to a complete stop, for in front me were three African American women.

I could see it in their eyes—they were guarded but curious. So I introduced myself and launched into my tale.

They told me that I'd interrupted their pre-dinner ritual. This mom, her daughter, and their neighbor, who was also a cousin, always share a beer and smoke a cigar to unwind from their workdays. As we talked, her teenage son and another cousin pulled up in a truck. The mom asked me to join them for a beer and we engaged in a conversation about race, the terrible public school system, jobs, and family. At some point, the mom told me not to worry; her son would load my bike in his truck and give me a lift to a motel in Jackson. The son nodded his head and smiled, assenting to her request.

That night at the motel I knelt down in prayer, as was (and is) my practice every night. I thanked God for protecting me and keeping me safe on this journey. I asked Him to watch over the two young people involved in the terrible accident I'd witnessed and I prayed for the well being of my own family and all the families I was so grateful to have met on this voyage.

The next day when I was checking out, I met and spoke with Marion, the hotel manager. Originally from Birmingham, Marion was living and working in Jackson. She'd had a full life with many lessons, but she lived her faith and set an example for people to live by. The conversation I had with her enriched, enlightened, and solidified my purpose.

Marion's Story

Marion grew up in a home with an alcoholic father who worked, so he drank only on weekends. But his drinking got worse—to the point where he would drink and then disappear for months. This created a lot of insecurities for his children. The last time he left there was nothing to eat in the house except potatoes.

Marion was the oldest of seven and remembers being 13 at the time. On that day, her father came home after he'd been drinking and was in a rage. "He started to beat my brother and then he was going to start in on me. My mother stopped him saying, 'I've put up with a lot from you but you will not touch my children.'

"I've always had a good imagination or perhaps you could say that out of my pain came the imagination, so I made this bowl of potatoes real fluffy and called everyone around the table and said, 'We're going to have vanilla ice cream.'

"Billy was one of my brothers—out of the seven of us, he's the only one who's deceased, and of a drug overdose. I remember Billy used to say, 'My sis can take a few grains of rice and some beans and make a gourmet meal.'"

In that moment, I realized that in listening to stories like this one, I had changed. I was filled with gratitude because of this new aware-ness. I am someone who's never experienced hunger. Her words took me into a new world where mashed potatoes became vanilla ice cream. In this story, I was able to experience the significance of food insecurity for a child.

Marion's eyes filled with tears as she said, "To this day, even though I may not want to eat the food I have stored in the pantry or the refrig-erator, I make sure that they are always kept stocked. I know what it is to look in the refrigerator and have no food. I know what it's like to have nothing to eat. I believe I'm secure about a lot of things and even though we get over those things, as I said, I always need to have the pantry full. It makes me realize how important safety and stability is for children when they are growing up. Security and safety became just nonexistent for us in our childhood and it went on for a lot of years."

Experiencing pain in her childhood turned Marion into the woman I met—a woman with the capacity to forgive. When her dad got sick with cirrhosis of the liver, he had nowhere to go and he came back to her. By this time Marion was healthy and strong, married, and in her 30s. She remembered sitting beside his bed as he was dying. "I can't say to you I had this daughter-father wonderful relationship, but I had compassion for him," she said. "I had sympathy because I thought 'he's laying here, he's old, he's got no one but me out of all the kids. I would not be in his shoes; he's got no one.'"

Marion confided that it was her faith that gave her the ability to love him and have sympathy for him. Faith led her through the choice to see that her life events made her a better—not bitter—person. "Long ago, my faith became my stronghold," she said. "I remember going to church alone and just digging into a relationship with God, Jehovah, or whatever you want to call Him. I believe there is a higher power, a higher being who is guiding us."

CHAPTER 9

Trading Old Life for New, and Bicycle for a Greyhound Bus

Let us not see today's troubles as a reason to give up;
let us see them as an opportunity for God to deliver.
~ **DILLON BURROUGHS** ~

My awareness that physical fatigue had set in lingered with me for a couple of weeks, and it grew each day. I was taking longer breaks and staying in motels rather than camping. My budget couldn't sustain that for much longer. Getting on the bike felt like a chore and the recent bad weather had not helped. My legs were weak—not as strong as they had been during my first cross-country journey—and were not bouncing back with recovered strength after a night of rest.

But my fatigue was not just physical—it was also emotional and intellectual. I felt mentally exhausted.

Jackson to Linden, Alabama

The narrow two-lane road I took out of Jackson was treacherous. The shoulder was almost non-existent and it forced me to pull over every time a lumber truck came into view, especially when two trucks approached from opposite directions.

The blaring horn of a lumber truck triggered an internal alarm and I responded by driving off the road and landing in a ditch. As I got up and checked for cuts and bruises, doubt set in, and I wondered, "What the hell am I doing out here on this country road in the middle of nowhere? Is this how it's meant to end for me?"

I checked over the bike, readjusted the handlebars, and secured the panniers on the rack. I pulled myself out of the ditch and pedaled another 40 miles to Linden, Alabama.

Dog tired, I turned into the first motel I saw, the Linden Inn. It was Thursday, June 5. An elderly African American gentleman sat on a recliner and smoked a cigarette at the entrance to the front office. I got off my bike, approached the window and noticed a sign that said, "Back in a Few Minutes."

I leaned the bike against a wall and reached for my water bottle. "If you're looking for a room you're going to have to wait."

"Thank you. I saw the sign."

"You a biker? Lots of bikers come through these parts. I'm in charge of room service. You looking for a room?"

"Yes. One with a bathtub because I need a good warm bath."

He told me that I was at the right place. Rooms were available, and they all had tubs. He told me that there was a Family Dollar Store a block away where I could pick up Epsom salts for $2.99. "People riding through here all the time, they tell me they like to sit in them salts. Say it's good for the muscles."

That night as I was filling up the tub, I heard a knock on the door. Pulling back the curtain, I saw the gentleman from "room service."

I opened the door and he asked me if I had a couple of dollars to spare. He wanted some food and his paycheck was due in a couple of days. I handed him five dollars. He thanked me and, as he was walking away, he said, "Tomorrow if you're looking to have a good breakfast, good home cooking, country fried steak, eggs, and biscuits, go to Screamers…about three blocks up the road."

One of the things I'd learned is that there is no such thing as chance or coincidence. Everything is connected. Carl Jung said it best: "It all depends on how we look at things, and not on how they are themselves."

The next morning I found Screamers and enjoyed a plate of country-fried steak, eggs, biscuits and coffee.

I was also listening to my body and researching locations on my phone for the nearest Greyhound bus station.

An elderly man was having breakfast at the table next to me. He introduced himself and said, "I'm not one to snoop but couldn't help but listen to the conversation you was having with the waitress." He'd overheard the ACE elevator speech overview—how the study came about, how it evolved into a national study addressing adverse childhood experiences, and why I'm on the road.

He told me that he belonged to the local Southern Baptist church and that they had a wonderful pastor who was doing great work with the community's youth. "I always learn something from his preachin'," the man said while pulling out his phone. "You mind if I give him a call? I'm sure he'd love to meet you."

Chad's Story...and My New Story

Ten minutes later, brother Chad, pastor of Southern Baptist church in Linden, walked over to my table. Chad was a large imposing man who overcame a congenital foot deformity to be the starting center on his college football team. It wasn't until the age of six, after having endured a series of painful operations in order to walk normally, God entered his life.

Lying on the operating table, preparing for a final surgical procedure, Chad became conscious that he was not alone. He understood that there was no reason to be afraid and knew that it was time for him to profess Jesus Christ as his Lord and Savior. In that moment, his whole life took on new meaning.

On hearing his story, I smiled; although I did not have to endure any operations, I too had been born with my feet slightly turned inward and had to wear metal leg braces for the first year of my life. Was it synchronicity or our shared physical childhood condition that bound us together for the next three hours?

At the age of 56, a full 50 years later than Chad, God expanded my consciousness, and my life. Thanks to Chad. We engaged in a powerful and personal conversation on faith, spirituality, and personal calling. Chad prayed over me as I chose and professed that Jesus Christ was my Lord and Savior.

It was a complex yet simple act that I realized gave context to my whole journey. I'd engaged in an act of personal vulnerability—professed my belief in an unseen energy, based on love, from a source unimaginable by the human brain.

It is this kind of vulnerability and belief that is needed in times when the idea of rugged individualism is celebrated—when people are shunned for being their brother's keeper. It's needed when people live in pronounced refusal to regard others with respect. When so many communities have become fragmented and infected with a coliseum-like, "lion's den" culture. In a time when there is little respect for truth, pure love and vulnerability must be valued. People just want simple answers that give them immediate gratification.

Chad and I spoke about the teachings of Jesus and the shared consensus that across all religious traditions there is a common belief: The inherent dignity of every person, including children. This is a moral imperative that many people in the world have lost sight of—dignity and respect for all. Chad said that as warriors in Christ's name, we must break the silence and speak truth by acknowledging suffering and reaching out with compassion to people who've been excluded and rejected. Chad quoted from the book of James, 2:15-17: "Suppose a brother or sister is without clothes and daily food. If one of you says to him, 'Go, I wish you well; keep warm and well fed,' but does nothing about his physical needs, what good is it?"

We discussed a concept, a figure of speech in the Bible—the concept of parrhesia (to speak candidly or to ask forgiveness for so speaking; freedom of speech). We spoke about accepting Christ as the savior to create a specific relation to truth through frankness, a relationship to life through danger, a relation to self or other people through criticism (self-criticism or criticism of other people), and a specific relation to moral law through freedom and duty.

We prayed together and spoke from our hearts. We asked God to allow us to be compassionate with ourselves and help us practice compassion with others. We asked Him to assist us in letting go of who we think we should be and to give us the courage to be who we are. We prayed for the vulnerability to live in this world and engage in truth telling instead of falsehood or silence, and, to demonstrate moral duty instead of self-interest and moral apathy. We prayed for God to guide us, strengthen our faith, and give us the courage to live with an open heart.

Then Chad removed his hand from my shoulder and we sat in silence for a while.

I remembered what Mother Teresa, one of my heroes, said when questioned about what one could do to promote world peace. Her answer: "Go home and love your family."

I realized that I had walked into the answer to the question I'd been asking for more than 50 years. God is in me. God is in all of us. Faith is less about belief and it's more about doing.

Rilke was right—you do not attain the answer you're seeking until you are ready for it. Years ago, when an acting teacher watched me struggle with my emotions, he told me that acting was not about feeling. It was about doing. In a moment of frustration with my work, he imparted an important truth that I was not ready to hear or understand. This teacher went on to tell me that if all people did was walk around feeling rather than doing, nothing would get done.

Karen Armstrong, author of numerous books on religious issues also wrote a memoir titled *The Spiral Staircase*. The following quote from her memoir expresses an important insight: "The religious quest is not about discovering 'the truth' or 'the meaning of life' but about living as intensely as possible here and now."

This quest I'd been on informed and changed me. It confirmed a powerful truth I now deeply understand and will preach—as well as walk in example of—for the rest of my life. All the great religions teach their own version. We call it the golden rule: "Treat others as you would like them to treat you."

The Golden Rule is ready to be expanded to the Platinum Rule®
as Tony Alessandra, Ph.D. has described. On his website, he writes:

> *We have all heard of the Golden Rule-and many people
> aspire to live by it. The Golden Rule is not a panacea.
> Think about it: "Do unto others as you would have them do
> unto you." The Golden Rule implies the basic assumption
> that other people would like to be treated the way that you
> would like to be treated.*
>
> *The alternative to the Golden Rule is the Platinum Rule:*
>
> *"Treat others the way they want to be treated." Ah hah!
> What a difference. The Platinum Rule accommodates the
> feelings of others. The focus of relationships shifts from
> "this is what I want, so I'll give everyone the same thing"
> to "let me first understand what they want and then I'll
> give it to them."*
>
> *A Modern Model For Chemistry*
>
> *The goal of The Platinum Rule is personal chemistry and
> productive relationships. You do not have to change
> your personality. You do not have to roll over and submit
> to others. You simply have to understand what drives
> people and recognize your options for dealing with them.*

My life serves to make me living proof that Adverse Childhood
Experiences have a lasting detrimental impact on a human being.
Children that experience violence and abuse do not experience
the Golden Rule (much less the Platinum Rule). If they are not
treated with love and respect they become adults who hurt themselves and they learn to hurt others. With a lack of love and care,

children are set on a path and will rarely be able to reach what Maslow's "Hierarchy of Needs" identified as the top of level of personal growth—self-actualization. Maslow knew that a person must satisfy lower level basic needs before progressing on to higher level emotional growth needs.

Children who experience ACEs are destined to exist cycling in the lower energies of their brain—the fight, freeze, or flight mode. They will—like I did—struggle to develop the top part of their brains, the frontal lobe area.

Personality exists in the frontal lobes. The frontal lobes manage emotions, problem solving, reasoning, planning, and several other functions. The brain's frontal lobes are linked to sensory and memory centers. Their primary job is to allow humans to think things through and determine how to use information located elsewhere in the brain. Unless we act on this newfound knowledge and insight, the cycle of violence passes from one generation to the next—forever.

Linden to Tuscaloosa, Alabama

My visit with Chad was complete but I asked if he was able to give me a ride to the bus depot. I told him that I was ready to go home.

Twenty minutes later, my bike was secure in the bed of his truck and we were on the road to Tuscaloosa, Alabama, 72 miles north of Linden.

While we drove, Chad said that he started out as a pastor at another church, one located in a very prominent community. One particular Sunday he decided to preach the parable of the wedding feast.

In that parable, a man planned a large banquet and sent out invitations. When the banquet was ready, he sent his servant to contact each of the invited guests, telling them that all was ready and the meal was about to start. One after another, the guests made excuses for not coming and so he told his servant to forget the guest list and go into the back streets and alleyways of the town and invite "the poor, the crippled, the blind and the lame."

A few days after delivering the sermon Chad received a call from the church elders inviting him to dinner. They asked if he was interested in continuing to preach at their church. Chad heard them say that he had a great future, but they needed for him to tone down his message. From their perspective, it sounded as if he was telling the congregation that all were welcome. They said that people might get the wrong idea about being welcome; the wrong idea was that African Americans were to be welcome.

Chad's head filled with questions. How would he provide for his wife and two young kids if he didn't do what they told him to do? Where could they go? How would they live? So, he thanked them and then told them it was exactly the message that he was trying to convey. He said to them that if Jesus were here today, the message that African Americans were welcome to worship in their church would be exactly what Jesus would be shouting from the rooftops. Chad reminded them that God judges people not by the color of their skin but by the content of their character.

That dinner experience was a turning point in Chad's life. As we pulled into the Greyhound bus depot Chad told me the news that he'd invited an African American bishop from his denomination to come to Linden and preach the Sunday sermon in a month. And it would be an event the town had never experienced until that day.

Meeting Chad was the best possible way I could have ended my bicycle journey. Filled with gratitude I stood next to the bike and waved goodbye as Chad drove away from the depot.

Tuscaloosa, Alabama to Pittsburgh, Pennsylvania

The bus ride from Tuscaloosa to Pittsburgh lasts 36 hours. If memory serves me, I changed buses twice: in Nashville, Tennessee, and Columbus, Ohio.

In Columbus, waiting in the Greyhound terminal for the connecting bus, I noticed that the woman sitting next to me was having trouble opening a packaged snack. I introduced myself and asked if I could be of help.

She smiled, thanked me, and pointed the package towards me. I opened it and placed it back in her hands while saying that I was waiting for the bus to Pittsburgh.

Roxanne told me that she was blind and that she was waiting for the same bus. It was due to arrive in an hour and a half. Time flew as we carried on a conversation.

Roxanne's Story

Roxanne had lived in Ohio for the past 20 years and was on her way to Pittsburgh to connect with her sister. From there the two were going to Virginia. Her sister's husband was to pick her up at the bus station and then drive the sisters to an annual reunion at the Virginia School for the Deaf and Blind.

Her son was in his late 20s and was going through a tough time. He'd lost his job and had to move out of his apartment. Roxanne allowed him to move in with her until he got another job. The problem was that he'd been drinking—when drunk he struggled with anger issues. Just before her trip, he'd gotten so angry that he got in her face and threatened to hit her. She was afraid of him, even though she loved him. She let him know that he needed to get help and if he hadn't done anything about it by the time she returned he would have to find another place to live. She admitted that getting an opportunity to spend time away from him was good for her.

But now she was trying to hold back tears. She felt his problems were all her fault. Her ex-husband, the son's father, was an abusive alcoholic. Maybe if Roxanne had left him sooner her son wouldn't have turned out as he did. On more than one occasion her son witnessed his father beating her and, towards the end of the marriage, the son stepped in between them in order to protect her.

I asked Roxanne if she would like me to find her some tissues. She shook her head 'no' while reaching into her purse to retrieve a handkerchief.

It's difficult to experience another's pain. It is difficult to share pain with others. Social and cultural norms teach us that sharing pain is a sign of weakness.

From the intercom we heard of the arrival of the bus to Pittsburgh. I offered to carry Roxanne's bag onto the bus. After hoisting the panniers over my shoulder, I lifted up her bag and followed. Due to her disability, we were granted priority while boarding. Roxanne made her way up the steps and into the front seat. I placed her bag on the seat next to her and, after depositing my stuff on the overhead rack, took a seat in the row behind her.

She fell asleep, but I thought about her struggle with her son. And then I couldn't help but recall when my family moved out of my mother's house, and I'd moved into that house, which led to the terrible confrontation with my father.

As the bus wheels rolled, I remembered the screaming and the sight of my mother on her knees crying, picking up pieces of shattered glass. Before I knew it, I was in my father's face, yelling at him at the top of my lungs, physically threatening to break his neck if he so much as laid a hand on her....

Did she forget to pay a bill?

Was she being too lenient with one of us?

Did he have a bad day at work?

Was she on the phone too long?

Did she spend money on something he considered stupid?

My sister ran into the room, screaming for us to stop. She caused me to back away and gave him the space to go into the kitchen.

When my father came out of the kitchen he was screaming in rage. A knife was in his hand. We froze, but only for a moment.

I was on my hands and knees, helping my mother and sister collect the pieces of broken glass, pieces of a German anniversary clock. But for the knife in his hand, we'd all danced this dance before.

It became clear that the knife was for me and not my mother.

My father said that he was going to kill me if I didn't get out of the house. He was screaming at me to get out of his house. My sister begged for him to stop and told everyone that unless we stopped, she'd call the police.

My mother got up off her knees and walked towards me. She begged me to leave. I stood my ground. I yelled back at him, telling him to go ahead, go ahead and kill me. My mother pulled on my arm. She tried to move me towards the door. She was telling me to leave for a little while until he could calm down.

The last thing I heard as I was walking out the door was my sister's voice as she screamed, "I'm dialing the police!"

My phone vibrated in my pocket. I answered it and heard my sister's voice. She told me that she was on her way to Pittsburgh from New Jersey. She was making good time but I'd still have to wait about an hour for her. I must have drifted off to sleep for a while, because the next time I opened my eyes the bus was pulling into the Pittsburgh terminal.

I helped Roxanne off the bus and made my way over to retrieve the cardboard box I'd crafted together in order to transport my bike. Inside the terminal, Roxanne introduced me to her brother-in-law. Her brother-in-law took a picture of us with my phone and I stood still for a moment to watch them fade from view as they exited the terminal.

I searched for a place to reassemble the bike after breaking down and disposing of the cardboard container.

Pittsburgh, Pennsylvania to New Jersey

My sister showed up in a car she'd rented and parked in the posted No Parking zone where I stood waiting for her. She popped the trunk open so I could put the bike in it, then she put my gear in the back seat. As we drove away from the terminal I gave her a kiss on the cheek. I was feeling deep gratitude for her selfless, compassionate, and giving nature.

After about 20 minutes, we stopped for dinner at an Italian restaurant in downtown Pittsburgh. It was there that we made the decision to stay overnight rather than attempt the six-hour drive back to New Jersey. I was grateful for the time that we were going to have together because we don't get to see one another very often, but I was also aware that the experience would leave me feeling unfulfilled.

One of the things that those of us who grow up in violent homes lose is the certainty of being loved, the open heart and natural confidence that we were born with. We learn to be on guard—if not completely shut down—at the emotional level. It's how we survive. When a child is consistently treated without respect and is in constant fear of verbal and physical abuse he or she does not learn how to express basic needs or feelings.

My sister had no problem driving 348 miles to pick me up, but she was unable to hug me or tell me that she loved me. I am unable to hold her and make her feel truly safe and loved; our early experiences have robbed us of this kind of loving connection. We are different from siblings who were fortunate enough to grow up in a healthy, loving, nurturing home; different than those who were taught and developed the skills to freely ask for and give attention and affection.

There is ample literature from the world of neuroscience that validates what I've just expressed in layman's terms. Neuroscientists have studied the brains of children who have experienced domestic violence and found in them the same quality of damage as in the brains of combat veterans. Both meet the diagnostic criteria for Post Traumatic Stress Disorder (PTSD). The feelings I had throughout most of my childhood and young adulthood—as if I was walking on eggshells, unsure about everything, an inability to form healthy attachments and meaningful connections—are the same feelings experienced and felt by combat soldiers with PTSD.

My sister suggested that we stop at Hershey's Chocolate World on the drive back to New Jersey to pick up some gifts for our mom and my brother's kids. I was never a fan of theme parks, amusement parks, or commercial entertainment venues but I know she enjoys them so of course I consented.

What she didn't know is that I kept an old photo of her in my wallet. She was a year old and was sitting in a bed of flowers wearing a frilly yellow dress, white patent leather shoes, and white lace socks

with yellow bows. I keep it because it reminds me of her fragility—
and our fragility. When I look at the picture I wonder what could
have been, what our lives would have been like if we had not grown
up with domestic violence.

It was Tuesday June 9, 2014 when we arrived at our mother's house
in New Jersey. My plan was to stay in the area for a couple of weeks.
Also, I was scheduled to speak at an ACEs event in Philadelphia on
June 26—a short side trip—but my main reason for being at home
was to spend quality time with family who still lived there. By this
time, my father had moved to Florida.

A few days later, my mother and sister took me to see Maria, my
mom's hairdresser, for a haircut—I hadn't had one since going on the
bicycle trip. During the haircut, Maria talked about how fond she was
of my mother and sister.

I shared with her the story of my second cross-country trip, my
mission and some of the stories I'd collected. It opened into a candid
and engaging conversation on the subjects of child abuse, sexual
abuse, domestic violence, and forgiveness. I asked Maria if she would
tell me her story.

She answered, "If I tell you my story and it helps somebody, sure,
why not?"

Maria's Story

I went to Maria's house for the interview and as I walked to the front door I noticed a package on the front steps. When Maria opened the door, I picked it up and handed it to her. "Oh, that must be my husband's work boots," she said. "How are you?" Come in, please."

Then Maria introduced me to her only daughter, Sarah, who'd just arrived home from college on summer break. Maria was very proud of Sarah. In their interaction, I saw the powerful bond between them. I asked Sarah if she would join our conversation.

"Sure. OK," Sarah said.

"She knows all that I'm going to tell you. I have never kept any of it from her," Maria added. Maria then told me that she would like to tell her story in English rather than Spanish; it would be easier for her. Telling it in English, she said, would not be as sad or as painful.

"The first time my mother beat me, I was three. We were living in Spain in an old house, but it was a new residence for us. We were in the kitchen and I was looking at my mother as she swept the floor. We were alone. I was sitting against the wall with my hands in my lap. I was so happy. I watched her and thought, 'Wow, my mom is beautiful, so beautiful!'

"All of a sudden she just hit me with the broom. I didn't know what was happening. She started laughing and I started crying. Then she hit me again and started making fun of the situation, like laughing. That was the moment I realized that I wasn't safe."

I asked Maria about her father. She told me that he wasn't around most of the time because he worked at sea as a fisherman. He was gone for six months at a time. "That was the nightmare—when he wasn't home. When he was home everything was fine. He never suspected what was going on in the house and I was terrified to share that with him because she made sure that I knew that I would have to suffer the consequences when he left, if I ever said anything to my dad."

Maria's father was a smoker and because of that she'd always loved the smell of cigarettes. She loved to snuggle up and bury her face in his fisherman's coat. It reeked of cigarette smoke but it made her feel safe. She wondered if that is why she started smoking when she was 13. "The first time I tried a cigarette I just loved it!" she said.

I listened as Maria recounted the abuse she'd endured throughout most of her childhood and early teenage years. She remembered being a child of 5 years when she was pulled out of bed one night while sleeping. "It was late at night and it was raining. My mother dragged me outside to the back yard and kept hitting me and repeating, 'I told you to be quiet! I told you to be quiet and you don't listen.' My older brother and sister must have been making some noise and, without bothering to ask who was doing it, she singled me out. I must have stood out in that rain for about half an hour, but it felt like much longer. I was so terrified to be outside in the dark. It was raining and thundering—to me it was an eternity."

Maria turned to Sarah and said that she was pretty sure there were good moments in her childhood. She paused to search back through the chambers of her memory, but was unable to remember any. I wondered if the bad moments were so extreme that she'd thrown away any good memories.

"A really bad moment happened on the day I was going to start first grade and I had just turned six. My brother or sisters broke the chain of the rubber sink stopper in the bathroom and blamed it on me. I remember my mother putting me on the bed and hitting me. She just went on and on and on and on, saying, 'Say the truth! *Di la verdad, fuiste tu*! (Say the truth! It was you!).'

"I kept yelling and screaming, 'I didn't do it! I didn't do it!'

"And she'd say, 'If you don't say the truth, I'm going to go to the kitchen, I'm going to take a knife and I'm going to kill you.'"

It was in this moment Maria learned that for her to be safe, she had to start lying.

Around this time Maria's older brother began to sexually molest her, a detail she had revealed during our initial conversation at the salon. He sexually abused her from ages 6 to 14. "What's really strange," she says, "is that a couple of days after my conversation with you at the salon, my brother reached out to me through Facebook—out of the blue! Then he called me and told me that Jesus Christ was talking to him, that he's so sorry for what he did. He went on and on and on, talking. I listened.

"I replied, 'I forgave you a long time ago. You don't have that over me.'"

After Maria married and conceived her daughter she put out of her mind the memories of sexual abuse by her brother. "I kept it a secret for a long time and that's a horrible feeling because it's s a feeling of shame that you keep. You feel ashamed for what happened to you because you feel that it's your fault, feel that you should have done something more, that you should tell people. But it was a taboo thing to talk about then even more than now. You didn't talk about anything that had to do with sex. I was born during the times of Francisco Franco, an authoritarian regime that existed in Spain from 1936 until 1975; talking about anything sexual led to a punishment. Telling my mother what my brother was doing, after all the beatings she gave me, was not an option."

When Maria was 15, it was the last time her mother laid a hand on her—having punched her in the face and bloodied her nose. "I remember running upstairs and locking myself in my room. Blood was streaming from my nose. My mother was outside trying to open the door and I remember looking out my window and thinking 'I'm not staying here for this.' I had a pink shirt on that my grandmother gave me, a fake Adidas shirt that now looked red because it was covered in blood. Outside my second floor window there was a mountain of gravel from some construction that my parents where having done. I decided that if I jumped and broke something my mother would at least have to take me to the hospital, so I jumped.

"Luckily for me I landed safely, ran to my grandmother's house, and asked her to take me to the police."

In the late 1970s in Spain, no one went to the police. But Maria did.

Maria told the police that her mother had bloodied her nose and showed them the shirt. She asked them if she could have her mother arrested; wondered if there was anything she could do about it. The police told her that there wasn't any law preventing her mother from beating her. Fortunately for Maria, it was a small town and she thinks her mother found out about her trip to the police station. "After that, she stopped beating me."

A couple of years later, Maria met a man from a Portuguese family and, after a fairly brief courtship, they married. "I saw that he was a hard-working guy and he was good-looking," Maria laughs. They moved from Spain to the United States, as he had family in New Jersey.

Soon after their move, another set of problems began.

"He came from a culture were the man is the boss; you have to do what the man wants to do. He was very nasty about some things, like money. He was always worried about the money. He was also physical but he didn't think it was wrong because he just pushed me. He didn't beat me because his father used to beat the crap out of his mother, so I guess he thought pushing was OK. I had a girlfriend who would confront him and say, 'Stop beating her! You push a woman against the wall—that's beating her.' It's not like I let him get away with it. I fought right back because after what my mother did to me I swore that nobody was going to do that again. But it was different with him because after he did something like that, a few minutes later, he cried and said he was sorry. I thought 'This guy is more screwed up than I am.' So I fought back because, like I said, ever since I was a kid, you know, I promised I wouldn't let anyone treat me like that when I grew up, so I called the cops on him a couple of times."

The second time in her life that Maria called the police for help was on Sarah's second birthday. "It was a Saturday morning and I had to get her cake—a Barbie cake. I asked him to stay home with Sarah and he said he was going to the gym—he went to the gym. So when he got home, I told him that on Monday I was going to go to a lawyer and get a divorce. His response was to go to the bank and withdraw all the money we had. He left me with nothing except my paycheck that I had not cashed— $300. That's when I decided that I wasn't going to take it because now he was threatening my ability to take care of my daughter and that was the last straw. If somebody does that to me, I'm going to fight like a lion, so I called the cops. I don't know how it came to me, I was just so angry, really, very angry."

It was a tense time for both mother and daughter. Maria continued: "A couple of days prior to Sarah's second birthday, I tried to climb over the fence in the back yard and fell. The fall left a huge bruise on my leg. So when these two cops arrived at my house and asked me what happened, I told them that he left and went to his mother's house. Told them that we started having a fight in the morning about babysitting my daughter and he kicked me. I showed them the bruised leg and they said, 'Wow that's pretty bad!'

"I said, 'I know, and on top of kicking me he took all the money out of the bank and left me without a penny. I have a two year old. What do you expect me to do?'

"Let me tell you, what happened next is one of the reasons why I believe in God and know that God is real. The two cops that showed up at my door knew him. I showed them his picture and it turned out they knew him. They knew my husband!"

The reason the cops knew him was because he had already been married to, and divorced, a young Portuguese woman who lived in the same neighborhood. "Anyway, it turned out that he beat the crap out of her a couple of times and these cops had already been involved with him. I'm telling you there are no coincidences. I had no problem getting a restraining order against him when I went to court because the cops and judge were in my favor. So to make a long story short he went to jail for a couple of days and I got a lawyer. And even though the lawyer told him not to contact me because he could get locked up for five years, that man kept calling and calling and begging for me to take him back.

"At that point, I weighed the good and the bad of a divorce. I wanted my daughter to have a father. I didn't want her, when she turned 18, to blame me for a divorce. I knew he was also a good provider and loved our daughter. So I decided to give him a final chance and we went to a marriage counselor. I picked a Portuguese psychologist, not an American one, because I knew that if I picked an American one he would not trust him as much. I picked one from his culture and his background, we went to therapy for a couple of months, and I saw that he did make an effort. I'm not going to tell you that everything changed from one day to the other because it didn't, but he tried, he was a little bit more understanding. If you asked him today he probably wouldn't admit it, but a couple of times he has told me that he is lucky and grateful that I didn't leave him."

Maria cried as she told me that deep down in her heart she feels she is a loving person now and was a loving person when she was little. The narrative about her life that she'd shared has not changed who she was and was born to be. She just thinks that without the trauma she would have been so much happier and so much healthier, but she also feels that her childhood trauma has not made her an aggressive person or vindictive person. She shared that when she talks to her mother about the times that she suffered abuse in her childhood, her mother tells her that she doesn't remember. "That kind of bothered me a lot because I felt that she didn't want to take any blame for it. At least say 'I'm sorry,' say something, you know...own it! Say 'OK, I didn't know how to be better. I had my own issues, I'm sorry that that happened.' I think that's what hurts me the most, that she doesn't remember, she doesn't remember anything negative."

But Maria doesn't want her mother to feel she was a bad mother. "I'm pretty sure in some moments she was a good mother. My mother did tell me a while ago that she should have put her priorities together. Just having her give me that little admission set me free. I also have my faith in God. It sustains me and it has taught me forgiveness."

Then it was time for her daughter, Sarah, to tell me her story. I asked Sarah how she thought her mother's experiences had influenced her life.

Sarah's Story

She said, "I think because my mom experienced what she experienced, she did everything that she could and everything there was to do for me to experience the complete opposite. Never in my life can I remember feeling unsafe, feeling unstable at all.

"If anything, it's been the complete opposite. She and my father have made it so that there have been no bumps on the road for me.

They've had their fights like everyone does, but I've never felt unsafe. I don't really remember half of my childhood. Maybe because it was so flowery and fantastic. I don't have the memories my mother has. I've been very sheltered. I feel because of the way my mom and dad raised me, I don't feel anything can stop me. My mom and my father are working-class people and they worked really hard to get me to where I am.

"For me it was never really an option not to go to college and now I'm a very driven individual. From the moment I started college I hit the ground running. In my freshman year, I got an internship. I've just finished my junior year and am doing very well. So, for me, whatever my mother's done, whatever my father's done, has put me on the road I'm on."

With that, my time with Maria and Sarah came to an end. I was grateful to have a story where an abused parent had not passed on the trauma to a child.

A few days later, I decided to call the mental health program for which I worked after graduating from college. I learned that a caseworker colleague of mine, Josephine Ruiz-Carpenter, was now the director of Harbor House, a partial hospitalization behavioral health service center in Paterson, New Jersey. It offers services such as outpatient or partial residential care for people age 18 and over who are dealing with serious mental illness, mental health issues, substance abuse disorders, and those struggling with PTSD. Josephine agreed to tell me her story.

Josephine's Story

"This is going to sound schmaltzy, but this work is what drives me as a person. It's my goal. It's my vocation," Josephine declared. She recalled that when she was in training as a rehab counselor she went to a hospital to do her internship and disliked it terribly because it was very strict, regimented, and very much a silo. "'If this is what it's going to be like,' I thought, 'it's not for me.'" After that experience, she was getting ready to pack her bags, get a master's degree in education, and "take my act on the road."

But her plan was not to be. One of her professors suggested that she go to meet with a man who was running an interesting program. His name was Bob Harvey, and he was the director of Harbor House. A week went by and she had not followed up on the suggestion. "Week two comes along, and again he asks if I'd met with the director. I told him no, so he says, 'If you don't follow through and meet with him, I'm going to give you an incomplete!'"

She told the professor that he couldn't do that. He said to just watch him do it. "I knew there must be something making him so insistent so I asked him why he was being so adamant. He said, 'I know this organization, I know you. I know you have what is needed to work there.' He used to tell me that I was earthy; he called me his 'diamond in the rough.'"

I had to laugh. Josephine did, too.

So Josephine went to Harbor House. She "walked in and saw maybe 25 clients, saw the small staff really getting down and dirty— they were cooking together, cleaning together. They worked on the apartments and ran the thrift shop together. They did this, did that, I witnessed the camaraderie, and the connection that I knew was essential. I observed it and I said, 'this is what I want to do.'"

Josephine knew—and knows—herself well. She said, "I knew that I could connect with them because I know that what drives me are the relationships that I have. I knew that the people being served were no different than myself! I did the interview and when I left I didn't even know what the job paid but when I got the call I didn't think twice and took it."

That was back in 1976 and she's never left. "I remember having this conversation with one of the Sisters of Charity, the group of nuns who run a local hospital. We went out to dinner had a few glasses of wine and we were talking. She said to me, 'Do you think that your being here is pure coincidence?'

"She didn't have to say anymore. I grew up here, came here [to Harbor House] when I was 24, met my husband here, got married here, had my two children here, they went to daycare across the street, this place is very much a part of who I am! For me, it was my destiny to come here."

Josephine explained that the funding folks and the programing people do not necessarily see the importance of this kind of story. They go to Harbor House and they're impressed by the external. The fact that the place is clean, that people from all walks of life, cultures, and religions are getting along, the fact that they rarely have violent or disturbing incidents. "They don't see the resilience of the people here, the love in their hearts," she told me. "That love is what gets to me. I have clients here who have absolutely nothing, have been through hell and back, and yet when something happens to someone else they have that extra part of themselves to give, that part of them that is concerned with others' well being. They are constantly concerned with me as a person—not a staff worker, but me, Josephine."

She said, "I'm talking about myself personally now. My mother passed away two months ago and they were phenomenal. I was fine with all my family, my friends, the wake, the funeral and all. I was fine—until I came in here and people started to give me their sympathy. They gave me so much love I couldn't hold it together. It amazes me, just amazes me!"

Harbor House is different from other such centers under Josephine's unique leadership. Here's one example. She said, "We are told you are not supposed to take any gifts from clients. They come and bring you these little things that mean the world to them. For me to say to them, 'I can't take that' because of rules and regulations? I mean that's such an insult to people, to their humanity! I come from a Hispanic culture. You don't do that to people. They're great, really great! They get up every morning and fight the fight and the love that they are capable of is so overwhelming, so overwhelming."

On another personal note, Josephine confided, "As a woman I've watched the women of my culture put up with so much stuff, domestic violence, abuse, not being given their due, always in the shadows, having to blend into the woodwork. Women like my mother. You see their struggle and what's more important you witness their selflessness! When you witness that unconditional love from another human being, it can make you feel small. For myself, my mother was a very bright woman, but my father never gave her the credit and validation. The way that it affected me was that the more he didn't give me recognition for what I did and accomplished, the harder I worked. It was more to show him that I could do it, despite what he said. I still did not get much recognition but it sure felt good to do it because I knew I could do it."

Harbor House was part of the de-institutionalization thrust in the late 1970s and early 1980s. Josephine witnessed that, too. "We were trying to teach people how to survive here in the community, give them a place to attend during the day, and help them get back on track. It was a place of hope where they could go back to school or work."

She reminded me that when I was at Harbor House in the early 1980s, what we modeled was from Fountain House in New York. It was a model that has been copied and used in many places throughout the world. Josephine explained, "We basically provided basic life needs according to Maslow's principals: a place to go, a place to live, and a place to work. Actually, our brochures were set up like that at that time."

In the 38 years that she'd been at Harbor House, at every assessment/interview she'd ever done, either the person has said, "I want to go to work" or when asked, "What do you want to do?" their response has been, "I want to go to work!"

Josephine feels that the society we live in defines a person by the job they have. "What you do is very important in regard to the social structure. When you ask a person with mental health issues what they do for work and they don't have a response, the usual response is 'you do nothing?' It's hard to live with that. The reality is that many don't work because they are suffering from this illness, their lives are being constantly interrupted, they don't get to finish school, achieve success on the job…the things you and I do."

There are many problems with the current system, but one of the big problems that Josephine identified is that most agencies have been set up to deal with only the specific issues that an individual is dealing with. Many services exist in their own individual silos. In the case of Harbor House, the service provided focuses on individuals with severe, persistent mental illness. "But the reality is that we focus on their specific illness and along with that comes a lot of other issues as well, which the person brings. They are no different than any of us! They bring their person, again no different than you and I, they bring all the issues that they've had in growing up, all the issues one has in living a life.

"We are not able to commit the time and the level of focus that we would like to because that's not what we get paid for," Josephine explained. "But they do have certain treatments that they do offer their clients that are not part and parcel of what the state funds and pays them for. Once we meet the needs or requirements of what we are funded to provide we then provide individuals with additional factors because we are invested in treating the whole person. We understand that the people we service are not disconnected from the neck down.

"For example, we started to use meditation as a form of treatment or coping mechanism, a tool that individuals can use to help themselves when they are no longer here and we are no longer available to them. If anyone is unable to provide them with support or guidance, they can at least use this tool to have the ability step back when they are struggling and have something that can help them center themselves again."

Harbor House dedicated one room that they call their meditation room to help clients practice mindfulness—a concept that anyone can benefit from no matter who you are, or what your position or station in life is. "That room is a place where people can go when they want to go on their own and in which we hold meditation groups throughout the week," Josephine told me. "We also have a place of worship or prayer—not particular to any religion but where someone can sit and pray to whoever they pray to for solace and guidance and support—little things that are beyond the vocational training programs that we offer."

Many people who come to Harbor House are broken individuals who are severely mentally ill. Along with the mental illness, they have secondary issues such as substance abuse. There is also a deaf community. Harbor House is able to serve the monolingual Hispanic population. "We attend to all of them using best practice modalities that are used here but we also understand that the person we are treating is a whole person. That's the problem. All types of things come up when they are in treatment here and we are not given the time or the funding to focus on them so we basically are made to focus on what we are only funded to do."

Like me, Josephine believes in giving witness to the stories people want to tell. "I've always concerned myself with the fact that there are many aspects to an individual. One must learn about the person, learn their stories, let them tell you their stories," she said. "We all have our individual stories, they are very unique, like our fingerprints. Our stories are very important and given the opportunity individuals are able and willing to share them. And when you hear the story one can't help to be amazed at how functional and resourceful individuals are prior to their having to go to the hospital."

Josephine went on to speak about the fact that medication has side effects that bring on metabolic issues. "The journals tell us that an individual who takes psychotropic medications on average shortens their life span by 25 years. So in addition to dealing with the mental illness, you are dealing with the secondary issues of the medication, such as metabolic issues, cardiac issues, and endocrinology issues such as diabetes. Again we don't look at it as a whole. We look at it in a segmented way. We treat the symptom but not the whole person. We need to understand that mental illness is not the person—the person happens to have mental illness, but it's not who they are!"

When she looks at the history of the people she has encountered and listened to their childhood stories she sees patterns. "People who grew up in domestic violence, alcoholism, intercultural violence, sexual abuse..." she said, "...these experiences compound the problem and stop the person from being able to develop themselves. They get stymied. Many yearn to go back to a point in their life to when they felt they where doing OK...a particular school, a job, a relationship. That's when they felt they where normal. And when I analyze it it's probably the worst thing they could do because part of their problem stems from what was going on in their life at that time and, for many of them, developed into the issues that they suffer from today. For example, they might have been abused at home or at school."

Yes, Josephine is right that the holistic approach is the best, but it costs a lot of money. When you look at the results it's well worth the money. The people making the policies, whether county, state, or federal, need to look at these tools, these life skills that we all need and can benefit from, and see them as essential. Meditation, good nutrition, exercise—things that can be incredibly important for individual health and well being—need to be supported through funding, whether it is from public, private or other sources that are yet to be discovered.

Camden, New Jersey, about an hour's drive from the home I lived in from age 11 until college, is one of the most violent cities in America. My mother went back to college when I was 16 in order to become a teacher. She attended what was then a satellite campus of Rutgers University in Camden. Since around 2000, Camden has been home to a unique nonprofit program for at risk youth called Hopeworks 'N Camden. Here is its mission statement: "Hopeworks 'N Camden uses education, technology and entrepreneurship to partner with young men and women as they identify and earn a sustainable future.

Together we seize the opportunity to heal and thrive in the midst of violence and poverty."

I decided to pay them a visit while I was in the area, and I found a Jesuit priest, Father Jeff, at its helm. He's the one who created Hopeworks 'N Camden.

Father Jeff's personal journey informed this vocation. He told me "Our vision at Hopeworks used to be 'creating a safe pathway so that people could have dreams.' It was the sanctuary model. After learning about the ACE study, the vision became 'creating a safe pathway so that people can learn their history and have choices for a future.' Hopeworks experienced lots of youth getting into school, getting a job and doing well, but we also experienced a lot of youth getting into school, getting a job and blowing it up."

As the program evolved, Father Jeff had to ask questions such as: "Why are some of our youth blowing it up? Why aren't they going to school? What's wrong with them? Why is there so much injustice? Why? Why? Why?"

He said, "Organizations like ours, that are working at helping people, that stand in opposition to what harms people, have to understand that trauma informed care is about the healing of people who have been harmed—the many, many, who are harmed from injustice in our world!"

Father Jeff's Story

Father Jeff doesn't remember a great deal of trauma in his early childhood although his guess is that it happened. But when he was around the ages of 9 or 10, a series of events occurred. He had been living in Florida but in the fourth grade he moved back to Kansas City and everything changed. "My father went to work at his dad's company and became a successful salesperson. He sold printing. Along with his success came pain. There was drinking and drugging, gambling, physical abuse, a lot of that stuff. We owned a boat and on the weekends we went to the lake. By the time I got to high school I refused to go because I hated it. I hated being trapped on that boat. I hated all that went with it, all the energy, the drama. So what happened in my family, the way they dealt with it, was to blame me. They asked, 'Jeff why are you being like that? If you would just change everything would be OK.' I got put into the persecutor role a lot. Instead of addressing the behavior or what was happening, the narrative was always around how to accommodate what was happening without naming it.

"The most important thing to know about how I am today is that when I was 21, my father killed himself. I was at a point in my life where it was literally life or death for me. I realized that if I was going to go on I couldn't continue to try to process his death with the tools I had. Up to then I had kind of figured out how to cope with all the craziness in my family growing up. But this was different. How I had coped wasn't going to work this time.

"The best way for me to describe what the event did to me is through an experience I had when I went to Mount St. Helens after the eruption of 1980. The initial approach to the mountain led us along a beautiful path but as we kept walking, all of a sudden, literally within yards, things started to change and as we moved on and trekked around the corner we were faced with complete devastation, the mountain was ravaged, just like the pictures. I stood there and started to bawl. It was like I was one with the mountain. It had exploded and left devastation. That was my own experience. My father's suicide, this thing that was done to me, was horrific and changed the face of my mountain. It wasn't like my life was gone, but in a sense my life was reconfigured very suddenly without my permission."

Father Jeff was in Belize when he got the news of his father's death. "I remember a dream that I had at that time. It was like being in a coffin and the lid was being put on me like this event was going to seal me away. But it didn't because in the dream I had a very powerful experience of Jesus reaching in and stopping that from happening, stopping that lid from closing on me. For me that was really hopeful, because I felt that there was some other way."

After that dream, Father Jeff had a series of experiences with important people in his life that helped him with the grief he was carrying. "For me, those experiences were not embedded in a person, they were embedded in moments. I remember a Jesuit asking me, 'How are you?' I was so relieved. People didn't talk to me about my dad because they didn't want to make me upset—I was already upset and their actions just made me angry. So when he asked me how I felt I don't remember what I said but I remember him saying, 'It's so really hard when your engines are all going different ways.' He comforted me. It was a moment; just a moment.

"Four months later a group of us were gathered together and another Jesuit asked me how I was doing. I told him and he replied, 'you know, we teach a milquetoast Jesus and that's wrong! Jesus got angry!' That was an incredibly powerful moment for me.

"Another time I was in philosophy studies and I had this amazing connection with a teacher who told stories. I ended up creating my own story about my dad's death—that I was being chased by it. Eventually I presented the story to the class, but when I read it I didn't tell the class it was about my dad. Afterwards, I needed to talk to the teacher, so I told him how important it was for me to read the story. He got really, really quiet. Then he said, 'That is how my dad died.' It made me feel normal, really normal. I thought, 'If it happened to him, this amazing teacher that I loved, it must then mean I'm OK.'"

Father Jeff went to several meetings of Adult Children of Alcoholics World Service Organization (http://www.adultchildren.org/). He said, "I remember showing up at that place and they asked me about my dad and I told them what happened and they said, 'that doesn't surprise us.' They were the first people to ever say that— and this was back in the 1980s, when suicide was still a huge stigma. Again, I remember being so relieved."

We talked about these moments of grace he'd experienced. For Father Jeff they were tangible. "Jesus entered my life through the times I had people caring for me—allowing me to name what happened to cause me pain."

To be able to name what happened to cause pain is transformative.

Father Jeff commented that his father's ACE score must have been very high. "I'm not sure anyone got to ask him what happened to him. I now have empathy for my father that back then I didn't have. Back then he was someone who hurt us and we just tried to deny the hurt. Now that I've been able to contextualize and have a new frame for understanding what happened to me, it's made it all make sense. Knowing my history, being able to understand all the craziness that went on in my family, all the things that I went through, has freed me."

Father Jeff shared his knowledge of the Japanese art of *kintsukuroi* –to repair with gold, or, the art of repairing cracked pottery with gold or silver lacquer and understanding that the piece is more beautiful for having been broken. *Kintsukuroi* is a powerful image for adversity and ACEs. In knowing your history, this kind of beauty is possible. Knowing your history, seeing it for what it was, facing it and working to heal it creates a path to your future, a place where emotional pain is neutral and no longer in effect.

Physical wounds heal by being washed, treated with antibiotics, and covered with bandages. Then they form scar tissue. In time, only a mark remains on the skin that shows the injury, but that mark no longer festers or bleeds.

Emotional wounds—especially traumas experienced during childhood—need a different kind of treatment. Each person must find their own equivalents of washing methods, antibiotics, and bandages. The "scar tissue" of an emotional wound becomes the mere fact of an ACE. A person can live with emotional trauma as a fact, like a physical scar that no longer festers or bleeds, when it is made inactive through any number of therapies or healing modalities.

Healing is like having the beauty of gold seal your wounds.

Father Jeff's experience taught him about the question anyone who is suffering needs to ask: "The question we need to ask," he said, "is 'What happened to you?' When we ask that question of a youth at Hopeworks, we help them realize the pattern, the dynamic that they have, which is what they carry into the school or the job or throughout their lives and engagements. They are led to understand that their history caused them to develop ways to compensate for their pain, and that those methods helped them to survive and get through their experiences. We ask if they are now using those same methods in new places because if they are, it doesn't work.

"It's powerful when you know what is causing you to make the choices you make. When you live in a world in which you are amped up all the time because you never know if something bad is going to happen—it's not good. When you are not sure if it's going to get you— it's unhealthy. It's like living around nuclear fallout, like Chernobyl. If you're around Chernobyl, exposed to radiation and don't realize you are being radiated, yet your hair starts falling out, you start to blame yourself. The radiation and its poison are invisible—just like emotional trauma."

At Hopeworks one of the tools used to effectively deal with the "invisible radiation" kind of trauma is the sanctuary model. Father Jeff explained that Hopeworks was in the process of being sanctuary certified. "The process is all about creating a healthy community so that we can be really attentive to what has happened and how our history is really present in our lives. Again, when we come to understand that what's happened to us is not a memory. The way we think about it it's more like a ghost; it's alive within the person. So when we are interacting with another person, their history is alive right then and there, and if things come up rather than to be reactive one can learn to be mindful, and that gives one choices.

"What's powerful about the sanctuary model is that it supports us in our desire for providing the youth with tools of self-efficacy. They are getting really good at saying, 'I feel unsafe, you make me feel unsafe.'

"What we are working on is: 'No, you have it wrong here. Feel angry, feel upset, we want you to have your feelings, but we want you to learn to have them without having a re-enactment.' The reality is that you can be as pissed off and as angry as you want, but I'm not your dad, or even more importantly, you are pissed off and I remind you of your dad, but I'm not your dad.

"So, for example, we all have our safety plan, which we all carry around our necks for self-regulation, throughout the day. Each plan is specific to that person's needs, to help that person with real detailed things that they have to do. We create acronyms to help us remember. My plan is T.I.P.S.E – Time, Intrigue, Prayer, Sleep, and Exercise. I need those things, and if I don't get them, I become like a damaged nuclear reactor and there will be fallout radiation. If I have my safety plan I learn to become more aware and present.

"When the individual takes care of self, then the community can ask questions of itself such as: What does that remind you of? Do you have a safety plan when you start to feel like that? What do you need to do to take care of yourself?"

Father Jeff told me that managing the clients at Hopeworks takes work. It takes sweat. "Hope is sweat, it's not something you just say; it is the exercise. Trauma informed care is an exercise. Safety is an exercise. It's not magic. It's also not a recipe. Let's take the analogy of a car engine and its need to have the oil changed every 5,000 miles. If I change the oil, my engine is going to run better. It doesn't mean my engine will always run, but it will run better. And if something happens to it my engine will be easier to fix.

"Youth need to be encouraged to realize that they are really good at survival. The choices they made based on what's happened to them have led to their survival. But in many cases even though the choices that they made were a result of what's happened to them, the reality is that the choices they make today are the same choices that prevent them from succeeding. They are adaptive, unreflective choices. Reactive choices to painful situations that used to help them get by, but now impede their growth.

"The hope lives in knowing that, through hard work and sweat, you can access another way of being. You can access tools that allow you to self regulate and work towards being the person you were meant to be. Life is tough, bad things happen, but isn't it great that when bad things happen you can emotionally manage it as opposed to having that feeling overwhelm you because what happened to you is still alive in you?"

Both Josephine and Father Jeff are fulfilling what seems to be their mission—assisting hurt people and keeping them from hurting themselves or other people. What they did in their own communities to address deep hurt and create resiliency contributes to the healing of all societies as the messages in their successes continue to expand.

CHAPTER 10

The Beauty of the Work:
Personal and Social

Though we travel the world over to find the beautiful,
we must carry it with us or we find it not.

~ **RALPH WALDO EMERSON** ~

After reaching New Jersey by bicycle, car and bus at the age of 56, I felt a small sense of accomplishment. But I knew that the trip signaled a beginning rather than an end. I felt that great work for me was just ahead and I still had much to do.

I was not yet ready to go back to Los Angeles. Guided by an inner voice, I moved toward a feeling of completion, and a new level of emotional healing. So I planned a visit with my father, now in his mid-80s, living a solitary life in Florida. My youngest brother drove me to the airport.

When I got to Florida and my father's house, the first thing I noticed about him was that he'd aged a great deal since I'd last laid eyes on him, three years before at my brother's wedding. He was glad to see me, and I him, but on the drive to his place I sensed that I was there less for myself and more for him. He needed me there.

Like many people his age, my father had a set routine that he conformed to, a daily ritual. He began each day in one of three churches at mass. Of course, I went with him. On the drive to each church he gave me his assessments of the caliber of the priests and the quality of their sermons. He knew who would be speaking at which church on what day and that dictated the churches we attended. After mass we went home and he made breakfast for us: fruit and quinoa, a food staple produced in Bolivia, our native country. We spent the rest of the day reading, listening to classical music, and visiting either the pool or the beach. After a light lunch and dinner, by nine o'clock we'd head to bed for a night of sleep.

As I lay in bed on the first night of that visit, a need arose in me to do something for him—something he was not expecting from me. I'd noticed that his home was in need of cleaning, especially his kitchen. I resolved to clean the kitchen after the next morning's mass. When my father sat in the living room listening to music and reading after breakfast, I got to work on removing months of grunge and grime from the stove, cabinets, and floor. Then I rewashed all the plates, utensils, and glasses in his cabinets. When I stopped to check on him I found him napping, an open book on his chest. I returned to the kitchen to empty out and clean the refrigerator.

The work was a sort of cleansing and renewal on several layers.

On the last day of my visit, we went to mass then to Starbucks. He knew I preferred their brand of coffee to his. As we left the coffee shop on our way back home for a bowl of quinoa, my father said he was disappointed that we'd not really talked much during my visit.

I asked, "What did you want to talk about?"

After a long pause he told me that he had so much he wanted to say, so much he wanted to share. Then he said, "I am sorry for having failed you. Sorry that I was not the father you deserved to have. I wish that things had been different, wish that I could have been a better father."

A moment of closure had arrived for both of us.

Karen Armstrong, a former Catholic nun, wrote about this moment in her book, *Twelve Steps to a Compassionate Life*. It is a moment that comes about when one has acquired the ability to love oneself and in doing so has attained the capacity to empathize, "... to identify with or understand another's situation or feelings," and the capability to have compassion or, "...to suffer with another."

I told my father that I knew he did the best he could at the time, and that he was the best father he knew how to be.

I did not tell him I forgave him.

The moment did not require it.

On the flight from Florida back to Los Angeles, the emotional depth in that moment with my father overwhelmed me. I realized that I'd arrived at the final stage of what philosopher and writer Joseph Campbell identified as "The Hero's Journey."

The time had finally come for me to leave the cave Plato described. I had come to the conclusion that the current social structures and institutions often do more harm to people rather than help them in the ways they need and want. Institutions can become silos—storage bins for energy that keep cycling and do not transform. Instead of supporting people in the procurement of emotional skills that lead to safety, stability, connection, resiliency, mastery and access to resources that allow them to create the lives they envision for themselves, some institutions merely house the status quo or offer only temporary relief.

Johan Galtung was a Norwegian sociologist, mathematician, and principal founder of peace and conflict studies. He defined the conditions of modern society as "structural violence." Structural violence creates an "…avoidable impairment of fundamental human needs." My hero's journey taught me that structural violence and direct violence are dependent on one another. They boil down to the acceptance and application of aggression and create "family violence." Family violence (lack of the ability to give or receive love, inability to be compassionate, a need to strike or create emotional drama) and childhood trauma then become an epidemic that breeds shame, stress, inequity, and denigration of the human spirit on the individual and societal levels. As the ACE's study identified it, this is an epidemic that leads to "early death."

Back home in the Los Angeles area, I searched for places that would provide tools for me to take action in support of my mission to inform people about ACEs and healing. Echo Parenting and Education was what I found. I had the great fortune to be one of three individuals given a full scholarship to enroll in Echo's yearlong Parenting Educator Certification program.

I was the only male in the class of 24 students taught by Ruth Beaglehole.

The class was a learning adventure and experience that integrated a nonviolent parenting philosophy and trauma-informed knowledge towards the creation of a true and lasting change: for us, our families, and for the global community.

Together we learned and explored the detrimental impact that the dominant, old paradigm of power, violence and control has had on our human development. We experienced what it was like to be part of a community of practice that lives out the new, nonviolent paradigm of shared power and cooperation. We learned to understand our feelings and needs, our histories, and how our childhood adverse experiences influenced the choices we'd made.

I don't know if my experience would have been different if more males had been in that group, but I am so grateful I was alone in gender. It allowed me the opportunity to develop affection for everyone and everything (I felt safe) and to have a sense of loving responsibility for the whole course of the world. It reinforced my faith in another way of being and doing; it reinforced my belief that together we can build an ideal society, a community of people who have been nurtured, loved, and are in healthy relationship with each other.

Ruth's Story

After one of the classes, I asked Ruth to tell her story, beginning with childhood. She sat in silence for a moment before she spoke.

"I had a really gorgeous moment today. But you probably want to talk about trauma don't you?"

I replied, "Not necessarily!"

"A few years ago I found myself at a pediatric trauma conference. I went because I was working with the parents of a little girl who had leukemia. I was helping them make books and other things, and as the two days wore on I realized I was not there for this little girl, I was there for myself. I'd never had a name; I'd never been able to put a name on my babyhood!

"I was the worst case of childhood eczema ever in New Zealand in 1943. My hands and feet were bound. I was bound for three years until my mother got the first troop ship out of New Zealand, after the war. It was 1946. She brought her four children on this troop ship all the way to see her parents, in Louisiana, where I got relief through antihistamines.

"So there are myths about my early years. I don't know if they are myths or truths: I never slept more than 45 minutes, I had allergies, could only eat bananas...."

To step away from her memory of childhood trauma for a moment, I asked Ruth about the "gorgeous moment" she'd experienced earlier that day.

"So today I'm outside doing a Thich Nhat Hanh walking meditation, repeating a chant that is all about having self compassion and releasing of suffering. And as I'm walking I realize that all everybody talks about is what a terrible traumatic childhood it was, how I destroyed the family, how I took all the attention away from my siblings...and there I was today—in my memory—right back in my father's arms! When I was a child, he would hold me all day long because it was the only way that I could sleep. And as I was walking, I felt this amazing connection to and compassion for my father. I felt his heartbeat as he held me. That man is where I learned my early lessons in compassion and empathy. My father would hold me and sing me, 'Lili Marlene.'"

Ruth's early years where consumed by her illness—and by drugs. She was on antihistamines for most of her childhood. She said, "I had terrible itching and the only way they knew how to deal with it was the drugs. It affected me in school because I had a lot of learning issues. I was drugged up on the medication and not able to focus in school. I felt unconnected and didn't do well."

Around the age of 13, Ruth's brother sexually abused her on many occasions. That violence "...turned into self hate and bulimia, my coping strategy. I was working then as a papergirl and delivering newspapers gave me an incredible sense of liberation. Every night I would deliver papers, 79 papers. I would deliver the papers and then go and stuff myself with donuts and whatever I could get. Then I'd go home and vomit. Then it would be dinnertime. I also got my period at age 10, before anybody else, and I had early breast development, too. There were so many ways that I just didn't fit in...I had no friends, was completely alone. I was this contaminated kid. I had this huge secret."

To add more background in her story, Ruth grew up in an academic family where the males were scholars. "One of my brothers was a historian; my father was a social anthropologist. My sister had a doctorate degree by the age of 22. Then there was me. The question everywhere was 'which Beaglehole are you?' Well, I was the first Beaglehole to fail a university unit, and I became a pre-school and kindergarten teacher. My father thought that was the greatest insult that I could bring upon the family—my job was like babysitting. I became a preschool teacher because I was trying to relive my childhood. I also felt becoming a preschool teacher was a way to make sure other children didn't suffer the way I did."

Ruth spent many years in therapy to deal with bulimia. When her mother passed away in 1977, she went back to New Zealand for the funeral. On her return, she stopped seeing her therapist because (through an interesting series of circumstances) found someone who could heal bulimia. Ruth tracked him down and worked with him. Of that experience she said, "The easiest part was to stop vomiting. The way he got me to stop was by saying 'if you hadn't been vomiting all these years, you wouldn't have stayed alive.' His technique was teaching me to fall in love with myself *as a bulimic*.

When Ruth's daughter was born deaf, she had to come to terms with even more of the self-sabotage. To overcome the idea that she deserved to have a deaf child, she had to work hard to overcome it—and she did. She said of her daughter's life and journey: "It was a tremendous gift in my life."

Talking about of all these things made Ruth realize that her journey had been long and difficult. But, she recognizes that having lived in Echo Park and starting her preschool in the 1970s (in the time of the rise of feminism in the U.S.), she'd created a community of women who gave her the strength, confidence and resilience to move forward.

During that time, Ruth met Kit, a woman who was the head of a daycare company. "Kit told me to come down to Echo Park, that there was an apartment for rent. It's where I met my daughter's father, where I met people who had been active in Berkeley—a whole enclave of activists. At a food co-op I met Renie, a former nun who had come out of the convent during the rise of liberation theology. She became my sister here! She was my sister! We started the center together. With these friends, I was doing some beautiful risk-taking; tapping into the creative part of myself, the passion I had for children and the energy to be an activist for children. In that time, I learned so much about love, compassion, and connection."

Ruth was able to put a name to the justice that she was seeking and create a school that was about the right manifestation of a socialist collective belief, a brotherhood and sisterhood. "I found parts of me that have brought me so many moments of pure joy. Coming to understand that my faith is my passion, my faith is my belief—the belief that we *can* create a heaven here on Earth. I live my divinity. Feel my divinity. I live my divinity with my children, with my grandchildren. I live it with all people. And sometimes I blow it! I'm no angel, but I've become aware that my spiritual guide is within myself. There is so much beauty here.

"My daughter is a rabbi. I am a profound, deep atheist and I have been on a spiritual journey with her. I go to every service she leads and I sit there and feel the music and the joy and look at my daughter and say, 'this is exactly who she should be.' My children have given me grandchildren and I want to share in the moments of spontaneous joy with them."

While working with Ruth in the class on my certification as an Echo Parenting educator, I studied for 40 hours to attain a credential as a certified domestic violence counselor—a requirement in the state of California. That endeavor connected me with two other individuals who influenced my thinking and provided me with tools: Alyce La Violette, M.S., MFT, and Kendall Evans. I met them at Homeboy Industries in Los Angeles while attending the 40-hour domestic violence training awareness and prevention training that they put together. Like Ruth, these women have been on a decades-long mission to end violence in families, communities, and the world.

Alyce, one of the people responsible for this mandate, had worked with abused women since 1978. She created one of the first programs for men: "Alternatives to Violence." She has been running groups for men who've engaged in violence against intimate partners. She is a consummate storyteller; she is passionate, poignant, humorous, and has a gift for conveying the complexities of the world of domestic violence.

I asked Alyce if she'd share her personal story with me for this book. She agreed to do so in the recess from the training program.

Alyce's Story

I was interested to find out that Alyce was born in Camden, New Jersey, in 1947. For the first five years of her life, she lived with her parents, great grandmother, and great aunts. Then, her parents bought a home with the help of her grandfather, who moved in with them.

Back then, the town was typical of small towns in the 1950s. Alyce described her memory of "the commons, the town square, everybody knew each other. If you got in trouble down the street there was some other mother who would parent you for it; it was a community."

When Alyce turned 10, her sister Eileen was nine, and their baby sister was quite ill. The family moved to Arizona for health reasons. Eileen had been battling asthma since the age of ten months; the attacks were so bad that she almost died a couple of times. The asthma medication was so horrible it made her hallucinate.

Alyce remembered this because during that time she and her sister shared a room. The day they left New Jersey, Alyce had a feeling of sadness wash over her because it meant that (in addition to all the family goodbyes) she wouldn't get to participate in the upcoming pie eating contest.

The world she found in Arizona was a harsher one. Bullies victimized Alyce while she was in school. When she was in fifth grade she stood up to the school bully and made her back down. From that point on Alyce was popular.

Her mother gave birth to a fourth child in Arizona, Alyce's brother. The birth sent her mother into a depression so deep that Alyce remembers her mother putting her head in the oven. Alyce's dad was a union man, and he spoke up for the union against the heads of General Electric in Phoenix. Blacklisted, he lost his job, and ended up with employment at the post office. Alyce was never aware of the fact that they didn't have money but in high school she held down three jobs.

She also remembers *wanting* to have those three jobs.

Her marriage at age 22 was the beginning of another set of struggles. After the marriage, her husband got drafted and they moved to Fort Hood, Texas. She didn't know it, but he lived a double life: he was having affairs with men.

At 24, Alyce had a miscarriage. It was a terrible experience and the people at Fort Hood did not provide any support. The next year, her husband got an early release. They moved to Long Beach and Alyce got pregnant again. The pregnancy was difficult because she had toxemia and no health insurance. She relied on a teaching hospital to get her through the pregnancy.

When her son was 18 months old, they were involved in a car accident. Alyce was pinned between two cars and her legs were broken, but she managed to shield her son. For the next three years she was living in chronic pain, her son was difficult to manage, and her husband was not helpful.

Being very depressed during this time, Alyce picked up her son in anger and threw him. Frightened by her actions, she called a good friend and asked her to take the boy for a short while because she realized she'd committed child abuse and needed help.

Even though she and her husband brought another child, a daughter, into the world, the marriage did not last and she raised her children as a single mother. After they were somewhat grown up, Alyce went back to school.

It was there that she found herself attracted to a woman. Alyce ended up moving in with her and it turned out that the relationship changed her life because it was this woman that introduced Alyce to the abused women's shelter that became the starting point of her career in the field of domestic violence.

There was irony in this new relationship. This partner became abusive. She turned out to be a batterer.

During her presentation at the training, Alyce shared information about an unfinished, undistributed documentary film that featured some men in one of her groups. The documentary had a strong impact on me, but in a more powerful way, the manner in which she talked about the men featured in the documentary moved me on a deeper level.

Alyce cared about these men! As she talked, I realized that it is the love and compassion she brings to her work that is the greatest factor in the healing and transformation of these men. She does not judge or shame them but rather holds them in her heart and provides them with the tools, will and desire to change *themselves*.

One of the men featured in the documentary was Dave. Nearly seven feet tall, Dave used severe aggression in a fit of rage and he broke his wife's neck. The crime put him in prison, severed his relationship with his children, and physically, emotionally, and mentally, damaged and traumatized his wife, the woman he at one time promised to love and protect. Dave struggled with his guilt and shame until he realized that what he'd done was irreversible. His remorse, sorrow, anguish, and pain were apparent in the documentary, but he was able to transform from that place into a powerful advocate against domestic violence. Dave went on to speak at schools, shelters, and programs for men who were batterers. He modeled and practiced restorative justice.

When the documentary came to an end, someone asked, "What happened to Dave?"

Alyce said, "Dave ended up getting throat cancer." She told us that throughout his treatment he continued his work. Part of Dave's tongue was removed; surgeons grafted skin from his forearm to rebuild it.

Later, Alyce got a call from Dave. He told her that his children called and wanted to see him. It was the one thing he wanted more than anything in the world—his dream. Trying to contain her emotion, Alyce told us that Dave died shortly after he saw his children.

Some of the men from his original group stood at his bedside to comfort him in his final moments. Alyce said that she couldn't bear to view him as he passed away.

Kendall Evans was the second facilitator of the certification program. Like Alyce, he was passionate and committed to the work because of his personal story.

Kendall's Story

Kendall grew up in a large family and experienced a very tumultuous and traumatic childhood. "I was the oldest of what eventually added up to 10 children; five adopted, three steps and a half-sister. My father was physically and emotionally abusive to my siblings, my mother and myself. My mother was distant yet controlling and did not have the skills to acknowledge or meet my emotional needs.

"I learned that my needs were secondary to everyone else's. I was expected to take care of myself after everyone else was taken care of and did not know that I could say, 'This is too much for me.' I remember doing a lot of the childcare and housework and recall I helped raise my sister Janelle and brother Enoch from the time they were infants."

His family moved constantly due to frequent economic chaos and/or poverty—13 different housing situations and 11 schools before Kendall was a freshman in high school. School was no place of respite from the trauma he experienced at home. "I was the class scapegoat in fifth grade and endured daily mistreatment from all but one friend. It was hell."

During sixth grade, for three months, Kendall had a paper route in the mornings and delivered 100 newspapers. His pay bought food to feed the family.

After eighth grade, Kendall attended a summer camp near Montreal. His father worked there, but Kendall was sexually assaulted and harassed. When the police arrived, they did nothing. A con artist ran the camp. Kendall's father found out about the scam and went into Montreal to expose them. Following that crisis, Kendall's father was fired and the family spent the rest of the summer "camping" (homeless) at a church campground.

As it does for anyone, Kendall's ACE score influenced the choices he made in his adult life. "As I said, my mother was distant and controlling and I learned before I had words to express it to bury my needs and feelings very, very deeply into my unconscious, to bury the awareness that I did not want my mother to literally or metaphorically hug me. I learned to create high emotional walls as a way of life."

There was a time when Kendall felt extraordinary privilege. "I got a full tuition scholarship to an all boys boarding school and as a result did not live at home. It saved me." Kendall maintained excellent grades throughout that period and was second in the class. Being first meant getting teased. As a result of Kendall's effort, he got into Harvard on a scholarship. Kendall graduated *cum laude* in 1971. He decided to continue his education and go to graduate school. In 1981, he graduated with a master's degree in psychology paid for by grants from the National Institute of Mental Health. "I was blessed with high intelligence and a good voice. Music has been and continues to be a nurturing force and an ongoing hobby."

Laurie was Kendall's first wife. They were madly in love but also very co-dependent. Laurie suffered from extreme anxiety. Kendall tried to make her better by overcompensating and doing half or more of the housework. The marriage did not work out and Kendall divorced Laurie in 1978 because she was physically and emotionally abusive.

Kendall credits his studies in school for helping him to come to terms with the fact that he was in an abusive relationship. Going through therapy at school as part of his own training as a therapist forced Kendall to be aware of how he actually felt. "Well, at least on the surface," he said.

A year after his divorce from Laurie was final, Kendall met Beth, and they married in 1979. A few years into the second marriage, questions arose in Kendall's mind and he told me that in 1981 he joined the Los Angeles Men's Collective. His studies in gender kicked into high gear. "I participated in advocacy/social change activities with the organization now known as Peace Over Violence, or POV," he said. "I also volunteered on the Los Angeles Domestic Violence Council and throughout the 1980s helped plan three California Men's gatherings that looked at men's roles and behavior. I became very critical of stereotyped male socialization and behavior. During this time I began to experiment with less conventional clothing as a means of self-expression—but not much because Beth did not approve. I was not happy, but I was trying to 'make it work' in my marriage by being a 'man.'"

When Beth and Kendall finally separated, he questioned his life. He wanted to find out the reason his two marriages ended. "It led to questioning my sexual orientation and identity. After several months of questioning, I attended a one-year 'coming-out' group at the Los Angeles Gay and Lesbian Center (LAGLC). Soon after, I attended the 'Transgender Perceptions' group at LAGLC. A year later, I started dressing in women's clothes. Today, after two years of attending a therapy group for male-to-female transgender people, I now have lived fully as a woman for two and a half years. I feel happy and at one with myself. I feel more whole. Before, I would look in the mirror and see a stranger. Now, I see me."

Kendall said that he had to adopt new patterns (such as being aware of feelings, rather than stuffing them) to heal. "Being emotionally shut-down worked while growing up; it did not in my adult life. I chose to be a therapist, which required me to become (gradually) more self-aware. I finally realized that I was only partly alive, and I needed to open up and change if I wanted to thrive. Ironically, I believe that surviving cancer and three other potentially fatal illnesses helped me value life more, and be less afraid of death or disaster. Also, I came to realize that life is harder than death, and if you do not give up, you can work through almost anything."

To learn to take care of himself, Kendall said, "I have been increasingly able to ask for help from therapy and support groups, and to be vulnerable in relationships. That change has come with a momentum of its own. Also, music, reading, and friendships, support my growth."

The skills Kendall used while raising her siblings were instrumental in teaching her about the art of loving; skills she uses in parenting her own child. Of her work as a psychotherapist, Kendall said, "My siblings and my child have exposed me to a life-long love of learning and self-examination, which I use to help both my clients and myself.

"I learned to be an agnostic by studying the Bible. Nevertheless, I have always intuitively felt that I am connected to all other beings and maybe to everything, period. I feel best when I feel most connected. That has always been true, even though I have also always felt somewhat separate. Music, helping someone, painting, appreciating a sunset or a cute baby, tasting good food, or a number of other experiences keep me connected and alive, even when I feel otherwise disconnected and separated from life."

Since transitioning to life as a female, Kendall feels solidly connected to herself, "…even when I am down, but I still feel nurtured by the experiences I have lived."

Kendall now works as a licensed marriage and family therapist providing services in West Los Angeles through Open Paths Counseling Center. Kendall founded Another Way, a program focused on stopping violence and abuse, helping abusers and survivors, as well as supervising trainees and interns learning the work.

Because of Kendall, who allowed me to co-facilitate two of her groups, I got certified as a domestic violence service provider and became able to lead my own groups. In California there are two parts to this certificate: a 40-hour training that takes five weeks to complete, and 100 hours of group facilitation. This training generally takes a year but I got clearance to do two classes a week and finished in six months.

Glenda Linares is another special person I met through the classes I took at Echo. Like Ruth, Alyce and Kendall, Glenda is great an example of the impact that "healers" have, one-on-one, on the life of another person. Unbeknownst to her, she began her career in early childhood development while still in high school, raising her daughter as a single parent and taking classes with Ruth Beaglehole, the founder of Echo. Over the last 15 years, Glenda has worked with children, youth, parents, families, and professionals at many levels. She oversaw community programs in the Echo Park area as the program manager at Echo Parenting and Education. In fact, she is the one who kept the program alive for seven years before taking a job as education manager for the Promesa Boyle Heights Best Start ELA Initiative in an industrial area of Los Angeles. Best Start ELA's vision is: "To ensure all children in our zone have access to effective schools and strong systems of family and community supports to prepare them to succeed in school and become dynamic and engaged citizens of the 21st century."

There was never a reason for Glenda to attend college. She learned valuable lessons through the reality of her own life. Her story is an inspiration to me. Glenda gave me the poem titled, "Stirrings," from the book, *Psalms of a Laywoman* by Edwina Gateley and told me that, for her, the poem "describes a series of moments, moments I have lived and felt."

Glenda's Story

Glenda knew violence in the form of war—the civil war that broke out in El Salvador during 1979 shaped her life. This war between rich and poor people destroyed the land, the crops, and…the people. It lasted 12 years and killed millions of innocents. Her memories of that war faded and her family refuses to talk about it. She said, "They want to forget it happened; they want to erase the fear, the terror. My family went through great sacrifices to escape this war. My uncles fled first, leaving family behind in hopes of a better future. My dad followed, leaving me, a heartbroken 3-year-old behind. Two years later, it was our turn, and in 1988 I left with my mother and sister."

They embarked on a month-long journey on foot and with little food and escaped to what they knew as *Los Estados Unidos* in search of the American Dream. Glenda learned that while she could escape war, the experience of war never escaped her. She said, "The memories get buried in your body; they shape the chemistry of your brain. You have to work a lifetime to heal from the harm. The fear stays too, gripping you tightly, sometimes paralyzing you. Other times, it makes you vigilant and hypersensitive. You are forever molded by war. That's what I discovered in my early years in the United States. When you grow up around violence, survival becomes your priority, and I learned how to survive."

Glenda's dreams of being reunited with her father and coming to a beautiful home were crushed. Her new home was the body shop where her dad worked. It was cold at night; there were no windows. She had to take showers outside with a water hose. "We were in America, but where was my home? My dollhouse? What broke my heart were not the conditions we had to live under, it was my father. It was as if the civil war I had fled found its way back into my new home."

The kind and loving father who left her behind in the war zone was now a bitter, sad, and angry man. An alcoholic, he medicated his wounds with booze and women. "He was the reincarnation of war. I don't remember the first time I witnessed my dad hit my mom, but I know it happened here in the United States, and I know it happened many times. By the time I was nine, I had witnessed my father beat, choke and hurt my mom far too many times. In El Salvador the fears were losing lives to the bullets and violence. In the States, my new fear was that I could lose my mom.

"One Saturday afternoon, I went over to my cousin's house for her birthday. My mom did not come because she had to work. My baby sister, who was less than a year old at the time, stayed with my mom. It was a great day; we went roller-skating, played with our Barbie dolls, and ate cake. I got to spend the night at her house. I was full of joy.

"Everything changed the next morning. I arrived at home and found several pictures frames broken. Things seemed out of place, as if two kids had been having a wrestling match. I learned that my father had come home drunk the night before and chased my mom up the stairs. She tried to run away, holding my little sister in her arms. When he caught up to her, he beat her. She had bruises all over her face. I cried when I heard what had happened, and promised myself never to leave my mom alone again.

School was the only place Glenda felt safe. "Learning, teachers and school work became my safe haven. I could escape in books. I could dream of a different life through someone else's story. I could try to forget the reality of my life. The teachers, unaware of my situation at home, saw an eager child, excited for learning and ready to soak it all up. The attention and the connection the teachers gave me helped me navigate a turbulent childhood.

"Unfortunately, in my teen years, my need for attention and connection were no longer met at school, and all the violence I had experienced started to impact my ability to learn. I fell behind and didn't know how to reach out for help. At that time the only help, attention and affection I found was from a classmate at school. Like me, he also had witnessed his dad hurt his mother. Our painful experiences connected us and we became sexually active. I was only 13 at the time, a desperate child trying to escape a nightmare that was my life.

"After witnessing my dad come home drunk yet again, I decided that if I got pregnant, I could escape the violence in my home. I could start over with my own family. I could create my own home, one free of violence. So, I became pregnant."

Glenda's fantasy did not last long. When she was eight months pregnant, her boyfriend hit her for the first time. She realized a few months after her daughter was born that like her mother, she'd ended up with a violent man. Her heart was shattered and her attempts to escape failed. She said, "Unlike my mother, I decided that I could not live that way. I wanted to live a nonviolent life. I would not raise my child in a household like the one I grew up in. I would not allow my daughter to grow up in fear."

Scared, unsure, and without any role models, she left. Glenda was 15 at the time and her daughter Kayla was just three months old.

In her search for a life without violence, she came in contact with Ruth Beaglehole, the director of the childcare center at the school she was attending. The center provided childcare and parenting classes.

In her first parenting class, Glenda learned about breaking the cycles of violence and its connection to parenting.

"This class was more than parenting; it was about a nonviolent movement. Ruth's message was that we could create nonviolent communities and nonviolent households by being intentional about our parenting approach. I didn't need much convincing that I was in the right place. Without hesitation I signed up for Ruth's teen parenting program." Glenda went to that parenting program every day for two years until she got her high school diploma.

"I learned that a nonviolent world begins with our children and our parenting. I learned about emotional intelligence, nonviolent communication, feelings and needs, brain development, child development, coherent narrative, and many other tools that would support me in my daily practice. It was through this form of parenting that I began to heal the wounds inside of me and break the cycle of violence in my family."

Glenda admits that it wasn't easy to raise her daughter that way, and many times she felt lost and confused. "Sometimes I wanted to give up, but the look in my daughter's face when I put her to sleep every night gave me strength. I craved that sense of safety as a child, the kind of security that allows a child to rest with ease and trust. Growing up with violence, I never had that experience. Unlike my daughter, every night I went to bed worried that my dad might come home drunk and beat my mom. Kayla did not have to worry. I made sure of that."

Her dedication to nonviolence paid off in her good relationship with her daughter, but also with her mom. Seeing Glenda's passion for raising Kayla in a different way—and her pursuit of nonviolence—inspired the grandmother and gave her the courage to change and to even get out of her own cycle of violence.

"Last month when we were celebrating Kayla's 16th birthday, I could see how the philosophy of nonviolence has shaped her. She has become the young lady I hoped she would. She is kind, compassionate and sensitive to the people in her world. She is resilient, and she has the ability to express her feelings in ways that I never imagined possible. She was raised with respect, love and nonviolence. She will have her own challenges in life, but her foundation is strong. Watching Kayla grow is a reminder that we, as parents, can choose a different way. My practice and commitment to eliminating violence in my life and the world continues to holds strong."

Glenda graduated from high school at the same time Beaglehole retired and opened up her own nonprofit organization, The Center for Nonviolent Education and Parenting which became Echo Parenting and Education. As a result of Glenda's deep commitment to nonviolent parenting, she went to work for Echo Parenting and Education. Few people get the opportunity to make a living and at the same time do work that is meaningful and fulfilling. At Echo Parenting, Glenda had the privilege to support thousands of people who wanted a better life. During her years at the center, she went from being a parent educator to a childcare supervisor and became a program manager and fundraiser. She was able to move up in the organization without a college degree, learning as she went, guided by her own journey.

CHAPTER 11

A Whisper to Action

Life is like riding a bicycle. You don't fall off
unless you stop pedaling.
~ CLAUDE PEPPER ~

Injustice anywhere is a threat to justice everywhere
and we are caught in an inescapable network
of mutuality, tied in a single garment of destiny.
~ MARTIN LUTHER KING, JR. ~

On June 26, 2014 while still visiting family in New Jersey, I was honored to speak at a gathering that Jane Stevens facilitated with Carolyn Smith Brown, a community manager of an ACE's Virtual Community group in Philadelphia. Carolyn, a woman of great compassion, and her partners, created this event in conjunction with my bicycle journey to allow the Philadelphia virtual group of over 30 people to meet in person. Jane has always felt that for the ACE movement to grow, people have to get opportunities to gather in person. The event was held at a Quaker Meeting House, Friends Center.

When I spoke at that ACEs Connection meet-up, the audience was filled with a variety of people. Child protective service workers, community organizers, domestic violence advocates, housing advocates, mental health providers, social workers, and others—perhaps individuals like myself—wanted to recognize the effects of ACEs and seek pathways for healing.

It was the first time I'd shared my story in this type of a forum, and the feedback I got was positive. Organizer Carolyn Smith Brown said, "Your story was a meaningful way to bring the group to discussion on Thursday and I was very happy at the networking that happened as a consequence."

From Tim Clement, another organizer: "I thought your story was captivating and energized the room. We truly are lucky to have had the opportunity to learn from you and hear of your experiences. Thank you for all that you did for us and the Philadelphia community that cares about ACEs and resiliency."

It is my desire to know that communities can come together like this one did in Philadelphia.

Reader, are you someone who'd like to see this kind of event happen in your community? Who are the leaders in your area who would want to create trauma-informed communities? What kind of a community awareness event would fit your locale?

There are so many topics to cover at events like the one in Philadelphia. I want to see more such events cover topics like the history of the ACE study, the ACE score information and how it is used to guide individual healing and attention to resiliency, how the ACE study should affect policy changes in healthcare, prison reform, education, and overall awareness of the Golden and Platinum Rules for individual responsibility.

In reference to a bicycle, the tool I used to travel two paths across the United States in search of myself, and to honor the work I've done and yet to do, I have this to say:

> *The wheels stop spinning when I stop pedaling.*
>
> *Your wheels stop spinning when you stop pedaling.*
>
> *Mending trauma's wounds to the human's spirit requires motion and energy in the process of moving forward, gaining ground and experiencing more joy.*

You can interpret these statements for yourself in many different ways. I believe that all of us have made mistakes. Rather than be destroyed by them, you can engage in healing and transformation.

We have all harmed or wounded others, especially those with whom we are close. We ourselves have been wounded—by parents, society and by those we ourselves have vowed to love.

In the book *Falling Upward: A Spirituality for the Two Halves of Life*, Father Richard Rohr restated an important truth—"hurt people hurt people"—because when people are in a state of emotional trauma, they pass it on to others. He also highlighted this truth: "'healing people are healing people."

People who feel that they have failed—who have fallen "down"—are also the ones who can understand what it means to "fall up." Those who have somehow fallen, and especially those who have fallen well (or who have seen the advantage in the fall) are the only ones who can grow spiritually and not misuse what it means to be "up." What looks like falling down can, with the right attitude and perspective, be experienced as "falling upward!"

In the Christian tradition, Saint Paul is the example of a sinner who experienced, understood and then taught that God does not hold misdeeds against humans! God is not interested in punishing—adding more hurt to the hurt. God is interested in loving, healing, and transforming people. Jesus did not tell people what to think. He showed them what to do through his loving kindness, acts of compassion and through his love for self and for all. Jesus lived a life and started a movement that he committed himself to—through his actions He showed people that love is about social change for the best and highest good of all people. He showed us how to love God—that mysterious force of love and creation behind all of the reality we perceive—above all. And then, after loving the mystery and majesty of God, and finding a similar kind of love of self, people are to love the other people in their lives.

In the Bible, John 13:34, is God's command: "So now I am giving you a new commandment: Love each other. Just as I have loved you, you should love each other."

And also in the Bible, Matthew 25:35-36, explains the act of love: "For I was hungry, and you gave me something to eat; I was thirsty, and you gave me something to drink; I was a stranger, and you invited me in; naked, and you clothed me; I was sick, and you visited me; I was in prison, and you came to me."

The gospel of Jesus is not a theory for reflection. It is a plan of action. His love will manifest itself when each one of us accepts the invitation to be a participant in this spiritual delivery system.

Saint Augustine said, "Without God I can't, but without me, God won't." God sent Jesus to show people how to fall upward.

Other religions have similar messages that address the fact that Earth is a place of duality. To know relief, pain must be part of the experience. And, to address the concepts of both pain and relief as necessary, belief in a power greater than you is something that is necessary to build on faith.

What is faith? It is the process of learning to trust through the cycles of pain and relief from pain.

Through my journey I have acquired the ability to live in loving relationship with myself, to have faith in it and in my belief in a power greater than any human being. I now deeply appreciate that each person is born to know love's cycle of giving and receiving—from the universal level of God all the way down to personal levels, such as the love I imagine that a snail may feel for fellow snails and its garden environment.

I have also learned a powerful truth: the absence of love is fatal. Human beings who have someone with whom to practice love are less likely to suffer in their lives.

Neuroscience teaches that the brain has plasticity and the ability to change throughout life by forming new connections in synapses. It can unlearn what has been taught and/or experienced. The brain can learn new ways of being. People are wired to heal and transform, to love themselves, to be present and live fully and, in doing so, heal and transform others.

In Corinthians 1:13 the message is, "If I speak in human and angelic tongues but do not have love, I am a resounding gong or a clashing cymbal. And if I have the gift of prophecy and comprehend all mysteries and all knowledge; if I have all faith so as to move mountains but do not have love, I am nothing. If I give away everything I own, and if I hand my body over so that I may boast but do not have love, I gain nothing."

Many of the world's religions ask people to live in simple truth:

- Christianity: Love thy neighbor as thyself

- Judaism: What is hateful to you, do not to your fellow man

- Islam: None of you truly believes until he wishes for his brother, what he wishes for himself

- Taoism: Regard your neighbor's gain as your gain, and your neighbor's loss as your loss

- Buddhism: Hurt not others in ways that you yourself would find hurtful

Living this simple truth is complex! Movement toward growth and understanding is usually always difficult and painful. Love moves toward hate when fueled by fear and hate moves back toward love fueled by courage.

Keep your feet on the pedals. Keep moving away from fear and toward love. Love is not an intellectual concept; it is an action supported by the energy of gratitude for all positive and negative forces that lead to what is always higher ground.

Martin Luther King, Jr. said, "Power without love is reckless and abusive, and love without power is sentimental and anemic." Then he went on to state, "Power at its best is love implementing the demands of justice, and justice at its best is power correcting everything that stands against love." And, "Injustice anywhere is a threat to justice everywhere and we are caught in an inescapable network of mutuality, tied in a single garment of destiny."

Oliver Wendell Holmes said, "For the simplicity that lies this side of complexity, I would not give a fig, but for the simplicity that lies on the other side of complexity, I would give my life."

Gandhi, Martin Luther King, Jr., Mother Teresa, and many other thought leaders, both known and anonymous, understood this complexity and were willing to die for the truth. In so doing, they truly lived and through their lives imparted the complex truth that love necessitates "action" and requires "courage."

Love requires that humans let go of the structures that they create around themselves that give a false sense of security; let go of the rules that make people harsh judges; let go of the habits that make people feel safe. True love asks for vulnerability.

In her book *Daring Greatly*, Brené Brown suggests that life is not about winning or losing, but about having the courage to enter the arena and "dare greatly." She wrote that if you are going to go into the arena you will get your ass kicked and that going into the arena requires you to be vulnerable because joy and creativity can't exist without vulnerability.

Adverse childhood experiences bring the complexity of every human journey into the arena by creating feelings that shut down good emotional vitality; emotions such as shame, anxiety, rejection, and uncertainty.

But know this: The feelings that shut people down and deny vulnerability can be mitigated and even overcome.

There are no magic pills. It takes time and effort, frustration and commitment, chaos and depth, and a myriad of other factors, including synchronicity and surprise. Know that by moderating the effects of ACEs among parenting adults, helping them build on their strengths and improve their ability to function and cope, ACEs are prevented in their children for generations to come. Healing the ACEs of current parents ends "the cycle of violence." Let us begin now.

Continuing education is important for those who are involved in social work and healing. As part of my plan, I want to do all I can to learn more tools and acquire more skills to keep addressing ACEs and healing from them.

After I finished a 10-week class on parenting without violence, I had a chance to speak with a young couple, Layla and Caesar, who are both working to end the cycle of violence for themselves and their beautiful 2-year-old son named Santos. Layla was a student of mine at Westminster Avenue Elementary School when I first started teaching over 20 years ago. She and Caesar shared their stories with me. I feel they represent the hope I'd wish to leave with readers of this book.

Layla's Story

A child born to young parents, Layla's mom was 19 when she was born. One of her first memories (around age 3) was anger over a broken bike. She threw such a fit her dad bought her a new bike, even though her bike could have been fixed. She said, "Other than that, I don't remember my father being around much when my parents were married. When he was around he was either drunk or high on cocaine, which led to a lot of arguing and he'd beat my mom for things she did or didn't do.

"The violence was so common that I remember getting mad at my mom for reprimanding me. I told her, 'I'm going to tell my daddy to hit you.' She was in the kitchen at the time and she just looked at me. She didn't say a word but I could see in her face that it wasn't something she wanted. I thought that my parents' behaviors were normal. I thought it was how it was in every home.

"When my little brother came along things went from bad to worse. We were living in Los Angeles. One day my dad came home and said that my mom had to sell all of our stuff. He said, 'I have a great job in Miami and I'm going out there to find us a place.' So my mom sold everything, sent him the money and took us to Miami. But when we got to Miami there was no job, no apartment and we lived in a motel for two weeks because he had spent the money partying with other women.

"After the two weeks in the motel he moved us into the ghetto and the women he was involved with followed us. They came to our door looking for him. One day my mom got some sleeping pills and put them in his rice at night so he wouldn't go out drinking. For the next couple of weeks he would eat, go to sleep and then in the morning go to work. When he got his pay, my mom packed us up and while he slept took us to the Greyhound station and bought tickets to Texas, which is the farthest ticket she could afford.

"To this day I hate Popeye's because that's all we ate. I'll never eat at a Popeye's ever again. Out of money when we got to Texas, we sat at the bus terminal for a couple of hours until she figured things out. With no money, my mom got us to the airport. I don't know how she did it, but when we were there she told someone at the airport her story and got us two tickets to get back to Los Angeles.

"For a short while we lived with an aunt. Not long after that, my dad followed us back to Los Angeles. He didn't stay long because he did not change and continued to be abusive. In fact, it wasn't until I was 21 and had a flashback that I realized that my father raped my mother at my aunt's apartment. I slept in the same room with them at my aunt's place and didn't know what was going on. I remember asking him if we were going to live with him and he told me to shut up and go to sleep. I thought he was choking my mom. After the flashback, I asked my mom about it and she said, 'Yes, he raped me.' He left soon after that incident; moved to Atlanta and started a whole new family. After my father left, my mom met my stepdad.

"My stepdad was a good man. He never laid a hand on us and was never abusive but he was not a very loving person. He provided for us, which is why my mom married him, but he made it clear that I was not his daughter and he was not my dad. We were OK for a couple of years and then it all began again.

"My stepfather and my mother had a fight. I must have been in school because when I got home that afternoon, my mom had us packed and I remember thinking, 'not again.' I was seven; my brother was four. We moved from Silver Lake to an apartment in North Hollywood and I ended up at a new school where I was bullied. Every day this girl who was around 11 would take my lunch money and threaten to have her homeboys beat me up. It went on until I stood up to her. It helped that my parents got it together and my stepfather came back in the picture. They went to the school to speak to my teacher (who I hated because she was really mean, which is probably why there were bullies at that school in the first place).

"My stepdad and mom got back together and my mom got pregnant with her third child. We moved again—this time to the Westside because my mom worked in Venice. There was a period of stability for about four years.

"I went to Westminster Avenue Elementary and had Mrs. Berger as my teacher. I remember being excited because she had to take some days off and I learned that you were going to be our substitute. You reminded me of Don Johnson from "Miami Vice" with your black shirt and matching suit. When you took over the class we all behaved and we didn't act out like we did with other substitutes. Mrs. Berger asked us to be good and with you we were.

"I really liked Mrs. Berger; she was probably my favorite teacher. She was nice, very sweet; she made me feel good. And also Mr. Robbins—the counselor. I loved him. I remember he split up a fight with me and some girl because by then I did not let anybody bully me and she was trying to punk me. I lost a lot of hair that time in that fight. The way Mr. Robbins broke it up I knew that he cared and after that I felt I could go talk to him about anything.

"I think that maybe those years at Westminster were the most stable: I was in a good school, no moving, no fights at the house, we had dinner together every night at six o'clock, life became normal... until my mom wanted us to have our own house.

"Then we moved to Lancaster and everything went to hell. Once we got there, I became responsible for the household functions because of my mom's long commute to work. I was 12 at the time, and I had to make sure my sister got taken to the sitter's, make dinner for everyone and make my mom breakfast before she went to work. I became a maid.

"Around this time, I started having anxiety attacks, but my mom didn't know it was anxiety. We thought I just had stomach issues because I couldn't stop throwing up. In fact I didn't know I had anxiety until I was 23, went to a doctor and he told me that my illness was the result of anxiety.

"It was in Lancaster that I attended middle school and high school, but my time in those schools really doesn't stand out for me. I was a good student. I did what I was told and got through. When I graduated, I saw my mom in the audience and after I got my diploma I walked over to her and handed it to her. I said, 'Here, this is for you.'

"When I was 19, my mom kicked me out of the house because she found out I wasn't a virgin. In Hispanic culture it's considered unholy—or at least not a good thing—to have sex before marriage. She told everyone...the neighbors...my dad...and then kicked me out. She even helped find me an apartment—we learned that one of my cousin's friends was also looking to move out. My mom found out on a Wednesday and I was out by Friday.

"It was after that I decided I didn't want to go to college. I got a job at Albertson's and was living my life. Even though my mom kicked me out of the house, she still wanted me to help with the younger kids—pick them up from school and drop them off and watch them. I told her that if she wanted me to do that, I would rather work because between helping her and working I had no time.

"My mom was a good mom and I am who I am because of her. She worked hard all her life to provide for me and my brothers and sister and taught me to survive—that you've got to hustle and you can't just expect things to come to you. Part of what keeps me going is that I have to do something big so that one day I can buy her a house with a big old tree in her yard and she can say 'fuck it' to the world, and just be left alone and not have to worry about anything."

When Layla was 20, she left Lancaster and moved in with her cousin's cousin in Los Angeles. The young woman roommate was "a petite, gorgeous girl who wore Dolce & Gabbana and had a whole different perspective on life. She opened up my eyes to things I had been sheltered from—she taught me to be reckless and free at the same time! While living with her I learned to be confident because up to then I didn't feel like I was good enough. Although she gave me a sense of newfound freedom she also introduced me to another side of life—partying."

Layla spent the next few years smoking marijuana and using cocaine. She also got involved in what she calls "an unhealthy romantic relationship" and then went into a deep depression. She said, "It was during this time that Caesar came into my life but I was so numb emotionally that we couldn't really connect. And not long after meeting him, not knowing that I was in a deep depression, I decided that it was time to check out because I had stopped caring about anything, even my family.

"One day while I was babysitting I walked over to the mom I was working for and handed her the baby. I said, 'I can't do this anymore' and left. I went home, smoked some weed and took an overdose of anxiety medication the doctor had given me, about 22 pills. Because I wanted to leave with humor I texted a friend and told her I was going to take the pills. My friend contacted my roommate. The last thing I remember was my roommate coming in and asking me what pills I had taken. Then I woke up in the hospital with all my family around me—everybody upset and fighting because they had found out I had been doing drugs. It was a mess."

When Layla got out of the hospital, her mom made her come back home. Layla found her stepdad and sister sitting on the couch crying and said, "I never thought that my stepfather would ever cry over me. The next day my mom and stepdad had to go back to work, so for the next couple of weeks my 16-year-old sister took care of me and wouldn't let me out of her sight."

During Layla's recovery, Caesar stayed in the picture. He was supportive, and when Layla felt well enough they started dating. She says, "We dated but I knew it was too early. I had work to do on myself and I think he also had things to work on because he broke up with me, and I didn't care. We didn't speak for a whole year after that and I'm glad, because it gave me time to heal and figure out what I wanted to do with life. It was during that time that I decided to go back to work and school. I also dealt with my anxiety in a healthy way, and it eventually all came together for me.

"My focus on school led to my getting my degree as a medical assistant. My life was once again on track and I felt secure and ready to take a call from Caesar. He'd been calling and I had been avoiding talking with him. He convinced me to go on a date and it led to us getting back together. He presented me with a plan; my man likes to plan! He had written the plan for me and it was this: 'I want us to date. I want us to move in together, and then we can talk about where we are going.'"

The plan worked. Layla and Caesar created Santos! Layla says that her hope "is that we make it 50 years down the road. I see me with a walker and him with a cane, fighting about something silly that annoys me! But I see our grandchildren living for only the good things that we hoped for when we were younger."

Caesar's Story

Caesar's story begins with his mom. He said, "My mom had my sister when she was really young. Real young. My mom got pregnant at age 10 and had her at age 12." When Caesar was 4, he lived at 102nd and Normandy in Los Angeles. His sister had a boyfriend named Mario. He said, "I remember hearing gunshots and screaming and everybody, all of us running outside. Mario's mom was holding him. He was shot five or six times, was stabbed, and his throat was cut. That was one of my first memories.

"The place we lived at was a big place—my mom and me, my sister and stepfather (Howard, an African American), my mom's best friend Teresa (who she met in juvenile hall) and her husband Manuel lived there at the time. And also these guys: Mickey, Moses, and Bird (Manuel, Jr.). I remember Teresa getting beat up and my mom and stepdad fighting. I had a father, Lalo, but I didn't meet him until I was about six. He was an alcoholic. When my mom got pregnant with me, he left and went back to San Luis Potosí, Mexico. He told my mom that he was going to visit his mom but what actually happened was he went back and got married to his high school sweetheart, and he took my mom's savings with him.

"I thought my stepfather, Howard, was my father until he and my mom told me the truth. One time Howard tried to hit my mom with a boot and she picked up a hammer. My sister doesn't remember any of this but I remember that day and my mom saying, 'You want to use weapons?' and Howard saying, 'Baby, put the hammer down, put the hammer down.'"

Caesar grew up with adults who fought with one another. He said that what went on between Howard and his mom was nothing compared to what he saw between Teresa and her husband Manuel. "He was a big time alcoholic and when he got drunk he beat Teresa and Bird really bad. My mom tried to hide it from us, but as big as the house was, we knew. In fact, when Manuel got really drunk my mom put all us kids in one of the rooms and it was like we were having a sleepover. The next day we knew what happened because Teresa's head looked like a balloon."

These issues, plus the shooting of Mario and the fact that Howard was in the military at the time, are why Caesar's mom moved the family from the big house to a house in Pomona. Caesar said, "The thing is the issues actually got worse in Pomona because Howard, who had always used drugs, got heavy with his drug use—rock cocaine. It got to the point that things started disappearing from the house. My mom would ask him, 'Where's our wedding rings?' He even pawned the electric piano I'd gotten for Christmas. I don't want to paint Howard as a bad father because even though he was using drugs he was still a good father. He took us to see the Grand Canyon. He also provided for us and supported my mother.

"When I was 7, my mom put me in a martial arts program, tae kwon do, with Master Plum. Every time she had some money, she'd pay for those classes. I loved it. But again we had to move because Howard's drug habit went through the roof. Mom started to use drugs with him. Even though she was doing drugs, she knew she had to take care of us. Before we moved she got her sister and mom to come live with us and help take care of us. After a while she started fighting with them, so when I was 10, she moved us to Lawndale and in with Teresa who had left Manuel and was now living with Gilbert.

"We stayed in Lawndale until Howard re-appeared and they got back together. Then we moved to Santa Monica and lived in the Pico neighborhood on Michigan Avenue. I was then age 13. Howard had not stopped using drugs; in fact he was now dealing. One day I came home from school and he was in the kitchen cooking. I thought he was making cookies and I wanted some. He told me they weren't cookies to eat; they were cookies to sell. That's when I learned to make rock cocaine; he also taught me to smoke it and sell it. He took me out around midnight to sell with him and then gave me $40, a lot of money for a kid."

There were scary experiences Caesar had around addicts in his environment that caused him to run away from home. He said, "I was living in a drug house and somehow I knew I had to leave. I just was tired, tired of fighting with everybody, so I took some stuff and left and stayed on the beach for a couple nights."

Leaving home changed Caesar's life because his best friend in junior high, William, found out he was sleeping on the beach. William asked his mom, Stella, if Caesar could stay with them. Stella picked up the boys after school, had a short conversation with Caesar and gave him a place to stay. Caesar said, "They didn't ask anything from me; gave me a room out of the kindness of their hearts. Will's family was like the television show "Leave It to Beaver." He had a mom, a dad, an older sister, and a younger brother. They ate dinner together, their dad, Pico, watched TV in the living room, Stella talked on the phone with her mom or sisters while the kids played games together. They all showed me what a family should be. Just by watching them together, I learned that there was another way of being with people you loved. They had their problems like anybody but I never heard them raise their voices or be violent with each other. They let me stay through the summer."

At Santa Monica High School, "Mr. G., or Ernest Garcia, came into my life." Garcia was Caesar's English teacher who helped him graduate from high school. "He knew about me and that I had issues at home and when I walked into his class, he took me aside and he asked me, 'What is it that you want to do with your life?' I told him 'I want to fight. I want to do martial arts.'

"Mr. G. told me that if that was what I wanted to do then I should show up after school and he would teach me martial arts. I laughed because he was this little guy, five-four or maybe five feet five, telling me—a guy with a big ass chip on my shoulder who at the start of freshman year weighed a solid 240 pounds—telling me that he was going to teach me how to fight.

"I showed up that Friday after school. He was there and the room was cleared, chairs pushed to the sides and a bunch of kids like myself were in the room. It turned out that every Friday after school he had a bunch of guys come to his class, troubled kids like me, and for two hours he taught martial arts. So there I am, facing him, and he tells me that if I beat him he will give me an A in every class for the next four years, but if I lose I have to attend all his English classes and do all his homework, and on Fridays he would train me along with everyone else. I looked at this guy and thought, 'OK. I'm not going to hurt this guy. I'm just going to throw a jab, maybe break his nose, and then I'm going to be gone and that's it.'

"I remember throwing the jab. He grabbed my wrist, pulled me forward, kicked my ankle, flipped me on my back! As he held my hand in a wrist lock and I laid there he looked me in the eyes, broke my wrist and said, 'Are you done?'

"I wasn't like most kids. I knew pain. So I got up and threw a punch with the other hand. He did the same routine. Then he broke my other wrist and said, 'Now you're done.'

"When I woke up he wrapped up my wrists and called my mom. She took me to the doctor to get my wrists set. For the next three months, Mr. G. had my teachers send him all my homework and assigned me a student tutor to help me with my homework.

"From that day on I faithfully attended his English class and his Friday lessons for the next four years. He was always there for me. In my sophomore year, my math teacher called me 'a future wife beater who wouldn't amount to anything but a garbage man.' I lost it. I yelled at her, punched the blackboard, broke the wall, punched a locker, and ended up almost getting expelled. When Mr. G. heard what happened he got other teachers to support me and speak on my behalf and then he helped transfer me out of her class and into another teacher's class.

"Mr. G. was my friend. He taught me about Socrates, Plato; had me read Dan Millman's *Way of the Peaceful Warrior*. He intervened when I had problems, even after I graduated from high school and until he retired! I was 23 by then, and I continued to go to his martial arts class on Fridays.

"Mr. G. helped a lot of kids. He wasn't like a normal teacher. The last time I saw him was at Santa Monica Medical Center where I was working as security officer. He was being treated for colon cancer, which he beat. The last I heard, he was in his mid-70s, cancer free, and still training and practicing martial arts."

After September 11, 2001 Caesar joined the Marines, but it was not a good fit for him. When he told his family they wondered what he was thinking. He says that he should have listened to them. The Marines had a culture that is very different from the one he grew up in, and they kept trying to break him, make him follow their rules, not what he had learned or been taught to do. Caesar endured a lot of conflict before he left basic training. On his way out, he took a beating from a bunch of his trainers.

He said, "I wasn't in good shape mentally and emotionally when I left boot camp and returned to Santa Monica. I needed to work so I got a job as a bouncer and that led to darker times because I got involved in dealing drugs, fights, bad relationships, and then, due to a violent incident, I had to leave the country. It was because I found out that the girl I was seeing at the time had gotten pregnant and had an abortion without telling me. I flipped. Flipped out, got drunk, went on a tear, got into six or seven bar fights that day.

"When I sobered up I called and talked to my mom and she said it was time for me to leave the area for a while. Apart from the training I received with Mr. G. I studied and learned from a couple of martial art experts and that's a whole story in and of itself but because of my training I was able to get work in Thailand. And so off I went to Thailand to fight as a professional, for money, and stayed there for about a month and a half. It didn't take long to miss being home and realize that I needed to go back and get myself together. I needed a job so I did go back to being a bouncer, but I told everybody that I no longer dealt drugs and that if they wanted to do drugs they couldn't do it in the club where I was working.

"Then, on September 9th, 2005 one of my brothers-in-law, Adam, an active Venice 13 gang member walked by the club while I was working the door. I remember seeing this dude running up with his black Raiders cap, blue leather shirt, long baggy blue jeans and it didn't register until I heard the first shot. I saw Adam go down. He got hit seven times. A lady who was driving by got hit on the shoulder and crashed her car into the corner. She was pregnant.

"As soon as I saw Adam get hit, I ran over, lifted his head onto my lap, took my shirt off and put pressure on the bullet holes. As he was lying in my arms he kept saying his daughter's name over and over. The ambulance arrived but they wouldn't let me go with him because they said I was 'not family.' Five or six cops had to restrain me.

"That was it, the end of being a bouncer for me. This time it took the death of a family member for me to change. It was then that I met Layla."

These two young adults, Layla and Caesar, are representative of many in our society. And, so is their child, Santos. It is a responsibility we all have to love each of them, to hold them in our hearts, and shepherd them.

Santos is the future.

Our collective future.

Layla's and Caesar's son holds our hope and represents what is possible. His hope, his future, lies in our understanding that caring for and serving each other is the foundation of a good society. By articulating and understanding the effects of their own ACEs, Caesar and Layla build on their strengths and improve their ability to function and cope with the everyday challenges. That means Santos' life experience will include far fewer ACEs than his parents'. The healing that takes place is mutual, it reinforces itself with the joy of discovery, and it means future generations will inherit—and cause—less adverse childhood experiences.

The concepts of "hope" and "understanding" stand on another simple yet complex truth: Every person is born with a gift, every individual is here for a reason, and every soul has a purpose.

Here is an idiom everyone knows: "Don't reinvent the wheel." It means to do or make something a second time when the first thing or act needed no improvement.

To ride a bicycle across the United States—twice—is to have a unique perspective on landscape, love and life. I believe my experiences over the long roads I've traveled did create a new kind of wheel—one that allowed me an adventure in healing.

But what I've discovered is that healing, for me, for others, is an ongoing process. Constant pedaling—with short breaks for rest, nourishment, respite and time to give attention to fellow travelers, to listen to, share in and appreciate their stories—is the only answer.

There are all kinds of systems in place to support emotional healing, but I'm now convinced that the most basic healing occurs outside any system—between two people, face-to-face, one-on-one. One body-heart-brain-spirit to another body-heart-brain-spirit.

And from there, healing can go on in groups of people, in communities, formed by people with natural leadership skills and abilities to manage group interactions. A majority of the world's population does not have access to, or ability to pay for, professional help to facilitate the processes of their own, their family's or their community's need for healing.

I believe there are ways to create a new wheel for healing in communities all over the world. These new ways await discovery, beyond this book. I've created a companion curriculum to this book, based on my own work with groups in my community. Teachers, social workers, community leaders and others who feel a call and a commitment may use the curriculum as a guide to facilitate health and healing in their landscape.

The basic truths are simple.

"Hurt people hurt people."

People healing themselves are also healing other people.

CHAPTER 12

Your Own Wheeling to Healing

Organizing your emotions reclaims
your power over any given drama. Nothing is
stronger than your own mind.
~ Jennifer Elisabeth ~

The following resources and references to experts in the fields of healing are here as a guide for readers who wish to have more information on the impact of Adverse Childhood Experiences and what is available in terms of healing bodies, minds and spirits. All are mere guides to individuals; none are advertisements, nor are any of them guarantees of healing.

If you've experienced a healing modality that has worked for you, please go to the book's website, www.wheelingtohealing.com, where you'll find a forum that allows for sharing healing experiences—from personal stories of triumph to types of modalities that soothe the embedded emotional impact of physical traumas and memories of psychological traumas.

Healing is possible.

Whether it is a bicycle trip, talk therapy, membership in a support group, hypnosis, reiki, tapping, Eye Movement Desensitization and Reprocessing (EMDR), the Emotion Code, acupuncture, holotropic breathwork, sound therapy, or any number of mainstream or alternative modalities, it is possible to lessen the impact of trauma and move into lives of less suffering, less emotional drama and mood swings and more emotional freedom to experience joy, love, compassion and the gift of one's own resilient nature.

Healing is a process and it is always possible.

That belief is the purpose of this book.

I want it for you. I want it for everyone.

Thank you for reading.

Resources

ACEs Connection

The home page is www.acesconnection.com/.

"The companion social network to ACEsTooHigh.com, ACES Connection is the most active, influential ACEs community in the world. Connect with people using trauma-informed/resilience-building practices. Stay current with news, research, events."

ACEs Too High

Find ACEs Too High at www.acestoohigh.com/aces-too-high-network/.

"ACEsConnection.com is for people who are implementing—or thinking about implementing—trauma informed and resilience-building practices based on ACEs research. If you join, you automatically receive a daily digest with summaries and links to the latest news, research and reports about ACEs research and implementation, plus a weekly roundup of activity within the network."

Adventure Cycling Association

A nonprofit organization in Montana empowers people to plan and take bicycle trips in North America.

The website is www.adventurecycling.org/about-us/.

Anda, Robert, M.D.

Meet Dr. Anda in a video titled, "Adverse Childhood Experiences (ACE), featuring Dr. Robert Anda." (The length of the video is 1:52:49 and it is described as "Childhood trauma expert Dr. Robert Anda, co-investigator of the Centers for Disease Control Adverse Childhood Experiences (ACE)

Study, spoken on 23 October 2012 at University of Alaska Anchorage on 'Adverse Childhood Experiences: How Can UAA Help Address ACES? What Do Future Leaders Need to Know?') www.youtube.com/watch?v=QLfUi4ssHmY

Castellino, Raymond, D.C. (retired), RPP, RPE, RCST®

Castellino focuses on the resolution of prenatal, birth, and other early trauma and stress and works to strengthen bonds between parents and babies. He works with midwife Mary Jackson (read an interview with her at www. http://birthinconnection.com/interview-cerelli/) to support the process of bringing a child into this world.

His website is http://www.castellinotraining.com/.

Chamberlain, Linda, Ph.D., MPH

Author of "The Amazing Adolescent Brain: What Every Educator, Youth Serving Professional, and Healthcare Provider Needs to Know" (2009) (See: www.instituteforsafefamilies.org, www.multiplyingconnections.org and www.advocatesforyouth.org); "The Amazing Teen Brain: What Every Child Advocate Needs to Know." American Bar Association Child Law Practice. (2009; 28(2):21-24) (See: www.childlawpractice.org); and, "The Amazing Adolescent Brain: Translating Science into Strategies." 2008. The Institute for Safe Families, Philadelphia, PA at www.instituteforsafefamilies. org. Chamberlain and Bruce Perry, M.D., Ph.D. are featured in this video, available on YouTube: www.youtube.com/watch?v=O4zP50tEad0

Cozolino, Louis, Ph.D.

This author has studied child abuse and authored several important books on the topic of healing, including: *The Making of a Therapist: A Practical Guide for the Inner Journey*, WW Norton & Company, New York. 2004. *The Neuroscience of Human Relationships: Attachment and the Developing Social Brain*, WW Norton & Company. 2006.

The Healthy Aging Brain: Sustaining Attachment, Attaining Wisdom, WW Norton & Company, New York. 2008. *The Neuroscience of Human Relationships: 2nd Edition, Attachment and the Developing Social Brain,* WW Norton & Company, New York. 2012.

The Social Neuroscience of Education: Optimizing Attachment & Learning in the Classroom, WW Norton & Company, New York. 2013. *Attachment-Based Teaching,* WW Norton & Company, New York. *Why Therapy Works: Using Your Mind to Change Your Brain,* WW Norton & Company, New York. 2015.

Felitti, Vincent J., M.D.

Author of "The Reverse Alchemy of Childhood: Turning Gold into Lead." Family Violence Prevention Fund newsletter (Summer, 2001).

www.futureswithoutviolence.org/userfiles/file/HealthCare/reserve_alchemy.pdf

Meet Dr. Felitti through this video tribute to him and his career: www.youtube.com/watch?v=q22Zt6aGwsA

Heller, Diane Poole, Ph.D.

Dr. Heller is an expert on the psychology of trauma and attachment in human relationships. Her website offers resources and workshops for counselors and others interested in learning more about what healthy attachment looks like and how to achieve it.

See www.dianepooleheller.com.

Iacoboni, Marco, M.D., Ph.D.

Marco Iacoboni is a neurologist, neuroscientist and professor of psychiatry and biobehavioral sciences. He is the director of the Transcranial Magnetic Stimulation Lab at the Ahmanson-Lovelace Brain Mapping Center at UCLA. The internet location of his lab is at http://iacoboni.bol.ucla.edu/. Dr. Iacoboni's work in empathy and mirror neurons may be explored on

YouTube in two parts: www.youtube.com/watch?v=UHqAY0UbzAI and www.youtube.com/watch?v=w4vdCNL01VE.

Levine, Michael

Author of *Walking the Tiger: Healing Trauma* www.amazon.com/Waking-Tiger-Healing-Peter-Levine/dp/155643233X.

Lyddon, Julianna

Author of *Raising a Happy Spirit*, MiniBuk.com (2012). This little book on parenting skills is available on amazon.com at www.amazon.com/Raising-Happy-Spirit-Wisdom-Parenting/dp/0615404715 for $4.95. It gives parents a how-to for teaching children about ideas and concepts such as: touch, self-soothing, imagination, emotions, role-playing, humility, compassion, forgiveness and truth.

Meet intuitive healer Julianna Lyddon, a marriage, relationship and family counselor at http://connectwithjulianna.com/meet-julianna/.

National Coalition Against Domestic Violence

At www.ncadv.org/ is a nonprofit organization formed to be the voice of victims and survivors. Its mission statement reads in part: "We are the catalyst for changing society to have zero tolerance for domestic violence. We do this by affecting public policy, increasing understanding of the impact of domestic violence, and providing programs and education that drive that change."

Nelson, Bradley, D.O.

Author of *The Emotion Code*. Wellness Unmasked Publishing, (2007). He offers a free eBook about this healing modality at: www.free-ebooks.net/ebook/The-Emotion-Code-How-to-Release-Your-Trapped-Emotions-for-Abundant-Health-Love-and-Happiness.

Newton, Michael, Ph.D.

Author of *Journey of Souls*. Llewellyn Publications, (1994). The Newton Institute also offers insight into a type of hypnosis that allows for a deep understanding of the nature of soul energy, relationships and life experiences. http://newtoninstitute.org/.

No Judgment Just Love®

A movement started by ShaRon Rea, a life and family coach, meant to shine light on the difference between judgment, discernment and the consequences of their actions.

See www.nojudgementjustlove.com/.

Office of Juvenile Justice and Delinquency Prevention (OJJDP)

A division of the U.S. Department of Justice (http://www.ojjdp.gov/about/about.html), the OJJDP's vision is "a nation where our children are healthy, educated, and free from violence. If they come into contact with the juvenile justice system, the contact should be rare, fair, and beneficial to them." As stated on its website, the mission is to provide "national leadership, coordination, and resources to prevent and respond to juvenile delinquency and victimization." The OJJDP supports communities in developing and implementing prevention and intervention programs. It seeks to improve the juvenile justice system to provide safety for the public, to hold youth accountable and to provide treatment and rehabilitation services appropriate for juveniles and their families. April is National Child Abuse Prevention Month OJJDP's supports ongoing efforts "to promote the safety and well being of our nation's children."

Find information about Restorative Justice Programs here: http://www.ojjdp.gov/pubs/implementing/contents.html.

"Paper Tigers" a film by James Redford

The premise of this documentary is that one caring, kind, loving adult can make a huge difference in the life trajectory of a child. The setting for this film is Lincoln Alternative High School in rural Walla Walla, Washington.

See http://kpjrfilms.co/paper-tigers/about-the-film/ for more information on how to view the film or host a screening.

Pasquale, Teresa B.

Author of *Sacred Wounds: A Path to Healing from Spiritual Trauma*. Chalice Press. (2015). This book deals with wounds inflicted by religion: religious authority figures, dogmas, etc.; spiritual pain in any form. Pasquale is Clinical Director of RECO Intensive, a trauma and addiction intensive and outpatient treatment program near Delray Beach, Florida. She is also a yoga instructor, meditation and retreat facilitator who brings mindfulness and healing into her work for social justice.

Perry, Bruce, M.D., Ph.D.

Psychiatrist and author Bruce D. Perry, M.D., Ph.D. is a Senior Fellow of the Child Trauma Academy in Houston, Texas. His work with author Maia Szalavitz resulted in the books, *The Boy Who Was Raised As a Dog And Other Stories from a Child Psychiatrist's Notebook* (subtitled *What Traumatized Children Can Teach Us About Loss, Love, and Healing*), 2008, and *Born for Love: Why Empathy is Essential—and Endangered*, 2010, will be helpful to social workers involved in seeing that ACEs are minimized when and where possible.

Phillips, Maggie, Ph.D.

Dr. Phillips is the author of *Finding the Energy to Heal*, expert in trauma, pain relief, energy psychology and hypnosis. See what she has to offer at http://www.maggiephillipsphd.com/ and also the video she's done about her work at www.youtube.com/watch?v=ZmgCBvg3O1U. A recent talk she gave was titled: "Polyvagal Solutions for Pain and Trauma: Where Self and Nervous Systems Meet." She is a proponent of avoiding re-traumatization.

Pratt, George, Ph.D.

Dr. Pratt is a licensed clinical and consulting psychologist who offers cognitive-behavioral therapy (CBT), clinical hypnosis, Eye Movement Desensitization and Reprocessing (EMDR), Energy Psychology and Mind/Body techniques. His depth of experience allows him to offer a free audiovisual relaxation DVD through his website. His book titled *Instant Emotional Healing: Acupressure for the Emotions* contains information on how to rid oneself of a range of negative emotions such as frustration, guilt, procrastination, and in this video, he demonstrates a technique for rapid relaxation: www.youtube.com/watch?v=fji9f8jI25c.

Real, Terry

Also a family therapist, speaker and author, Real is the founder of Relational Life Institute, http://www.terryreal.com/. In this blog article, he describes how to work with what he calls "carried feelings" http://www.terryreal.com/main-pages/blogs/articles/carried-feelings.

Siegel, Dan, M.D.

Over the span of his career, Dr. Siegel has done much to cultivate human well being and the practice of mindfulness. His website, http://www.drdansiegel.com/home/ offers a multitude of resources on topics ranging from neuroscience to education for counselors to parenting to "The Healthy Mind Platter."

"The Place of Refuge: Calming the Storm of Divorce"

Larry King is the commentator for this documentary film that gives insight into native Hawaiian practices for healing families who are in turmoil.

The producers of this film offer a website that promotes the best interests of children whose families are in the process of divorce: http://www.makingtheworldabetterplace.org/

van der Kolk, Bessel, M.D., The Justice Resource Institute's Trauma Center

One of the world's leading experts on psychological trauma, Dr. van der Kolk is the founder of the Trauma Center. The website includes a wealth of resources, including "Common Responses to Trauma - And Coping Strategies," by Patti Levin, LICSW, Psy.D., at http://www.traumacenter. org/resources/pdf_files/Common_responses.pdf

"Wounds That Won't Heal" Video

A ten-minute video by Cavalcade Productions, Inc. (2005) about child abuse and neglect in the voices of victims and it includes clips from speeches made by doctors Felitti and Anda. www.youtube.com/watch?v=tMXtOxXBCRo. Although the title indicates otherwise, *healing is possible.*

Some Alternative Healing Modalities to Explore

In addition to the faith-based methods of relief and the sciences of psychology and psychiatry, there are many alternative methods that involve both "science and spirit" toward emotional healing and self-discovery:

Alternative Healing Modalities — The most comprehensive list of non-allopathic healing modalities may be found on the internet at http://altmedworld.net/alternative.htm. The Indian Board of Alternative Medicines in Kolkata, West Bengal (India) took the time to write descriptions of therapiest organized in an alphabetical list: acupressure to herbology to lymphatic drainage massage to prolotherapy, Rolfing and yoga.

Emotion Code — The name of a technique for finding and releasing trapped emotions. A free eBook is available at www.free-ebooks. net/ebook/The-Emotion-Code-How-to-Release-Your-Trapped-Emotions-for-Abundant-Health-Love-and-Happiness.

Energy Healing Modalities — Energy healing involves the person and a practitioner who assists the person with neutralizing memories that seem to either attach themselves to body parts and cause pain or reside in the emotions ("heart") and prevent the person from living with joy and ease. In this book, Sherry Anshara is given as an example of an "energy healer." She's unique because she works as a team with a medical doctor, Anup Kanodia, M.D. The two support the use of a person's own physical and spiritual energy fields to start or continue a healing process.

There are many practitioners of "energy healing" and if a reader is interested in pursuing this kind of therapy, its history, and the way it is taught to practitioners in the state of California, please see Energy Medicine University's website at http://www.energymedicineuniversity.org/.

Energy Medicine University, established in 2006, is the distance learning school of the Academy of Intuition Medicine in Mill Valley, California, founded in 1984. Also, for advice on how to hire and work with energy healers, see http://www.the-energy-healing-site.com/choosing-a-healer.html.

For centuries, aspects of healing have alternated between external science and internal energy. Perhaps the time has come for aspects of science and spirit to be united instead of divided. Only the individual human being can make sense of what is true regarding this balance.

Enneagram — A personality assessment tool that allows you to understand yourself, your motivations and your relationships in a clear way. Russ Hudson teaches (on youtube.com) how using this method enhances communication. For more information and a free test, see www.eclecticenergies.com/enneagram/test.php.

Eye Movement Desensitization and Reprocessing (EMDR) — Information is available about this therapy using eye movement to process trauma (pioneered by Francine Shapiro, Ph.D.) at http://www.emdr.com/. Also see www.emdria.org

Holotropic Breathwork™ — A technique of paying attention to and modulating breath to produce an opened state of mind that allows healing (pioneered by Stanislav Grof).

See http://www.holotropic.com/about.shtml for more information.

Hypnosis — Much has been written about hypnosis, but the Mayo Clinic offers information about it here:

http://www.mayoclinic.org/tests-procedures/hypnosis/basics/definition/prc-20019177.

Reiki — A Japanese technique for stress reduction that involves mind/body plus a giving/receiving process.

See http://www.reiki.org/faq/whatisreiki.html.

True Colors — A personality assessment tool best used by high school and college students for insight into self, others and relationships.

Find more information here: www.truecolorsintl.com.

About the Author

 James Encinas, a former actor and grade school teacher, is a parent education specialist, teacher trainer, public speaker and author. He wrote *Wheeling to Healing... Broken Heart on a Bicycle: Understanding and Healing from Adverse Childhood Experiences* to illustrate that healing from Adverse Childhood Experiences (ACEs) is possible when the heart is open and the mind is willing to embrace healthy ways to maintain peace, honor and respect for self and others.

Children and adults reflect the reality in which they were raised. To avoid the shame, anxiety and uncertainty created by ACEs, people learn to armor up and shut down which traps them in unhealthy and even dangerous patterns. The workshops James teaches use a variety of tools and exercises (e.g., breath work, coordinated body movements, Emotional Freedom Technique (EFT), acupressure, meditation) to open individuals up to their pure, undamaged souls and give teachers new ways to reach into the minds and hearts of students. Clear communication, combined with active listening, is key for healing to begin and healthy relationships to be maintained.

Safe environments, especially in healing communities, allow members to recognize who they are, what they can become, and grasp the idea of a spiritual force greater than the self and its interconnection in all things. This type of awakening is key to letting go of the trauma left behind after ACEs, and preventing future emotional abuse and domestic violence. Workshop graduates bring non-judgmental behavior to their home/work/school, and this healthy paradigm is what changes communities for the better.

James is one of the founders of the Westminster Avenue Elementary School Endowment, a not-for-profit focused on strengthening ties with parents and the community at large. He is a certified Echo Parenting Trainer. James is a Fellow from the first class of the Aspen Teacher Leaders Fellowship and is a member of the Aspen Global Leadership Network. He is in the process of becoming an interfaith minister.

CPSIA information can be obtained
at www.ICGtesting.com
Printed in the USA
LVOW11s0250170817
545343LV00003B/349/P